Literacy for Young Children

Second Edition

Terry S. Salinger

Merrill,
an imprint of Prentice Hall
Englewood Cliffs, New Jersey   *Columbus, Ohio*

Library of Congress Cataloging-in-Publication Data

Literacy for young children / Terry S. Salinger.—2nd ed.

    p.   cm.

Rev. ed. of: Language arts and literacy for young children. c1988.

Includes bibliographical references and index.

ISBN 0-02-405272-8

1. Language arts (Primary)—United States. 2. Children—United States—Language. 3. English language—United States—Composition and exercises. 4. Reading (Primary)—United States. I. Salinger, Terry S. Language arts and literacy for young children. II. Title.

    LB1529.U5S35   1996

    372.6—dc20

                                                 94-47494

                                                           CIP

Cover art: Jack Disbrow

Editor: Bradley J. Potthoff

Production Editor: Alexandrina Benedicto Wolf

Photo Editor: Anne Vega

Design Coordinator: Julia Zonneveld Van Hook

Text Designer: Ed Horcharik

Cover Designer: Ed Horcharik

Production Manager: Deidra M. Schwartz

Electronic Text Management: Marilyn Wilson Phelps, Matthew Williams, Karen L. Bretz, Tracey Ward

This book was set in Bookman by Prentice Hall and was printed and bound by Quebecor Printing/ Book Press. The cover was printed by Phoenix Color Corp.

© 1996 by Prentice-Hall, Inc.

A Simon & Schuster Company

Englewood Cliffs, New Jersey 07632

Earlier edition, entitled *Language Arts and Literacy for Young Children,* © 1988 by Macmillan Publishing Company.

Photo credits: pp. 1, 10, 13, 17, 41, 103, 125, 131, 153, 160, 187, 227, 230, 235, 257, and 268 by Anne Vega, Merrill/Prentice Hall; pp. 54, 96, 194, 198, and 271 by Terry S. Salinger; p. 27 by Tom Watson, Merrill/Prentice Hall; pp. 35, 45, and 156 by Barbara Schwartz, Merrill/Prentice Hall; pp. 67, 87, 109, 113, and 146 by Scott Cunningham, Merrill/Prentice Hall; p. 78 by Dan Floss, Merrill/Prentice Hall; p. 83 by Todd Yarrington, Merrill/Prentice Hall; and p. 139 by Julie Tober, Merrill/Prentice Hall

Printed in the United States of America

10 9 8 7 6 5 4 3 2 1

ISBN: 0-02-405272-8

Prentice-Hall International (UK) Limited, *London*

Prentice-Hall of Australia Pty. Limited, *Sydney*

Prentice-Hall of Canada, Inc., *Toronto*

Prentice-Hall Hispanoamericana, S. A., *Mexico*

Prentice-Hall of India Private Limited, *New Delhi*

Prentice-Hall of Japan, Inc., *Tokyo*

Simon & Schuster Asia Pte. Ltd., *Singapore*

Editora Prentice-Hall do Brasil, Ltda., *Rio de Janeiro*

For
Richard A. Cole
and
Audrey D. Williams, in memoriam

PREFACE

The first edition of this book started with these words: "This book began to take shape in 1970 when I faced my first first-grade class, wondered why I had decided to become a teacher, and picked up a book to read to them." The process of revising the book has caused me to think back on the children in that class—most notably the little boy named David who is introduced in the first chapter—and to remember the excitement and satisfaction I experienced with those students and with subsequent classes of eager young learners. So much in the fields of early childhood education and literacy instruction has changed during the past twenty-five years, but what has remained constant is that helping young children become literate and love books is an exciting and satisfying endeavor. The terms *whole language, naturalistic,* and *authentic* approaches to instruction are all jargon until one actually observes the intensely intellectual methods young children use to explore how reading and writing work.

To young children, reading and writing are merely extensions of listening and speaking, more advanced and structured forms of the communication strategies they have been refining since birth. Though this may sound naive, it is a powerful instructional principle because it attests to the motivation children have for learning new ways to communicate with those around them. Children who are convinced that they can master literacy will take charge of their own learning when they find themselves in supportive, nurturing, literacy-rich environments.

This book discusses the knowledge base teachers must have to support children's inherent interest in communicating with others. The emphasis is on what children do as they explore reading, writing, speaking, and listening and on how teachers can strengthen children's natural explorations of literacy behaviors. An underlying principle of the book is that teachers are willing to assume the role of resource person and model for young learners—they are the experts who are always ready to share what they know with the novice literacy users in their classes. This is a new type of role for many early childhood teachers; teachers must place independence at the top of their list of goals for their students.

TEXT ORGANIZATION

I have written this text to help teachers explore ways to reach these instructional goals. The text therefore is divided into three sections. Chapters 1 through 5 provide information about the knowledge teachers need to create classrooms that fully support children's learning in reading, writing, speaking, and listening. Chapters 6 and 7 discuss what children themselves discover about language and literacy and suggest ways teachers can help young learners expand their discoveries toward greater and greater understanding. Chapters 8 through 10 present information on classrooms that support literacy learning for children from pre-kindergarten through grade three, and chapter 11 shows how children's literature can help teachers tie their instructional strategies together for active, exciting learning.

Activities at the end of each chapter challenge individual students and groups of students to think more deeply about children, classrooms, and instruction. Students are encouraged to keep a log of their ideas, reactions, and questions during the time they are reading this book and to share those logs with others. Part of learning about emergent literacy should be social, just as social interaction is vitally important for young children who are learning to read and write. Appendices at the end of the book are designed as references for both preservice and in-service teachers.

This book is not intended as a prescriptive "how-to" text; instead, its purpose is to help teachers reflect on children's learning and learn to make the decisions needed to create classrooms where *all* students can experience themselves as confident, capable, excited, successful learners. In such classrooms, teachers grow as professionals by experiencing the deep satisfaction of being a part of children's emerging literacy.

ACKNOWLEDGMENTS

No writing project is ever completed in a vacuum, and I wish to acknowledge the following people for their help and support. First, I thank Sharon Suskin and Naomi Drew of the South Brunswick, New Jersey, School District who graciously opened their classrooms to me; they are wonderful teachers, true models of what early childhood educators should be. The children whose lives they touch are truly blessed. Ted Chittenden has refined my concept of "kidwatching," and Willa Spicer demonstrates what the term "teacher empowerment" can really mean; my thanks to them for being challenging colleagues. The comments and suggestions of the following reviewers are greatly appreciated: Ruthanne Atkinson, Edinboro University of Pennsylvania, Virginia R. Beidelman, The University of Texas at Tyler, and Laura Palka, Niagara University.

My thanks also go to Gail Keating for her kindness and her unfailing humor, to Sally Jaskold for her excellent editing, and to Alexandrina Wolf, the skillful production editor at Merrill. The voices of Richard Ward, Maralee Gorter, and Carolyn Kidder echoed throughout the first edition of this book and are heard in the revision as well. Finally, thanks to Dick Cole, as always.

Terry S. Salinger

CONTENTS

CHAPTER 6

Making Progress with Communication Skills   109

CHAPTER 7

Awareness of Print   131

CHAPTER 1

Understanding and Applying
Research on Literacy
Development

Views of how children learn to read and write have changed during the past twenty years, and many early childhood teachers have begun to adopt new approaches to supporting children's acquisition of literacy. Current views suggest that many children gain considerable knowledge about literacy long before they encounter formal reading or writing instruction. Youngsters seem to pursue information about literacy as part of their normal development, a natural "next step" after learning oral language. Almost from infancy, children are surrounded by written communication, even if their own parents do not read or write much themselves. They see billboards, signs, logos, package labels, mail, newspapers, and scores of other examples of print; gradually, they piece together a rudimentary understanding of how print functions and why it is used. In many ways, learning about literacy is an extension of children's play and free-spirited investigations of their world.

Children's own learning—their accumulated knowledge—becomes the core upon which teachers build as they support children's continued curiosity about and investigations of reading and writing. The instructional approach based on this core stresses that all language processes are related and mutually reinforcing; it builds on children's curiosity about communication systems and their need to make sense of the world around them. The premises of this approach—that children learn much about literacy on their own and are motivated to master *literate behavior*—underlie the discussions in this book. A brief look at the history of literacy research and instruction during this century will place this view and the recommended approach in perspective.

HISTORY OF LITERACY INSTRUCTION

The history of literacy instruction is a story of twos: two theoretical points of view, two approaches to instruction, and two distinct literacy behaviors recently brought together.

Two Theories

The two theories on reading instruction became most pronounced around 1925 and represented opposing attitudes that are still voiced today (Smith, 1965).

One theory maintained that children gain reading ability by repeated practice of sequential skills through lessons that have been *carefully planned and structured by adults.* By 1925, complete basal reader series or instructional packages were widely used. Tracy Kidder (1989), a writer who studied life in one classroom for a year, captured much of the essence of basal readers in the following description of the classroom he observed:

> [The basals] were more than reading books. They were mountains of equipment, big charts for teaching what was called "skills lessons," and big metal

frames to hold these charts erect, and workbooks for the children to practice those skills, and readers full of articles and stories that did not fairly represent the best of children's literature, and for each grade level, a fat teacher's manual that went so far as to print out in boldface type the very words . . . any . . . teacher anywhere should say to her pupils so as to *make* them learn to read (p. 29, Kidder's italics).

Some form of the basal approach still dominates many elementary classrooms because basals are well organized and easy to use. The emphasis in this approach is on *teaching a collection of skills that together amount to reading.*

The second theory maintained that the *search for meaning* dominates reading and that children should be taught with meaningful material. As in oral language acquisition, children are curious about communication and seek meaning from literacy contexts. The children's own knowledge base allows them to begin to understand what they read; this understanding is strengthened by experiences with topics that interest them or that they want to learn about (Edelsky, Altwerger, & Flores, 1991; Shannon, 1989; Smith, 1965). Early in this century, proponents of progressive education had children dictate "experience" stories for teacher transcription. These stories became children's personal reading texts.

This second theoretical perspective has continued to be refined and expanded. Many educators now accept the premise that reading involves an active process of constructing meaning from text (see Goodman, 1990). According to this view, readers bring a certain knowledge base to the text, to which is added the meaning found in the text itself. Readers draw upon many different kinds of knowledge: personal experiences, prior reading, vocabulary, grammar, the structure of different kinds of texts, and the strategies needed to read efficiently. These sources of knowledge help readers translate printed words, anticipate what the text will say, and monitor whether their construction of meaning is making sense. Reading is also influenced by context and purpose; for example, reading at home for pleasure is different from reading in school as a learning exercise.

Writing is also a process of constructing meaning by orchestrating many aspects of text. What is constructed must make sense to the writer, but the writer must also consider the extent to which his or her readers will be able to access the meaning that is intended.

Two Instructional Approaches

Two approaches to the teaching of reading have been dominant in the current century: the sight-word, or whole-word, approach and phonics instruction. The **sight-word approach** begins with presenting the visual representation of whole words so that children develop a "sight vocabulary" enabling them to read simple material almost from the beginning of instruction.

Essentially, children acquire a visual memory for words, from which they generalize letter–sound correspondences. Gradually, their skills for analyzing words increase and they can figure out unfamiliar words on their own.

Phonics instruction stresses the importance of teaching letter–sound correspondences so that children can "sound out" words as they begin to read. Some phonics programs recommend that first graders learn sounds in isolation from words, so that they make automatic connections between letters and their sounds. This is usually considered inappropriate, however, because it is not the individual sounds that work together with other sounds to produce words we can recognize (Adams, 1991). In some of the more rigid programs, no sight words are introduced until most sounds have been mastered, so young learners gain very little experience with or pleasure from actual reading activities. In many phonics programs, motivation can lag before children's usable storehouse of phonics rules is large enough to allow them to read independently.

Both sight-word and phonics approaches depend primarily on commercial materials. Teachers follow directions in a manual or guidebook and sequence instruction, practice, and children's activities with reading according to predetermined schedules. The quest for meaning is subordinated to the accumulation of skills and to lockstep progress through prescribed materials.

Two Processes: Which Comes First?

Reading and writing make up another set of two. Until recently, these were treated as virtually unrelated processes. Children were supposed to learn to read well before being expected to write. Currently, researchers stress that the two behaviors must be considered part of a developmental continuum—children learn first to communicate with gestures, then with oral language, and finally with print. This end point of the continuum involves communication with print by means of both writing and reading, either of which may develop first. Children construct meaning *with their own print* as they write, and they construct meaning *from others' print* as they read. Combining reading and writing instructionally in early childhood acknowledges this continuum and capitalizes on children's early explorations of literacy.

The integration of reading and writing, along with emphasis on listening and speaking, constitutes a particular approach to beginning literacy instruction.

DIFFERENT VIEWS OF CHILDREN'S LEARNING: CURRENT RESEARCH

During the past century, some research has been guided by specific questions and governed by precise research procedures, whereas other efforts have been more open-ended (Kamil, 1984). Methods for open-ended research allow investigators to look carefully at what children do, to make inferences about what children are thinking and how they are motivated, to make sense of the "products" that children produce (such as recordings of oral reading), and to systematically analyze what they, the researchers, have seen. Such research is grounded on an understanding that classrooms are complex, dynamic places and that students are individuals who approach learning in their own distinct ways. Both methods have value, but open-ended research has been most influential in reshaping views about how children acquire literacy.

Researchers reevaluating the traditional view of the way children master literacy have focused on what children discover about language and how they develop and test language rules. Recently, the research community has expanded to include more and more classroom teachers, who pose questions and raise points of inquiry about their teaching situation. Teacher-researchers use the results of their investigations both to further their own knowledge and to improve conditions for their students' learning (Goswami & Stillman, 1987; Olson, 1990; Patterson, Santa, Short, & Smith, 1993). Bissex (1987) suggested that "a teacher researcher may start out not with a hypothesis to test, but a wondering to pursue" (p. 3). Often, teams of elementary schoolteachers and university professors work in collaboration to research topics of mutual interest.

Kidwatching

Common to most of the recent research is a technique that has been called *kidwatching* (Goodman, 1985). **Kidwatching** means observing children to see how they go about the process of learning. It involves listening carefully to children's words, analyzing their explanations and frustrations, and trying to identify and understand their logic. Kidwatching can be especially productive in environments where students are encouraged to investigate objects and ideas.

Kidwatching requires respect for the cognitive efforts children bring to their self-motivated investigation of reading and writing. Researchers often have to infer or to make educated guesses about why children perform specific acts, make specific statements, or ask specific questions. From analysis of observations of many children, often during extended periods of time, patterns of behavior emerge to substantiate these inferences. Of course, confident teachers engage in similar behavior all the time, without realizing that they are conducting their own classroom-based research.

The importance of teachers as researchers is discussed more fully in the next chapter, and chapters 2 and 3 elaborate on the importance of kidwatching for the classroom teacher. Many of the examples cited in this book present the voices of teacher-researchers who have talked and written about their early childhood classes.

The following is a summary of one year of my own kidwatching; Figure 1.1 shows written work from the fascinating child whom I watched.

An Example of Kidwatching: One Year with David.   David entered my combined first- and second-grade classroom at the beginning of my fifth year of teaching. I had taught his older brother the previous year, and I knew and respected his family. David's brother had been a model student: well behaved, motivated, very creative, and self-confident. David, the mother told me, was not the same; in fact, he was virtually opposite to his sibling except in regards to a high intelligence and a sense of belonging to a warm, supportive family. The first thing I noticed about David, besides his booming voice and wiry movements, was that many of the other children who had been in kindergarten with him were either afraid or in awe of his outrageous behavior. David seemed to recognize the power he had and probably was determined to gain control of our classroom as soon as possible.

David and I battled too much the first few weeks of school for me to watch him extensively. He tried to terrorize the children through noise and aggression, and I fought back the dreaded words "Why can't you be like your brother?" The best way to keep him under control was to keep him close to me, and he became my shadow. David held my hand, sat next to me, and even stayed in and ate lunch with me from time to time. Rather than resenting this attention, the other children seemed to realize that they were being protected. David especially liked to be near me during storytime so that he could see the pictures and print close up.

David refused to do much of the independent classroom work, so he stayed close by during all small-group instruction. My rationale was that he would learn through repeated exposure to the material and that he would not be on the loose to bother other children. As I finally was able to begin to watch this fascinating child, I noticed his intense interest in whatever I and the children said and did. Because the class had both first- and second-grade children, David was bombarded with instruction, but he followed along with all the lessons, contributed to story dictation, and even began to volunteer answers to questions. The twinkle in his eye as I handed him a book to "look at" was heartening. He was clearly very interested in "real" reading instruction.

After about a month, David began to write notes for me. He "delivered" his first note by crumpling it into a ball and hurling it, baseball like, onto my desk. I can't remember what the note said, and I didn't keep that first effort. But I do remember being amazed at the clarity of what he wrote. David had used "invented spelling," a powerful behavior common to young children, and although the spelling was not standard, it did approximate the letter–sound correspondences of traditional English. Clearly, David was

Figure 1.1
David frequently annotated his drawings and wrote many letters to communicate his ideas to me. (Not all of his letters to me were as complimentary as this one!)

learning and was trying to show me his progress. I was impressed and vowed to watch his literacy behaviors more closely.

David obliged my interest by writing profusely. He continued to sit close to me through all reading and language arts instruction, participating when he wished and doing an increasing amount of independent seat work, silent reading, and writing. Throughout the year, he loudly maintained that he "couldn't read," but frequently he curled up in the library corner "just looking at books." On the test at year's end, he scored considerably above grade level in reading.

My management of this child was untraditional and stemmed from a desire to not spend my time scolding and disciplining him. I still wish I had been able to incorporate him more successfully into the overall classroom activities, but I believe that he did gain in two ways. First, he learned to read and to write well. Second, he left first grade feeling good about himself as a user of written language, confident that he had academic skills as good as anyone else's. That success strengthened his self-concept enough that he seemed more willing to accommodate himself to the requirements of his second grade. (I left the school that year, sad that I would not be able to follow him further.)

David taught me many things, not the least of which was the value of looking very closely at children's behaviors. He reinforced an idea that was already emerging in my mind—that the environment rather than direct instruction will often "teach" children literacy skills. He also shared his progression in invented spelling with me, almost as though *he* wanted to tutor *me* to be more interested in this common early childhood behavior. By watching David and by studying the work he did for me, I discovered new dimensions of children's learning strategies and was influenced to alter my approaches to literacy instruction.

Important Findings

Several important findings have emerged from current research. Most important, what children learn about print production and use becomes part of the background knowledge they bring with them to school. Much of children's early learning occurs as part of **literacy events**—that is, situations in which young learners attend to some aspect of literacy or participate in some event that requires reading or writing. Literacy events may be planned, as when an adult suggests that a child write her own list to take to the grocery store. Alternately, literacy events may be spontaneous, as when a child queries a parent about the content and purpose of the grocery list the parent has prepared. Whether initiated and hence controlled by adults or children, literacy events strengthen children's conceptualization of literate behaviors (Cochran-Smith, 1984; Harste, Woodward, & Burke, 1984). Table 1.1 lists the kinds of activities classified as literacy events. Because they spring from the everyday fabric of children's lives, they are authentic and are highly meaningful to young learners.

Another important finding is that teachers in early childhood classes need to create **literate environments** for their students—that is, classrooms should be full of books and other print materials, and situations should invite students to read and write. Time must be allowed each day for children to talk among themselves about literacy so that their "own social concerns may come to infuse school literacy activities with social meaning" (Dyson, 1989, p. 13). How teachers accomplish this goal is explained throughout this book.

Furthermore, children learn best when learning experiences are personally meaningful. The term *authentic* is often used to describe the best kinds of activities to foster literacy skills. To understand this concept, one should think about how children learn oral language. In most cases, language learners

Table 1.1
Examples of Literacy Events

Parents involve children in literacy events when they do the following:

- Suggest that the children write a letter to send to a grandparent
- Encourage children to prepare and take their own grocery list to the supermarket
- Ask children to find a specific book in the bookcase (children will use the cover as a whole to recognize the book)
- Allow children to follow along in a recipe or instruction sheet as the parent does something
- Point out what a street or traffic sign says
- Ask a child to "read" a familiar sign or label

Teachers encourage literacy events when they do the following:

- Ask children what a street sign says during a neighborhood walk
- Provide appropriate printed material for children's learning centers (e.g., travel brochures to consult in a travel agency center)
- Ask children to "read along" on a parent letter and add their own comments
- Encourage children to pick out favorite books by "reading" the covers
- Ask children to read their beginning writing efforts and discuss the contents enthusiastically
- Listen to children retelling stories that have been read in class

Children initiate literacy events when they do the following:

- Ask what a sign or label says
- Point out that a word "begins like my name"
- Ask an adult to "read" a scribbled message
- Ask an adult to transcribe a story on a painting or drawing
- Scribble within the lines on junk mail or other forms as a kind of "writing"
- Experiment with reading or writing behaviors and ask for confirmation of what they are doing

---

learn by really using language, not by going through exercises in artificial language-like activities. Just as babies learn to talk by really talking, by really asking for more water (not practicing so they can then ask for more when they're older), children learn to read by really reading . . . and to write by really writing. . . . They don't learn by "practicing" reading and writing. Nor do they have to wait to use written language until they have "mastered" the [necessary] skills. (Edelsky, Altwerger, & Flores, 1991, p. 16)

To illustrate, consider how two first graders followed through on writing assignments. The first account is of a girl who had been a user of written language since the age of three (Harste, Woodward, and Burke, 1984, pp. 183, 184). She was given the assignment of making a Thanksgiving "book" by copying and illustrating the following line:

When they got to America they found corn and saw unfriendly Indians.

The stated objective of the activity was to use "writing" to support reading by having children attend to print. According to Harste, Woodward, and Burke, the child perceived the objective as neat handwriting: "Because of the lined school paper [she] tried to be extra careful . . . concentrating on letter forms she got worse rather than better [and produced] a carefully done maze of crowded letters and words."

Learning to read involves independent work as well as collaboration with others. When young children share books, they freely swap literacy strategies. They explain to each other how they go about the task of making sense of text.

At home, the same day, the girl drew a snowman in a pilgrim's hat and wrote the following:

THE POGROMS HOD A LONG WOTH AND BOLT SNOW MON AND WON WAS A POGRAM MAN SNOW MON THEE END.
[The pilgrims had a long winter and built snowmen and one was a pilgrim snowman. The end.]

The child's writing a story at home affirmed that she had things to write about and the skills needed to express herself. Had her teacher wanted to structure the assignment to take full advantage of her first-grade students' emerging literacy skills, she would have invited the children to write an original sentence or two for their Thanksgiving books. This would have been a *structured literacy event*—the teacher and children could have discussed what they might write and draw and how the book might be bound together at completion. As children wrote and drew, the teacher could have circulated among them for individual conferences. She might have rewritten the children's sentences in conventional spelling or transcribed dictation from children who did not choose to write themselves. When children had finished, they might have been asked to read their stories and could have shown drawings to each other for yet another valuable sharing of literacy efforts.

The second instructional perspective is summarized from Salinger (1988). The child was a first grader in one of my former graduate students' classes. Although some of the children spoke Spanish at home and were just beginning to communicate easily in English, the teacher required all students to write in their logs on a daily basis and invited them to write stories regularly. In the weeks before Thanksgiving, she used English to tell stories and read books about the Pilgrims and Plymouth Colony as part of her social studies work. After teaching background information about the first Thanksgiving, she asked the students to write and draw appropriate pictures. One child, who had only begun to communicate fluently in English and had been writing in Spanish, wrote the following:

The May Flower salud and salud in to thay land it. sum indyns hulpt the pelgrems the men owse sher food. they pray to god they Love itsh uchu
[The Mayflower sailed and sailed until they landed. Some Indians helped the Pilgrims. The men always shared food. They pray to God. They love each other.]

The teacher had demonstrated respect for students as language users and welcomed their efforts. This child felt safe and valued in the classroom; he had something to say about Thanksgiving and took the risk of writing it in English.

In addition to providing a well-supplied, print-rich classroom and ample literacy events, teachers assist children in acquiring literacy through **modeling** and **scaffolding.** Teachers are models—they demonstrate how to do certain things, and they model values, appreciation, and attitudes toward literacy. Even in preschool classrooms, teachers who read and write in the children's presence and take obvious satisfaction from their own mastery of literacy demonstrate adult behaviors for young learners to emulate. Teachers who set aside specific times during each day to read to students and clearly value and enjoy this activity send the message that sharing books is fun, worthwhile, and meaningful.

The concept of scaffolding has its roots in the interaction between infants and their parents as the parents strive to establish some kind of "conversation" with preverbal offspring, perhaps using structured games such as peekaboo or "This Little Piggie" so that the child learns to participate. The term has become common in early childhood instruction, where it refers to teachers' attempts to provide a verbal framework, or scaffold, to help children understand processes they are attempting to master. As children gain skill and competence, teachers gradually remove the scaffolding so that children can function independently.

INSTRUCTIONAL IMPLICATIONS: EMERGENT LITERACY

For many years, early childhood literacy tools have consisted of commercial worksheets and workbooks (full of drills and practices) and "reading books" in which language is false and stilted. These are hardly meaningful to young learners, especially those who, from earlier experiences, are accustomed to real children's literature. Dependence on such material has reflected the so-called prime myth in reading, which is that "instruction should consist exclusively of teaching phonics, vocabulary, and grammar . . . [even though] there is little evidence that children learn their working vocabularies from reading exercises." Reading should be "a way into worlds unheard of and undreamed, the worlds of Maurice Sendak and Dr. Seuss, of Snow White and E.B. White, even of the comics and the television advertisements" (Bruner, 1984, p. 194).

It is fortunate that many teachers now reject the traditional approach and the myth that it reflects. However, another myth persists in many schools: the importance of presenting activities that are supposed to teach "reading readiness."

The term *readiness* has diverse definitions and uses, often representing a "recurring theoretical and practical tug between two primary concepts: readiness to learn and readiness for school" (Kagan, 1990, 1992, p. 48). *Readiness to learn* connotes a point in time (differing from child to child) when children become "ready" for formal reading instruction (Clay, 1979). Inherent in this definition are the ideas of a developmental sequence and an accumulation of necessary skills and concepts. The definition does not designate a specific age by which children must be declared "ready" for literacy instruction but instead leaves room for individual developmental patterns and timetables.

Researchers have found that the long-held assumption that children need to be able to read before they can start to write is simply not true. Even very young children will often begin to write independently and enthusiastically. The children's writing shown in this book has been collected from classrooms where the children were expected to write each day.

Readiness for school is most often equated with readiness for reading. Teachers in kindergarten and first grade often speak of "teaching readiness," meaning that they present concepts and skills deemed necessary for beginning reading and reinforce their instruction with activities and worksheets emphasizing such ideas as directionality, sameness and difference, whole–part relationships, left and right, and so forth. This type of reading readiness curriculum suggests that teachers can influence children's literacy acquisition, which is indeed true. However, this conceptualization of reading readiness and readiness activities is flawed.

Current research on literacy acquisition points to the need to broaden the concept of readiness to reflect the entire continuum of language growth. An updated concept of readiness would stress that children can take command of much of their own literacy learning because they want to understand and use varied forms of communication; it would view literacy acquisition as a natural progression in learning the communicative processes.

New Terms

The term **emergent literacy** acknowledges the importance of children's attention to the varied uses of print in the environment. It emphasizes the continuum of language growth from oral language through mastery of reading and writing and focuses on what children themselves do to become literate. Children progress at their own pace through specific developmental sequences as they form, test, and refine their ideas about the world. Testing ideas about producing and reading print is part of this process.

The second term refers to what teachers can do to support emergent literacy. Instead of the traditional concept of readiness, teachers might think of Lev Vygotsky's **zone of proximal development**. Vygotsky (1962) used this term to describe the "discrepancy between a child's actual mental age and the level he reaches in solving problems with assistance. . . . What the child can do in cooperation today, he can do alone tomorrow. Therefore, the only good kind of instruction is that which must be aimed not so much at the ripe as at the ripening function" (pp. 103–104).

Emergent literacy is indeed a "ripening function." Bombarded by print and curious about how it works, young children seem to develop their own readiness curriculum. Their questions and experiments attest to their search for "cooperation today" so that they can solve problems "alone tomorrow." This suggests that children are nourished by their surroundings and in many ways "grow into the intellectual life around them and are stimulated by it" (Kagan, 1992, p. 49).

In terms of instruction, the zone of proximal development refers to the **appropriate teaching point.** This point represents the period during which children are tottering on the brink of understanding, when they are wrestling with new ideas or expansions of existing ideas. Instruction at this point supports children's efforts to make sense of what they are learning—to take ownership of new concepts and skills in purposeful ways. Instruction does not push children; instead, it responds to their attempts to construct meaning as they merge abstractions and practical skills. Sensitive, responsive teachers lead children to figure out the next step, idea, procedure, or concept necessary for new understanding, and they support children in assimilating new knowledge into existing schema.

Vygotsky (1978) also stressed the *social* dimensions of learning. He maintained that social connections—talking to and interacting with others—form the basis for the development of higher cognitive learning. This means that knowledge is socially constructed as learners engage in meaningful, authentic tasks (Englert & Palinscar, 1991; Palinscar & Klenk, 1992). The effectiveness of literacy events shared by young children and skilled literacy users demonstrates the power of social learning: the child asks, observes, talks with, and listens to someone who is demonstrating what literate people do. Social interaction helps the child construct an ever-expanding understanding of how reading and writing work.

Appropriate classroom work builds on what children know, and today's children know tremendous amounts about writing and reading. Instruction at the appropriate teaching point balances planned, formal lessons with spontaneous responses to difficulties children encounter in solving literacy puzzles. Teachers capitalize on literacy events and avoid instruction that would encourage rote memorization or employ unauthentic literacy activities, even though, as Vygotsky (1962) cautioned, such teaching often seems to produce more immediate "results." Teachers recognize that a "highly structured instructional system that focuses on mastery of one rule or skill before another loses sight of the complexity of learning written language. It oversimplifies what children really do learn and focuses some insecure children on insignificant and often erroneous principles about learning" (Goodman, 1984, p. 109).

Of course, accepting these ideas about readiness and literacy learning in general places more responsibility on teachers than traditional approaches ever did. In some ways, it places the burden of readiness on teachers and schools. Teachers must make their classrooms welcoming and inviting to children and supportive of them. Instruction must acknowledge and build upon whatever children bring to the learning environment. Rather than focus on whether children are ready for school, we must make sure that *schools are ready for all children*, no matter what their language background, economic status, or preschool experiences might be.

SUMMARY

Current research findings on literacy instruction should strike a chord of liberation in the hearts and minds of creative, caring teachers. Accepting that most children are interested in literacy and enter school with ideas about reading and writing already formed, teachers need not lock themselves and their students into predetermined curricula that may be appropriate for only a few children in each class. Instead, teachers can build on children's inclination to form hypotheses about literacy behaviors, test them through their own experimentations, and use these ideas as the base for refining reading and writing skills.

Children realize a lot about the way written language functions, but understanding will vary from child to child. If instruction is to be meaningful, teachers must assess how much each child knows and teach to that knowledge base. Kidwatching helps here. Teachers must trust that the real impetus for literacy learning lies in children's interest in communicating in an "adult" fashion and their need to do so; it does not lie in methodological considerations like basal reader series, workbooks, or ditto masters. Early childhood teachers who respond to children's needs and interests and help them test and refine their ideas about literacy contribute to children's natural progression in positive, supportive ways.

QUESTIONS AND TASKS FOR INDEPENDENT OR COLLABORATIVE WORK[1]

1. Be sure that you can define each of these terms:

   - sight-word, or whole-word, approach (draw on what you know already)
   - phonics instruction (draw on what you know already)
   - kidwatching
   - literacy events
   - literate environments
   - modeling (as a teacher behavior)
   - scaffolding (as a teacher behavior)
   - zone of proximal development
   - emergent literacy
   - appropriate teaching point

2. Begin a journal in which you record ideas, thoughts, and observations about literacy instruction. Record responses to any questions or tasks found at the ends of chapters; also record responses to any material listed in appendix A that you may read. Keep the journal as a record of your own emerging sense of early childhood literacy learning and of ideas you may want to try in your own classroom.

3. Develop a detailed definition of *kidwatching*. List the characteristics you think an adult should have to be a genuine kidwatcher. After you have done so, compare your definition and list with those of a peer. Revise your ideas as needed.

4. Visit an early childhood class (in later chapters you will be asked to make additional visits). You may want to start a section in your journal to record your observations. Observe and interview the teachers; determine the extent to which kidwatching is common and cite examples of kidwatching that you observe or that the teachers mention. What do the teachers do to help children refine their literacy skills? What more could they do?

5. Begin to read one of the books suggested in appendix A. Respond to it in your journal.

---

[1] Some questions and tasks at the end of each chapter are designed for students to complete independently, whereas others should be done in collaboration with other fellow students. Whenever possible, collaborative questions and tasks should be discussed in class so that students can benefit from the perceptions and experiences of others.

Classrooms for Literacy Growth

What are the characteristics of a teacher who can help young children reach their fullest potential in literacy learning? A graduate student who wrote the following essay imagined his first day of teaching:

Once upon a time, there was a brand new teacher for the kindergarten. He had just finished school and was ready to try some new ideas about working with children. His classroom had two neatly done bulletin boards up on the wall. One was entitled "All Words Are Made of . . . " and had letters with velcro backs on a felt board so that children could spell words on the board. The other board was "Numbers Are. . . . " In the play area, cartons containing specific items were stacked and labeled in the corner. As far as labeling goes, the objects in the room were all labeled. Labels with students' names were even neatly taped to the desks. The reading area was a circle. An easel stood next to the teacher's chair for the big books and other instructional charts the teacher had prepared. Plus, there were three shelves of books for the students to enjoy by themselves or with the teacher. Everything in the classroom could motivate the children to tell stories, from the blocks in the play area to the picture books in the class library. . . .

This new teacher was aware that children know that the spoken word is a useful form of communication and that children need to know writing and reading are important extensions of communications. . . . He dreams of the wonderful involvement in the reading group. He will begin with the books he has carefully selected for his classroom—wordless picture books, picture books, caption books, and big books, all of which can stimulate writing. . . .

The teacher is prepared to take children's dictation, to help them write their own books, and to have each child begin a "word bank" of personal sight words. When children dictate a story, the teacher will write it down on a big tablet. The teacher will use the children's investigative abilities by asking, "I don't know how to spell that word, do you think you can find it in your word bank for me?" After the story has been written, the students will color pictures to illustrate it. All of this writing is done so the children will realize the importance of the written words. . . . After each art project, the students will be encouraged to write a message. Even if the story doesn't look like traditional script, it will be ok, and the children will be asked to read what they have written.

Thinking back to his field experiences, this teacher remembered that children seemed to enjoy learning if it was a game. He [was] determined to let the children play with language as much as possible so that they would explore and find out about reading and writing themselves. He also remembered how valuable talk was to young children and decided to encourage peer teaching and conversations as much as possible. He wanted his classroom to be full of language—and not just his own.

All of a sudden, the first bell of the first day of his first class rang. Brought back to the real world by the loud noise, the new teacher opened the door and greeted his 15 new students with a smile and "Good morning."

The rest of this chapter discusses planning and structuring the classroom to create a supportive environment for learning to read and write. The basic model is of a literacy (reading/writing) workshop. To implement a workshop effectively, teachers must consciously assume the three roles discussed next.

TEACHERS AS KIDWATCHERS, DECISION MAKERS, AND RESEARCHERS

The essay in the previous section presents a new teacher's theoretical stance, enthusiasm, and values. It also exemplifies the three complex roles that all teachers should play: kidwatcher, decision maker, and researcher.

Kidwatchers

As suggested in chapter 1, kidwatching involves observing children's work, behavior, affect, and accomplishments. **Kidwatchers** constantly take in information, collate it with what they already know, evaluate its importance, and make decisions about children and instruction. As they observe, teachers "need the patience to stand back and watch and listen, and trust that in response to [their] patience, children will in fact reveal . . . what they know, what they are struggling with, and what they want to learn next" (Siu-Runyan, 1991, p. 102). Kidwatching results in rich, deep understandings of individuals and groups of children. It allows teachers to align direct instruction, classroom activities, pacing, and overall curriculum with students' needs.

Decision Makers

James Britton (1987), a noted British scholar who has observed many teachers, stated that "in the course of interacting with individuals and classes, a teacher must make a hundred and one decisions in every session—off-the-cuff decisions that can only reliably come from their inner conviction" (p. 15). Teachers who think of themselves as **decision makers** begin each school year—not just their first year of teaching—by making decisions about the structure of their classroom, the activities they hope to offer students, and the curriculum. These decisions do not negate the existence of mandated curricula but instead reflect how teachers align their own styles, goals, and expectations with whatever guidelines they must follow.

In making decisions, teachers draw on their knowledge of reading and writing and of appropriate instructional methodology for helping students learn. Harste (1990) has suggested that teachers possess "a practical theory of literacy instruction—a theory developed from observation of how language is actually learned" (p. vi). Throughout the school year, teachers alter their decisions, changing instruction and ways of interacting with students and evaluating each decision against this practical theory. For example, teachers ask questions about the following issues in students' experiences:

- Readiness to participate in a literacy workshop
- Previous experiences with workshops and with literacy
- Expectations for school
- Independent work habits
- Levels of maturity and development
- Language development and language dominance (for second language learners)
- Home support for literacy learning
- Needs of mainstreamed students
- Personal problems that may sidetrack learning
- Interests that might be used to motivate learning

Also, teachers make decisions about the following:

- When and how to introduce the workshop approach
- The amount of choice students will have
- Pairings and groupings of students
- The balance between independent, small groups, and whole class time during each day
- The amount of direct instruction to be offered
- Adjustments to long- or short-term plans that become necessary through the year

Researchers

Britton also wrote that decision making "requires that every lesson should be for the teacher an inquiry, some further discovery, a *quiet form of research,* and that time to reflect, draw inferences, and plan further is essential" (1987, p. 15, emphasis added). This suggests that teachers should think of themselves as **researchers** who actively endeavor to find out about their students. Chapter 1 suggested that many teachers have adopted this stance.

Teacher-researchers pose questions about students, seek to answer them by investigating students' behavior, and adjust the classroom environment, their teaching methods, or instructional approach on the basis of their investigation. The questions that teacher-researchers pose often invite descriptions of student behavior and teacher practice. Hubbard and Power (1993) suggested that "often questions for research start with a feeling of tension. . . . Teacher researchers look for questions to research that can lead to a new vision of themselves as teachers and their students as learners. These questions often involve seeing their students in new ways" (p. 21).

Over time, teachers may record observations and reflections in case studies of one or more students or of the whole class. They may write short vignettes, such as the ones that are used throughout this book, to illustrate points about teaching and learning. Or, they may focus their attention on some problem in the classroom that they want to investigate in depth.

The role of early childhood teachers is multifaceted. In kidwatching, decision making, and researching, teachers display the "inner conviction" mentioned by Britton, a theoretical stance about literacy, an understanding of child development, and pedagogical expertise. Recognizing the nature of their role enables early childhood teachers to take on the complex tasks involved in providing young learners with a literacy workshop environment.

LITERACY WORKSHOPS

There is no single, definitive picture of the environment that supports a **literacy workshop,** and there are no exact directions for establishing such an approach in a classroom. But there are common philosophies, assumptions, and attitudes that underlie the approach (Weed, 1991). Of great importance is how "the teacher views and treats children. Trust, responsibility, support, and high expectations must be generously and genuinely present for all children" (Routman, 1989, p. 27).

Perhaps the most important aspect of a successful literacy workshop is that all activities included during workshop periods (and indeed during the entire school day) are **developmentally appropriate** (Bredekamp & Rosegrant, 1992). The following list summarizes guidelines for developmentally appropriate practice in early childhood literacy workshops as suggested by the National Association for the Education of Young Children (NAEYC):

1. Age-appropriateness: instruction and activities reflect what is known about how children learn and develop.
2. Appropriateness for individuals: instruction and activities accommodate the developmental levels and patterns, interests, and cultural background of *each* child in the class.
3. Reasonable expectations: teachers' expectations for all children are realistic and attainable; teachers recognize that children can attain knowledge and skills most easily at different times during the year.
4. Active learning: teachers recognize the power of children's own, active learning in their construction of knowledge.
5. Exploration and inquiry: teachers encourage children to explore their environment and to ask questions; the focus is on active construction of knowledge rather than on "right" answers.

6. Authentic contexts for learning: teachers provide meaningful, authentic situations for learning (rather than artificial means such as workbooks) to encourage children's development of conceptual understanding.
7. Choice: within a supportive environment, children are allowed to make choices about what they will do and about how they will use their time.
8. Socialization: social interactions among adults and children are encouraged.
9. Multiple goals: teachers establish goals in the social, emotional, cognitive, and physical domains and encourage children to develop positive feelings and dispositions toward learning.

Physical Concerns for a Workshop Approach

An early childhood classroom where reading and writing workshops take place may look and "feel" different from a more traditional classroom, even if the basic trappings, such as work tables and centers, are evident. One source of difference may be the arrangement of space to accommodate several different kinds of work. A "rug area" will be prominent in most classrooms; it is where teachers and students meet for stories, mini lessons, and general discussion and sharing. Weed (1991) described her classroom as follows:

> As you come into our classroom, you see desks in groups, shelves and dividers providing "corners," walls filled with student work, and charts of one kind or another. Though to some it may appear cluttered, there are reasons for all of this. The desks are in groups to encourage and provide the opportunity for conversation between kids. . . . The arrangement also provides quiet private areas for students to be, whether it's to work independently, with a partner or small group, or to just be alone. Our classroom is very small, so the "get away" corners are very important. Shelves which separate the areas contain all the materials children may need in their daily work. (pp. 84–85)

In establishing a workshop environment, teachers must help students understand that there are definite work areas in the room—places where they can work with others and places where they can work alone. Students must also understand the "traffic flow," noise level requirements, and dynamics of the room and their share of responsibility for keeping their classroom a lively yet orderly learning environment. Table 2.1 lists the basic areas of classrooms where literacy workshops are successful, along with suggested materials and supplies for students' learning. Figure 2.1 offers possible floor plans.

As Weed suggested, it is important to set aside areas for independent writing and reading—corners or centers where students can work privately and quietly. For many children, especially those who do not have much privacy or many

Table 2.1
Suggestions for a Literacy Workshop Environment

Use of Space in a Working Environment

Places for conferencing:
Needed because conferences should be held in relatively private places where normal conversational tones can be used
Possible locations:

- By the teacher's desk
- In a corner
- At a worktable away from other work areas
- In a hallway

Room for group work:
Needed because many groups, both large and small, will be working together during workshop time
Possible locations:

- Around tables in several parts of the room
- In learning centers or library corner
- In hallways

Room for private reading and writing:
Needed because students need time to work quietly by themselves
Possible locations:

- In corners of the room or library corner
- At a specially designated table
- In nooks and crannies created by file cabinets or bookcases

Room for storage:
Needed because many books, print material, and other supplies should be organized; students will produce many different kinds of work, including journals, papers, projects, and so forth
Possible locations:

- File cabinets
- Closets
- Bookcases and revolving book racks
- Students' desks or cubbies
- Bins for work folders or portfolios
- "In" and "Out" baskets

Room for display and reference:
Needed because students' work should be "published" for classmates to see; students benefit from prominently displayed references such as word lists, punctuation rules, and calendars
Possible locations:

- Bulletin boards
- Chalkboards
- Hanging from the ceiling

continued

Table 2.1, *continued*

Materials for an Early Childhood Classroom

Furniture
- Desks or tables and chairs for all children
- Teacher space, either at a desk or table to work privately with children
- Movable furniture to provide private and open spaces

Printed material
- Books of all types
- Magazines, catalogues, junk mail, and so forth
- Reference sources

Environmental print/display space
- Calendar
- Teacher- and student-produced charts
- Commercially produced charts (only if appropriate)
- Signs and labels designating areas of the classroom
- Notices to students and parents
- Many samples of students' work
- Artwork with dictation or written comments
- Letter charts and other graphic reference materials

Text production supplies
- Various kinds of paper and writing tools
- Staples, tape, and so forth for book binding
- Computer (not absolutely essential)
- Typewriter (a nice extra)
- Stamp pads and letters that can be physically manipulated
- Pocket charts that allow students to manipulate word cards and create sentences

Other supplies
- Interesting things to observe and write about
- Materials for experimentation that can be written about
- Art supplies
- Equipment for other content areas
- Easels to hold chart tablets, charts, big books, notices, and student work
- Tape recorders

Figure 2.1a

Floor Plans for Early Childhood Classrooms: Primary Self-contained Classroom

Source: T. Salinger. *Models of Literacy Instruction.* Columbus, Ohio: Merrill/Prentice Hall, 1993.

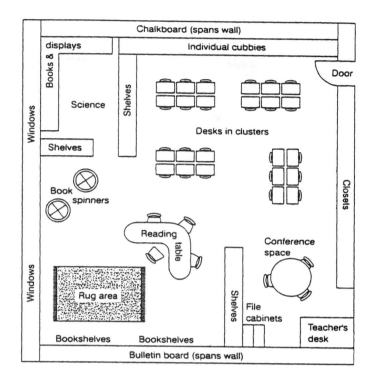

books at home, this time alone may be the only time they experience reading and writing as independent, pleasurable, free-time activities. Having this experience early can establish lifelong reading habits for them. Books such as *Evan's Corner* (Hill, 1991) can help children understand the importance of privacy.

The writing area may be as simple as a table labeled "Writing Center" and placed away from the traffic flow. Paper, pencils, other writing supplies, and reference materials (such as a dictionary) should all be readily available. If there is a classroom computer, it might be placed in the writing area for word processing.

Absolutely essential, even in preschool, is a library area with many books kept within easy reach. There also should be comfortable chairs for sitting and rugs and pillows for sprawling. The library should have a prominent place in the classroom and be attractive and inviting. Listening stations or centers where children can listen to a tape and follow along in a storybook are also beneficial. Commercial book-and-tape sets are available, and teachers can make their own tapes of children's favorites. Children benefit from the repetition of a read-along story, whether they are merely gaining familiarity with book handling or building their sight-word vocabularies.

Some teachers position a rocker or other comfortable chair in the library area as a special place for them to read to their class. It is unfortu-

Figure 2.1b
Floor Plans for Early Childhood Classrooms: Depart-
mentalized Language Arts
Classroom

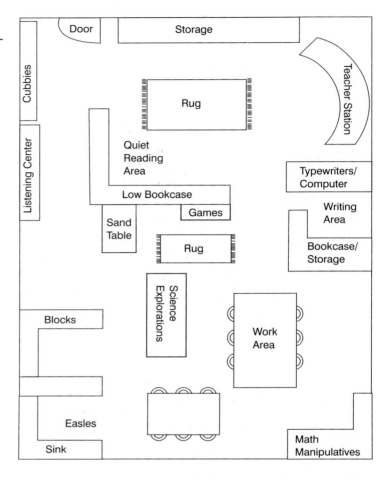

nate, however, that this limits the number of children who can gather around during storytime. The rug area often provides an alternate locale for book sharing.

The ideal classroom is a "total environment alive with print, displaying all its functions, from things as simple as signs and labels right through to literature" (Holdaway, 1979, p. 71). Such a classroom is full of words, many of which are charts and lists of words and phrases that have been developed jointly by the teacher and students. Children's writing and artwork should also be displayed as much as possible. Weed wrote, "Very little teacher-prepared and no store-bought materials cover the walls. I believe that kids' own work is more meaningful to them" (1991, p. 85).

The classroom library and displays of print reinforce children's understanding that print communicates meaning. Abundant writing supplies let children explore their emerging ideas about print production. By demonstrating that reading and writing are purposeful tasks and by allowing children to engage in these tasks at their own rates, teachers help children strengthen their emerging literacy skills.

Interpersonal Components

The acquisition of literacy is a social endeavor, so no matter how full of books and print their environment, young learners need contact with other literacy users—both adults and children. The arrangement of space in the classroom is one way by which teachers facilitate social interaction. Additionally, teachers must find time to talk about literacy with their students and must let them talk about reading and writing among themselves. As will be discussed throughout this book, conversations may take place during student-teacher conferences, peer conferences, small group meetings, or whole class instruction. Through such conversations, children expand their vocabularies to include words such as *read, write, word, story,* and so

Joy and enthusiasm for literacy are important goals for early childhood instruction. This child clearly feels comfortable sharing a draft of a story with his classmates and will probably incorporate their comments into his work as he continues writing.

forth—all the school-related terminology and concepts needed if they are to act on their belief that they can learn to read and write.

Another important interpersonal component of a successful workshop approach is a general recognition that students learn through trial and error and by taking risks. The workshop approach fosters this understanding by creating an atmosphere in which teacher-student relationships "are based on expertise and knowledge *to be shared or developed* rather than held by the authority and on the *desire to help individuals acquire or construct knowledge*. [Teachers in such] learning settings attempt to pass on rather than to retain their expertise" (Marshall, 1988, p. 14; italics in original). In such an **expert–novice relationship,** teachers assume the role of literacy experts, and students are the novices who learn from contact with the more experienced literacy user. Nonjudgmental feedback on errors and support for risk taking foster the novices' growth both academically and emotionally. Students are not afraid to make mistakes because they sense that the teacher recognizes that errors are essential for learning. Indeed, kidwatchers use students' mistakes diagnostically and fine-tune instruction accordingly.

Finally, it is essential that young learners feel competent about what they are doing. Commenting on a carefully structured, highly successful literacy workshop, Dyson (1989) wrote: "In the children's world, competence—know-how—was important, and part of being competent was knowing what they were supposed to do" (p. 45). The teacher in whose classroom Dyson conducted her research communicated high standards to the children and provided them with an environment in which they felt safe. Workshop routines were predictable, which "helps a child feel empowered and in control because she [or he] knows what comes next and what her [or his] choices will be" (Ford, 1993, p. 66).

GETTING STARTED WITH A LITERACY WORKSHOP APPROACH

Increasing numbers of early childhood programs are adopting a workshop approach, but teachers would be foolhardy to assume that children fall into this manner of working without some training and repeated explanations of expected behaviors. Here are some aspects to be considered in planning for literacy workshops:

- *External requirements:* These include grade, school, district, or state curriculum guides and mandated standardized tests that (however inappropriately) determine promotion.
- *Teacher expectations for curriculum:* Teachers draw upon their ideas about what students should bring to class and what they should learn in any grade.

- *Resources:* Included here are resources available in the classroom and others that must be donated, purchased, or "scrounged." As a minimum, a classroom should have a varied, multilevel library of books and other print materials, along with ample writing supplies.
- *Time:* A major advantage of the literacy workshop is that students can pursue their work in extended blocks of time—so long as such blocks are available. Teachers should allow one and a half to two hours for workshop activities. It is probably better to have a long workshop three times a week than a short one each day.
- *Teachers' own style, tolerances, and interests:* Teachers must ask themselves how much control they are willing to relinquish and how much noise and seeming confusion they will be able to tolerate.
- *Nature, needs, and interests of students:* Even more than in a traditional setting, workshop teachers must attend to individuals' personalities, needs, and interests and help students reach their maximum potential. The individual and small group interactions common in a workshop enable teachers to get to know their students well and to meet individuals' needs successfully.

Aspects of teachers' own styles and tolerances should not be overlooked in planning literacy workshops. Clearly, if teachers want to initiate this approach, they subscribe to a particular view of reading and writing and hold a specific stance toward instruction. But they may not realize the extent to which they must give up certain kinds of control as the class becomes centered on students as well as on literacy. Teachers' tendencies to be nurturing and supportive must be balanced by their desire for children to become independent learners. The pursuit of literacy by individuals and groups is the common thrust of the classroom. Teachers must be resource persons, guides, models, and managers, as well as nurturing providers of security for their young students.

Teachers in a literacy workshop try to keep track of each student's progress, but often the flurry of learning and activity that surrounds the children means that teachers will not have as clear-cut a notion of what each child is actually doing as in a class with similar work assigned to all students. Weed (1991) confessed, "Sometimes I get so caught up in the routines of each day that I lose the opportunity to reflect on why I do what I am doing" (p. 94).

Teachers in workshop environments have a holistic sense of how students are progressing in both their acquisition of skills and their attitudes toward literacy. This knowledge comes from mini lessons, daily check-ups, small group work, and individual conferences, all of which are discussed in this chapter. Little comments, often written on Post-it notes, help teachers keep track of patterns of student behavior during work time. Chapter 3 discusses how to put this all together.

Inherent in this approach is student collaboration, as groups discuss what they are doing, seek to solve problems together, and share ideas. Collaboration produces noise. Working with students to moderate the conversational levels and carefully structuring the physical arrangement of the room both help cut the noise level. To cite Weed (1991) again, "Yes, we do have rules about listening to the teacher or to anyone else who is speaking to the class. And yes, we work on using quiet voices so the noise level is not a distraction for students or teacher. These are life skills necessary within society, but opportunity to talk with each other is essential in striving for a happy medium. Self-discipline rather than teacher control is the goal" (p. 85).

PLANNING STUDENT ACTIVITIES

Literacy workshops do not just happen—careful, thoughtful planning on a daily basis as well as for the long term is essential. Teachers' knowledge base about literacy, child development, and pedagogy helps shape their expectations and informs their long-term plans for the school year. In developing long-term plans, teachers balance specific school, district, and state curriculum mandates with their informed understanding of the literacy behaviors, skills, experiences, and attitudes that are appropriate for students at a given level. They may plan for four or five specific thematic units (as discussed later in this chapter and in chapters 10 and 11), or they may set specific goals to be accomplished during the year. In either case, they are guided by the need for developmentally–appropriate activities, materials, experiences, and expectations.

Still, it is essential that teachers remain flexible in their expectations so that they can accommodate each young learner at his or her level. As suggested in chapter 1, teachers may ask themselves how ready students are to undertake the learning they, the teachers, have envisioned; but they must also ask how ready their classroom is for each student. Because teachers have thought through their plans and expectations (as did the teacher who wrote the essay at the beginning of the chapter), they are able to tailor activities during the initial weeks of school to help ease students into a new work orientation, new classmates, new patterns of interaction, and new sets of expectations for themselves and their teacher.

Teachers must, of course, develop plans for short periods of time as well. They approach instructional planning as a practical and ongoing exercise that parallels their emerging knowledge of the individuals in their classes. In a workshop, where students often work independently on self-selected tasks, planning can serve a dual role. Teachers try to guide students toward appropriate, purposeful activities and also use plans as a means of keeping track of students' activities and progress. Routman (1991) stressed that plans must be kept flexible; she illustrated her point with teachers who develop broad weekly plans but supplement them with comments written on Post-it notes. These small notes can be moved from day to day as children's work progresses. Routman quoted a first-grade teacher: "Our class projects and successful motivational activities stem from our daily shared reading experiences. The planning of these experiences often hinges upon the previous day's efforts, so that planning for the next session happens at the end of each day" (p. 431).

Activities for the Literacy Workshop

In a literacy workshop, students are encouraged to progress more or less at their own pace, with the teacher constantly monitoring to ensure that students are learning to their potential. Teachers offer instruction and support as needed to foster learning and to "nudge" students to each successive level. Teachers rely on their sense of what students should learn or their expectations of learning outcomes and on their records of how each student is proceeding (see chapter 3 for details about portfolios, checklists, and observations). Activities performed during literacy workshops include five kinds of behaviors: mini lessons, small group work, teacher–student conferences, sharing time for whole class meetings, and independent work.

Mini Lessons.   Many educators recommend **mini lessons** as the core of a workshop structure (Atwell, 1987; Routman, 1988, 1991). Mini lessons are brief instructional sessions, presented at the very start of a workshop period. At the beginning of the school year, teachers use the mini lesson time to explain and build consensus about classroom expectations and routines. Gradually, the mini lessons become more academic, although teachers still use the time to check on students' progress and clarify behavioral expectations.

During a mini lesson, which may be as brief as five minutes, teachers can check up on students by requesting a short statement about what they plan to do each day and recording this on a daily or weekly form (see appendix B). After checking up on students, teachers can alter plans and, as needed, determine who might be abusing the relative freedom of a workshop environment by not committing themselves to particular tasks. This overall summary of what students plan to do can be compared periodically with what they actually accomplish, and discrepancies can be attended to before serious problems develop. Teachers may have to help students evaluate their work realistically or learn to manage their time more effectively.

Teachers also use mini lessons to present a short, focused, single-topic lesson. Topics for mini lessons are suggested in Table 2.2.

Small Group Work.   Teachers in literacy workshops make good use of group work. The social nature of literacy learning is the major reason to

Table 2.2
Mini Lessons for a Literacy Workshop

Procedural Information and Rules about Life in the Classroom

When used: Primarily at the beginning of the year; throughout the year for reorientation

Purposes: To orient students to teacher's expectations, give students opportunities to voice their own expectations, and suggest consequences for violating expected behavior

Content: Procedural information

Advantage: Encourages students to take ownership of expectations for behavior

Instruction in Specific Skills and Strategies

When used: Throughout the year

Purpose: To present focused instruction on skills or strategies that teachers think students need to know

Content: Reading, writing, or thinking strategies that will be helpful to all students in their work; instruction in use of the library and reference materials; information that will help students build background knowledge; strategies or skills in which some students seem deficient and that other students can meaningfully review

Advantages: Creates a sense of instructional unity that fosters cooperation rather than competition; provides efficient means to introduce, review, and reteach skills and strategies

Instruction in Author's Craft or Literature Study

When used: Throughout the year

Purpose: To show students the craft of writing or to share a specific piece of literature

Content: Any of the techniques that writers use (e.g., methods to think of ideas or opening sentences; editing strategies; editing marks; use of specific conventions such as descriptive language, direct or indirect quotations, etc.; paragraphing; structure of different kinds of discourse; letter writing; and so forth); teachers may also use a piece of writing to demonstrate revision strategies; in short, the content will be determined by students' abilities and needs; there will be much overlap with mini lessons on skill and strategies, but the focus here is primarily on writing; a specific book or story may also be shared as a starting point for discussion

Advantages: Instruction is focused on one particular aspect of writing; students can put what they learn into practice immediately.

---

group students. Criteria for grouping students include immediate academic need, perceived readiness for instruction, and shared interests. Table 2.3 contrasts the different kinds of student groups that are used in a literacy workshop classroom.

As will be discussed in later chapters, small groups are the ideal environment for taking language experience dictation, sharing big books with students, and working with students who need extra help. Students frequently work independently in small groups, doing shared reading or writ-

Table 2.3
Student Groupings for a Literacy Workshop

Whole Class Interaction

Advantages: Develops a sense of community, cohesion, and sharing; provides efficient means for communicating procedural information and focused instruction, especially through mini lessons; allows teacher to check on progress of all students quickly

When used: At the beginning or possibly end of class

Small Group Interaction

Advantages: Allows students who share interests or needs to work together; builds collaboration and sharing of literacy knowledge; fosters use of oral language in literacy learning; helps students develop awareness of and sensitivity to multiple perspectives

When used: During workshop period; sometimes for small group conferences

Who: Students assigned by the teacher or self-selected; teacher may or may not participate

Activities: Group reading; conferring about writing; working on projects; and so forth

Pairs of Students Working as "Buddies"

Advantage: "Two heads are better than one" in solving literacy puzzles and completing work

When used: During workshop period

Who: Usually students who have elected to work together

Activities: Most often working on projects of mutual interest; conferring about writing; shared reading

Cross-Age Groupings

Advantages: Young learners receive special attention from older literacy users, who, in turn, enhance their own skills; participants become more enthusiastic about reading and writing

When used: During workshop or at any other time

Who: One or more young learners and a student from an upper grade or a visiting volunteer

Activities: Sharing books; going over rough drafts of stories; working on projects involving reading and writing

Teacher–Student One-on-One Interaction in Conferences

Advantages: Allows for quiet, intense interaction, often serving a diagnostic or assessment purpose; upon detecting a problem or misunderstanding, the teacher can provide immediately useful instruction to forestall additional problems or confusion

When used: Spur-of-the moment interchanges or planned reading or writing conferences

Students Working Alone

Advantage: Student can focus on his or her own interests or needs

When used: During workshop period

Who: Single students who have elected to work alone or who have been given assignments by the teacher

Activities: Possibly working on individual projects; reading or writing alone; preparing for conference with teacher

ing, working on thematic units, or completing some activity that extends their understanding of what they have read. The smallest possible grouping is two students working together, either on a shared project or engaging in "buddy reading."

Conferences.   Conferences between teachers and individual students provide opportunities for skill modeling and immediately useful, focused instruction. As teachers circulate around the room, they conduct impromptu conferences about students' independent reading and writing work. They may take dictation, help with a particularly puzzling writing task, discuss a book very briefly, suggest an additional book a student might like, and interact in countless other ways.

More formal conferences should be scheduled in advance, and students should expect to come to them prepared to read to the teacher or share a piece of writing-in-progress. If students continually come to conferences unprepared, they may temporarily lose their opportunity for this quiet, personal time with the teacher. While conferencing, teachers check up on a student's progress. They may uncover difficulties a student is having with literacy and then offer help for that particular difficulty, make suggestions for further growth, suggest reading or writing topics, and generally encourage the student to take risks to improve her or his skills. Conferences provide an important means for assessing student growth, as well as time to get to know students as individuals. Refer to Table 2.3 for more information on the different kinds of conferences that will be discussed throughout this book.

Sharing Time.   An important part of any literacy workshop is sharing time. Teachers may take dictation from the whole class about a shared experience, conduct a literacy-related discussion, read a book to the class, or allow students to share writing. When students share their own writing during this time, the work should be in a fairly advanced draft because the *primary* purpose of sharing in this forum is group enjoyment of what one student has composed. When all classes in an early childhood program are using the workshop approach, group sharing offers a time for visitors from other rooms to share their writing, a book they have enjoyed, or some other aspect of their literacy work. For example, students from first or second grade might be invited to share their stories with or read to a kindergarten class.

Students' Independent Work.   After the mini lesson and while the teacher works with individuals or small groups of students, other students work alone or with one or two classmates in an independent, self-directed way. Of course, they must understand what independent work is all about and must know specifically what they are supposed to do each day. Routman (1991) suggests giving students lists of required assignments, along with suggestions or "invitations" for other work that students might want to

Reading to children each day is an essential part of the early childhood literacy curriculum, but teachers often need to be tolerant as children squirm, fidget, and carry on their own conversations. Involving children in the story itself, with props or signs that repeat parts of the text, can often increase attention and make the experience even more enjoyable.

do. Students must understand that "assigned" means "required," and that their first responsibility is to complete these tasks. These activities must be challenging and truly worthwhile; they are not the same as the drill and practice "seat work" that so long dominated students' days in school. Appropriate kinds of assigned and invited work for preschool, kindergarten, and early grades are discussed in detail in chapters 8, 9, and 10.

INTEGRATED CURRICULUM IN EMERGENT LITERACY CLASSROOMS

Time spent in the literacy workshop is not the only time during the day when children use their emerging reading and writing skills. Strong early childhood teachers tie the curriculum areas together, with the use of reading and writing skills as a unifying thread. Opportunities for students to use their skills in authentic, meaningful ways flow easily from an **integrated curriculum** and **thematic units**.

The idea of integrating the curricular areas rather than thinking of them as distinct, separate subjects is based on a constructivist view of learning: no matter what the content area, learners draw skills and knowledge from many areas and unify them to construct new meaning. The integrated curriculum also recognizes that knowledge and skills in the real world are rarely fragmented. People use language arts skills, math skills, and knowledge from other content areas in integrated ways as they confront real-life problems.

Thematic units consist of activities clustered around an important central topic or "big idea"; a book list usually accompanies thematic units to spur students' reading. Thematic units often incorporate the use of the arts and other subject areas so that language arts are integrated with other subjects. Learning within areas such as social studies and science is promoted by thematic activities.

This approach sounds very productive, but unless the core of the unit is the teaching of big ideas and important concepts, the technique can lead to superficiality. Routman (1991) commented on a thematic unit on bears: "Teachers and students read lots of books about bears, write stories about bears, make bear cookies, draw bear pictures, and so on—all very entertaining and delightful. However, such a unit is not designed to develop important concepts and provide opportunities for transfer of skills" (pp. 277–278). The study of bears could more appropriately be part of a unit on animal adaptation, along with study of other animals that hibernate, bird migration, human adaptive behaviors, and other similar topics. Bears could also be included in a unit on animal habitation, with their construction of cozy dens highlighted.

For thematic units to be truly productive, they must be intellectually rich and challenging; topics must be relevant to students' lives and invite developmentally appropriate levels of inquiry and research. They must also help students understand relationships—the connections among facts and ideas that help them organize their knowledge and make increasingly sophisticated sense of their world. In planning thematic units, teachers should consider both the content they will ask students to explore and the learning that should result from students' work. Teachers can use a "web" approach to planning to ensure that relationships will be clearly illuminated. To develop a web for a thematic unit, teachers should brainstorm about all possible connections and interrelationships across the content to be studied, determining what aspects are most appropriate developmentally and logistically for the students in a class. The full range of topics and ideas that could be included in a thematic unit must be evaluated against students' knowledge and experience base, available resources, and time limitations. As students become accustomed to working on thematic units, they may be involved in determining the many "spokes" of a curriculum web. Figure 2.2 shows a content web and a learner outcome web for an early childhood thematic unit. Thematic units are discussed in more detail in chapters 10 and 11, along with information about how even young students can begin to master the research skills that make work in thematic units all the more challenging.

During literacy workshops, students often work on activities stemming from thematic units, but this is only one aspect of an integrated curriculum. Teachers, always watchful for opportunities to advance students' literacy skills, encourage them to write about their content learning as well as their own experiences. For example, in keeping with the standards of the National Council of Teachers of Mathematics, math learning can be enhanced by making up and solving "story problems" and talking about and graphing mathematical relationships. Science and social studies units not tied to larger thematic units provide similar opportunities for students to read, write, talk, and think about what they are studying. At an important beginning point in their lives as literacy users, students gain understanding that reading and writing provide valuable tools for enhancing their learning.

SUMMARY

Teaching is hard work, and teaching in the context of an early childhood literacy workshop can be especially taxing. But through careful planning, thoughtful organization, patience, and respect for students, teachers can successfully work toward such an approach. The real secret to success may reside in going slowly at first; progressing in measured, thoughtful steps; and ensuring that students understand and value their role in this classroom approach. Going slowly also allows teachers time to reflect on what they are doing and to make necessary adjustments to the environment and their instructional planning. They can become researchers, seeking the best ways to enhance their students' learning and to increase their own professional expertise and satisfaction.

QUESTIONS AND TASKS FOR INDEPENDENT OR COLLABORATIVE WORK

1. Be sure that you can define each of these terms:

    - kidwatcher
    - decision maker
    - researcher

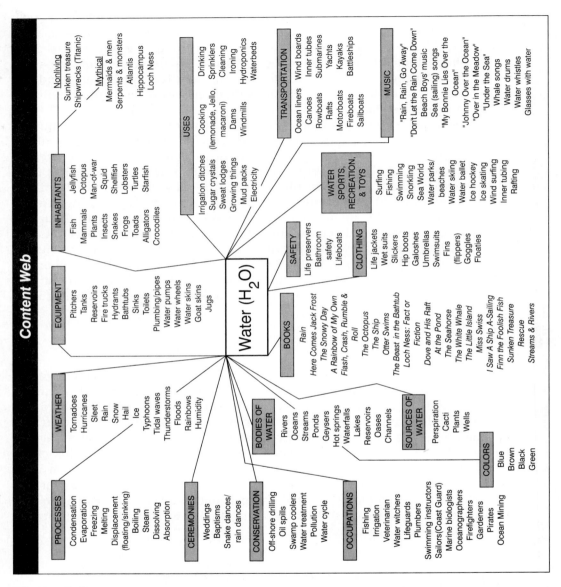

Figure 2.2
Webs for Thematic Lesson Planning

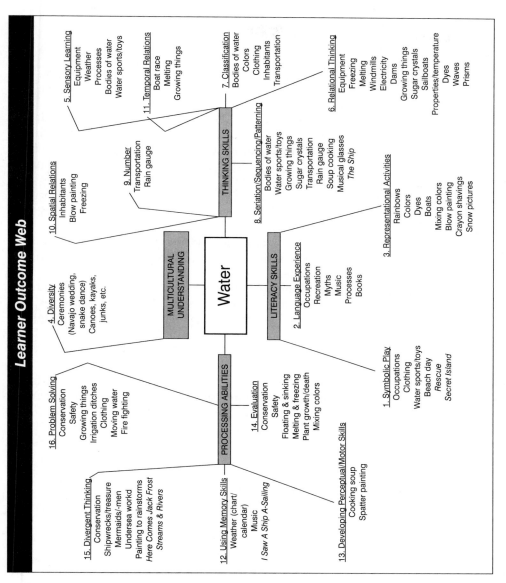

Learner Outcome Web

Water

THINKING SKILLS
MULTICULTURAL UNDERSTANDING
LITERACY SKILLS
PROCESSING ABILITIES

5. Sensory Learning
Equipment
Weather
Processes
Bodies of water
Water sports/toys

11. Temporal Relations
Boat race
Melting
Growing things

7. Classification
Bodies of water
Colors
Clothing
Inhabitants
Transportation

6. Relational Thinking
Equipment
Freezing
Melting
Windmills
Electricity
Dams
Growing things
Sugar crystals
Sailboats
Properties/temperature
Dyes
Waves
Prisms

10. Spatial Relations
Inhabitants
Blow painting
Freezing

9. Number
Transportation
Rain gauge

8. Seriation/Sequencing/Patterning
Bodies of water
Water sports/toys
Growing things
Sugar crystals
Transportation
Rain gauge
Soup cooking
Musical glasses
The Ship

3. Representational Activities
Rainbows
Colors
Dyes
Boats
Mixing colors
Blow painting
Crayon shavings
Snow pictures

4. Diversity
Ceremonies
(Navajo wedding,
snake dance)
Canoes, kayaks,
junks, etc.

2. Language Experience
Occupations
Recreation
Myths
Music
Processes
Books

16. Problem Solving
Conservation
Safety
Growing things
Irrigation ditches
Clothing
Moving water
Fire fighting

14. Evaluation
Conservation
Safety
Floating & sinking
Melting & freezing
Plant growth/death
Mixing colors

1. Symbolic Play
Occupations
Clothing
Water sports/toys
Beach day
Rescue
Secret Island

15. Divergent Thinking
Conservation
Shipwrecks/treasure
Mermaids/-men
Undersea workd
Painting to rainstorms
Here Comes Jack Frost
Streams & Rivers

12. Using Memory Skills
Weather (chart/
calendar)
Music
I Saw A Ship A-Sailing

13. Developing Perceptual/Motor Skills
Cooking soup
Spatter painting

Figure 2.2, *continued*

Reprinted from "Curriculum Webs: Weaving Connections from Children to Teachers," by S. Workman and M. C. Anziano, 1993, *Young Children* 48(2), pp. 5, 7. Copyright ©1993 by the National Association for the Education of Young Children. Used by permission.

- literacy workshop
- developmentally appropriate
- mini lesson
- expert–novice relationship
- integrated curriculum
- thematic units

2. Working with one partner or more, analyze the floor plans presented in Figure 2.1 (See pages 25 and 26). Discuss the advantages and disadvantages of various ways to arrange furniture and to provide space for storage, privacy, display, instruction, and conferencing. What changes would you suggest?

3. Observe at least one teacher who has developed a workshop approach in the classroom (even though he or she may not refer to it by this term). Look especially for evidence of the teacher's awareness of personal style and needs and for evidence of an expert–novice relationship between teachers and students. Decide how comfortable you yourself would feel in the classroom.

4. Draft a list of expectations for teachers and students at preschool, kindergarten, and early primary grade levels. Analyze the list for reasonableness in terms of child development and pedagogy. Compare your list with those of others in your class to develop a workable master list. In what ways do master lists differ at the different grade levels? What developmental strands can be identified?

5. Develop a definition of *teacher-researcher* based on your knowledge of schools and teachers' tasks. Update your definition as you think more about the teaching of literacy.

CHAPTER 3

Assessment of Literacy

I n recent years, considerable attention has been directed toward the issue of early childhood testing. Educators and researchers have been contending that too much testing is done, too many erroneous decisions about young learners are made because of test data, and too little credibility is afforded to classroom teachers as assessors of young children's learning. (See *Young Children,* July 1993; Meisels, 1987.)

Teachers must be given (and must take) a major share of responsibility for literacy assessment in early childhood classrooms, and children should be involved as well. Placing teachers and students at the center of the assessment process relegates external measures and tests to their proper functions.

THE DEBATE ABOUT ASSESSMENT

Although many forms of assessment have been carefully scrutinized, standardized testing has received the most vehement criticisms. The National Association for the Education of Young Children (NAEYC) has proposed several important principles about the use of such instruments. Most important, the NAEYC stresses that children's entry into school should be determined by their chronological age and legal rights, not by their scores on screening tests. As stressed in the previous chapters, schools must be ready for children, not the other way around. Additionally, decisions about promotion or placement in special or remedial education should be based on multiple sources of evidence, never on a single test score. Teachers' observations, their analysis of students' classroom work, and parents' comments must all be considered valid documentation, and this is especially true if such evidence seems to contradict a test score.

The arguments against testing young learners concern the tests themselves, the nature of children's learning, and the nature of young children themselves.[1] In general, the criticisms include the following:

1. Young children are frequently not good test takers. Tests and testing situations do not give them opportunities to show what they know and can do; hence, measurements of their abilities are often inaccurate.
2. A test score obtained by a young child may be highly influenced by the child's ability to sit quietly and communicate without shyness with strangers, behaviors that are highly atypical for many young children. Further, scores may be influenced by test takers' ability to make marks in the correct place in test booklets, attend to strange tasks, answer questions beyond their immediate experience, or perform other unfamiliar tasks on command.

---

[1] Many of these arguments are equally valid in discussions of testing and assessing the literacy progress of older students.

3. Young children grow and learn almost daily, so an appraisal of what they know and can do that is based on a single test may be highly inaccurate at a later point in time. Appraisals based on single measurements can lead to inappropriate labeling or diagnosing of young learners.
4. The range of achievement and development that can be considered "normal" is very wide for young children, and single measurements often do not accommodate the range.
5. There is no such thing as a culture-free test. Many children are thus disadvantaged by tests that do not accommodate language variations, cultural differences, diversity of background, and physical or academic disabilities.

An additional argument concerns teachers, who seem to be left out of the process of assessing young learners (Hills, 1993; Pearson & Valencia, 1987). Whether they realize it or not, most early childhood teachers are assessment experts. They can state, with high degrees of reliability and validity, how well their students are progressing toward mastery of literacy. By looking at a piece of a student's writing and listening to his or her reading, they can tell what the student knows and how to help the student continue to grow. In short, teachers can easily be the primary sources of assessment data about young children's literacy growth.

Good assessment strategies include the following characteristics:

1. Tasks that students are asked to perform are as close as possible to what they actually do during their regular school activities. The tasks are appropriate for students' developmental level.
2. Tasks allow students to show what they actually know and can do.
3. Assessments are not dependent upon students speaking in a particular way or being familiar with a large amount of extraneous or experiential information.
4. As much as possible, students are involved in determining how they will be assessed.
5. Teachers are involved in interpreting assessment results and play a major role in reporting results to all stakeholders.

The key to understanding these characteristics is in the distinction between testing and assessment. **Testing** involves using instruments to gather data about children's performance on single occasions. These are developed and scored by commercial testing companies or state agencies. **Assessment,** on the other hand, implies an ongoing process that results in richer, potentially more useful, and varied information about students. Although specific instruments or tasks may be used, the ultimate purpose of assessment is to present a cumulative portrait of learners' strengths, weaknesses, and capabilities that will enable teachers to help each student learn more efficiently.

In many ways, appropriate "instruments" and "tasks" already exist within functioning, literacy-rich early childhood classes. Chittenden (1991) has referred to these elements of classrooms as the "database for literacy assessment." This database, he says, is "potentially a broad one indeed." He adds:

> As teachers incorporate greater variety of activities and materials into their reading program, the base can become that much more solid. It is true, sometimes, that teachers worry that they won't know "where the children are" when they shift from a single-dimension basal program to a more variegated literature-based approach. But these same teachers, it seems to me, are now in a position to know much more about the child as a reader—interests, choices, strategies, skills—because the opportunities for assessment have multiplied. (p. 28)

When this "database" is used effectively, the majority of assessment procedures develop from inside the classroom, under the teacher's control, and with input from the students themselves. Assessment can actually reinforce sound teaching practices, and students can gain a sense of ownership in the evaluation process. In a way, students get to tell their own stories about their progress.

CLASSROOM-BASED ASSESSMENT

The merger of assessment and instruction fits perfectly with the concept of teachers as researchers and decision makers. **Classroom-based assessment** results in a focus on the processes students use rather than merely on the product of their learning. To make sense of processes, teachers (as kidwatchers) must observe students continuously and carefully analyze work samples to document these observations. These actions give teachers' assessments validity and emphasize that teachers are skilled decision makers who should be guiding the curriculum in their classrooms. Observation and analysis lead teachers to refine their instruction and the classroom environment to better meet students' needs and interests.

Many methods recommended as classroom-based alternatives to traditional assessment depend on the collection of various kinds of evidence to document what students have accomplished and are trying to do. This evidence may include "artifacts" of students' efforts in school, such as work samples selected by the students, pieces of work assigned by the teachers, audiotapes, drawings, and other records of accomplishments. Teachers' notes or records of observations, conferences, and interviews with students also count as valid evidence of student accomplishments. Evidence may result from routine class activities, as when a work sample is placed in an assessment portfolio, or it may be collected through more standardized means, such as oral reading samples from a predetermined set of books.

Keeping track of so much information may seem a monumental task—in truth, establishing a mechanism for alternative assessments takes an initial large commitment of time and energy (Salinger & Chittenden, 1994).

Good assessment methods are based in everyday classroom activities. As teachers work with students, they note areas of strengths and areas that need additional instruction.

The key is to think of a *system* and a *timetable*, a routinized method for *collecting, storing, evaluating, collating, and synthesizing* information about students' emerging literacy. This chapter will present ideas for developing both a system and a timetable. The order of discussion will reflect practical considerations: finding time for assessment; observing, interviewing, and conferencing with students; keeping running records and asking for story retellings; and creating portfolios.

FINDING TIME FOR ASSESSMENT

When teachers take on responsibility for student assessment, they must find the time to accomplish their goals. Thinking through an effective timetable is among the first steps teachers should take in establishing a classroom-based assessment program. The constraints of a school marking term or scheduled parent conferences will probably influence the timetable, but some definite period of time should be decided upon. A sample six-week evaluation/monitoring cycle is outlined in Table 3.1.

Within any given cycle, teachers will use three different levels of assessment: keeping track, checking up, and finding out (Chittenden, 1991). **Keeping track** is what teachers do all the time as they watch students, interpret behavior, and make notes about whom to nudge forward, whom to help on the spot, and who needs reteaching. Often, teachers carry this information in their heads, although it should be recorded briefly in some useful format as part of the overall assessment procedures (Lamme & Hysmith,

Table 3.1
Sequencing of Classroom-Based Assessment in Early Childhood Classes

This schedule is based on a six week cycle that can easily be modified according to teachers' needs or the evaluation period of a school district. To accomplish this kind of assessment successfully, teachers must balance instructional and assessment time by using some of the instructional interactions with students as part of the assessment cycle. This requires teachers to refine their kidwatching skills.

Week 1: Observations

- Observe students as they work.
- Interact with students informally, looking and listening specifically for students' understanding of what they are doing, their ability to talk to each other and to the teacher about their work, and their level of confidence and ease in their work.
- Hold impromptu conferences with students as they work.
- Throughout, make notes on observations, interpretations, and hunches, and later collate them for future use.

Weeks 2 and 3: Reading

- Hold conferences with individuals and small groups.
- Interview students about their reading, asking specific questions about students' work—for example, ask a series of questions about content or strategies students have used.
- Collect running records.

Weeks 4 and 5: Writing

- Eavesdrop as students write, listening for indications of the strategies they are using and their feelings about writing.
- Sit in on peer response groups or paired editing sessions to hear how students discuss the processes they have used and to determine their level of sophistication and understanding in thinking and talking about writing.
- Hold writing conferences with individual students.
- Collect writing samples, often asking students to discuss them in conferences or to annotate them with brief notes about their significance.

Week 6: Repeat Reading Procedures

- Concentrate again on reading, perhaps by focusing more intently on students identified as having problems.

At the conclusion of the cycle, teachers should have accumulated an immense amount of useful information with which to make informed decisions about future directions for instruction and about which to report to parents.

1991). Many teachers use Post-it notes for initial comments about students and later use these comments as they plan for students' future work.

The process of **checking up** on students is more structured and includes focused activities and procedures that result in accumulated documentation about students' progress. As teachers conference with students, look at their work, and listen to them read, they are checking up. As they do so, they gather much assessment data about each student.

Activities that allow teachers to keep track and check up on students are common within a strong emergent literacy program, where children consider reading and writing to be meaningful aspects of their school routines. To turn students' activities into sources of assessment data is not difficult if teachers begin to take control of classroom assessment practices. Teachers may have to become more organized and write down more notes about specific students' behaviors, but the benefits of achieving this organization are tremendous. Strategies for observing and for creating portfolio assessments, discussed later in the chapter, help teachers to organize effectively.

The final level of student assessment, **finding out,** involves interpretation of accumulated data. For this level of assessment, teachers may pose specific tasks or assign all students to complete a common activity to gather equivalent work samples from all class members. Teachers can also analyze existing documentation, such as their anecdotal notes about students or the contents of students' daily logs. The purpose at this level is for teachers to analyze, interpret, and often compare students' work against standards that specify what is usually accomplished by a particular developmental level. These standards are drawn from teachers' knowledge of the sequence of literacy development (an internalized and logical scope and sequence) and from knowledge of the needs, characteristics, strengths, and weaknesses of each individual child whose work is being evaluated.

Because the criteria for evaluation are derived from multiple sources, including teachers' knowledge about literacy acquisition and child development, this highest level of evaluation is more truly reflective of what students are accomplishing than any externally imposed testing program could ever be. Contextualized within the classroom, it gives a broad and meaningful portrait of students' achievements. Teachers need to be alert for the opportunities each day presents for assessing students' progress. As will be discussed next, teachers can gather assessment data as students work independently and in small groups and by posing specific tasks that reflect what students do as part of their routine reading and writing work.

OBSERVING, INTERVIEWING, AND CONFERENCING WITH STUDENTS

Because literacy learning should be a social endeavor, full of talk and discussion, the best means for assessing young children also involve verbal interaction. These methods situate assessment in real-life, authentic contexts and capture what goes on as literacy learners engage in purposeful reading and writing tasks.

When investigating specific questions, university-based and teacher researchers often select focal groups of children for close observation. In their role as assessment experts, teachers use a similar strategy. Depending on what they want to know, they direct their observations toward three focal groups: a single child; pairs or small groups of children; or the entire class. Teachers need to schedule times periodically to step back and observe students in all three groupings. Teachers might, for example, plan for all students to work independently or in small groups for fifteen minutes of workshop time twice a week. During that time, teachers can observe individuals or pairs of students; or they can walk around the room, taking notes as they look over children's shoulders, talk to individuals, or listen to conversations. Teachers seek specific kinds of information, not just a general sense of how students are functioning at a moment in time; and their notes are real assessment data. Teachers might want to see who is reading or writing independently, who seems to be doing the same things day after day, or who seems to work best in collaboration with a peer. As teachers observe, they form a record of what individual students or the class as a whole can do in a given situation. This behavior shows teachers as real kidwatchers and gives them data for their role as classroom decision makers. Reviewing the notes provides teachers insight into behaviors of individual students and into the dynamics of the entire class. Patterns of behavior emerge from this analysis—such patterns contribute to instructional planning, suggest ways to regroup students, and point to further inquiry about students' learning. From these observations may spring questions or concerns to guide ongoing teacher research.

Teachers may also conduct **interviews** with students. Again, teachers need to set aside a specific portion of time at regular intervals to conduct interviews (and conferences) without interruption. Interviews should be structured around a predetermined set of questions that will yield information about students' work, attitudes, and approaches to literacy. During an interview, teachers take notes about students' answers so that they can better meet students' needs. Sample interview questions are presented in appendix B.

One specialized interview is the sort recommended by Marie Clay (1979, 1985). Through these interviews, when used in their most formal and systematic way, teachers gather information concerning students' knowledge about books and other print material. Such interviews represent Clay's *Concepts about Print Test* (1979). Teachers use two small books, *Stones* and *Sand*, to check students' concepts about the directionality of words and letters, punctuation, inversion of print and pictures, and so forth. For example, some of the pictures and print are upside down. Students who can recognize this have advanced further toward initial mastery of reading than those who cannot see the difference.

The Concepts about Print is a standardized test, but teachers can gather similar information in a simplified form by following these steps:

1. Select a simple picture book with clear, straightforward illustrations. Keep it aside from the class library so that it is unfamiliar to students.
2. Present the book to a child and observe how he or she handles it:
    *   Is the book held upside down?
    *   Does the child open the book from the back or front?
    *   Does the child readily leaf through the book?
    *   Does the child seem to be differentiating between print and illustrations?
3. Ask the child to show you the part of the book that tells the story; probe if necessary to determine whether the child knows that the print conveys the gist of the story.
4. Ask the child to try to "read" the book to you and determine the extent to which he or she can make sense from the illustrations.

Observation of children performing these simple tasks gives teachers a preliminary indication of how familiar the students are with books and print. A child who seems confused by the tasks or the questions needs more opportunities to handle books and to share stories with more experienced literacy users.

Conferences give teachers opportunities to check up on their students by talking about reading and writing, often through discussions of something a student has read or a piece of writing the student is working on. In conferencing with students, the focus is on a literacy task or work sample, and teachers do not frame discussion with a predetermined set of questions. Needless to say, valuable assessment information can be obtained during conferences, and teachers should take care to include such data in records on students.

As part of their assessment procedures, teachers keep observational records, conduct focused interviews with students, and make notes and tallies about the specific independent or collaborative activities that engage students. Teachers may record information on checklists or observation forms or keep notes in a notebook, on cards, or on Post-it notes that can later be affixed in a more permanent fashion. A word of warning is necessary, however, if teachers plan to use checklists of any sort. The content of a checklist should parallel what actually happens in the classroom as much as possible, rather than merely reproducing a generic list of behavioral indicators of literacy growth. This means that teachers should ask themselves *what evidence* they want to see to indicate growth and *what specific kinds of behaviors* will be evidence of that growth. Often, teachers find that single statements of behaviors are not rich enough to describe what beginning literacy users do. Brief narrative records written by teachers in a kind of shorthand are often superior to simple checklists. Sample recording forms are presented in appendix B.

RUNNING RECORDS AND STORY RETELLINGS

Running records and story retellings are specific forms of verbal interaction that can turn a reading conference into an assessment opportunity (Clay, 1979; Glazer & Brown, 1993). A **running record** is labor intensive, as suggested by the outline presented Table 3.2, but it is invaluable for the breadth of information that it can provide. Running records are an example of a standardized task that all students can complete. They are developmentally appropriate because students read from books that are at their correct difficulty level. Usually, teachers keep a set of graded books separate from the classroom library to use for running records; in this way, the books are unfamiliar to the students so that no one has the advantage of already knowing a book when he or she reads it to the teacher. Teachers should set aside time to collect frequent running records as part of their routine assessment procedures. Running records make visible the strategies students use to guide their reading and provide real insight into how the students go about constructing meaning. As the teacher guides the student through reflection and self-report after reading, patterns of strengths and weaknesses, use or lack of strategies, and understandings and misconceptions about reading become apparent.

Story retellings give information about students' comprehension abilities. As suggested in Table 3.3, students should be asked to retell a story very soon after hearing or reading it. Teachers may prompt the retelling but should note when prompting is necessary. Some children may enjoy drawing their retelling or putting it in writing.

Running records and story retellings give teachers solid evidence about what students do and don't do during reading—in short, real assessment data that can have immediate use in instructional planning. Both of these strategies are examples of the "finding out" level of classroom-based assessment because teachers must analyze and interpret the data that result. Analyses of running records and retellings collected at several different times show students' development in terms of real behaviors. Teachers can see the growth of reading strategies and can also identify weaknesses before they become habitual. Such data are far more powerful than test scores could ever be.

CREATING STUDENT PORTFOLIOS

Portfolios are compilations of students' work samples and thoughts about their work, collected over a period of time to profile what and how students have learned. Different from a work folder, a portfolio can be a tool for assessing student growth—in effect, teachers and students analyze and reflect on what is included in each portfolio and on what the contents mean collectively. Many early childhood teachers now use a portfolio assessment

Table 3.2
Simplified Procedures for a Running Record

The Passage(s)

1. Select one passage or more for students to read; if there are more than one passage at the same level, students may be given a choice of what to read.
2. Determine the levels of the passages according to the vocabulary and concept loads and the extent to which prior knowledge is needed for comprehension.
3. Prepare a photocopy of the material for your use.

Initial Interview

Talk to the student about literacy use in general; establish rapport and gain insight into how the student thinks he or she should go about constructing meaning.

Oral Reading

1. Listen while the student reads the selection orally.
2. Either tape the reading for later coding or transcribe it as the child reads (easier to do with simple material).
3. Use relatively straightforward markings to note the following:
    *   Substitutions: record substitution above the word in text
    *   Omissions: circle words
    *   Repetitions: indicate with letter *R*; write additional word repetitions; use multiple check marks for multiple repetitions
    *   Insertions: mark with caret and write inserted word
    *   Corrections: indicate with letter *C*; underline the text that is corrected; write in student's original word(s) and circle

Retelling

1. Ask student to retell what he or she has read.
2. Aid student as needed:
    *   Unaided retelling, during which teacher may give support such as, "Good. What else?" but does not provide content
    *   Aided retelling, during which teacher responds to unfinished sentences as much as possible without providing what student should be saying
    *   Cued retelling, during which the teacher tells student that there is more to say about the reading and essentially encourages student to fill in gaps

Reflection

1. Ask students to reflect on reading, possibly by asking first, "How do you think your reading went? How was the retelling?"
2. Ask more specific questions about parts that went well and those that did not.
3. Return the book and ask students to locate specific words and parts of the story; an example would be to tell student that he left out a particular word and ask him to try to figure it out.

Analysis of Miscues and Follow-up

1. Later, analyze the miscues to see the extent to which students changed meanings, and the extent to which they showed strengths and weaknesses.
2. Plan additional instruction as indicated.

Table 3.3

Simplified Version of Story Retellings

Selection of Materials

1. Determine a sequence of books that are graduated in difficulty—that is, books should range from very easy to more difficult. Try to find books that the students will not have encountered in other settings.

2. In making the selection, evaluate traditional measures of difficulty such as number of words, vocabulary, and sentence length, but also think about the background experiences needed to construct meaning, the relationship between text and illustrations, the extent to which illustrations make the book easier to read, students' possible familiarity with the story type and text structure, and the overall attractiveness of the book for students.

3. Keep these books separate from the regular class library to use for assessment purposes.

Kinds of Retellings

1. Students may retell stories orally, as drawings, or in written form.

2. A combination of drawing and writing eases students toward more sophisticated methods of expressing themselves.

Levels of Learning

Very Young Learners

1. Read one of the books to the whole class or read it to a small group of four or five students.

2. Very soon after reading the book, engage the majority of the class in productive activities that they can perform independently or with supervision from someone other than the teacher. During this time, take students aside one by one and ask them to retell the story in their own words. Prompt them as needed by asking about the following:

   - The beginning of the story
   - The characters and setting
   - The plot or story line
   - The middle of the story
   - The conclusion

3. Make notations about the thoroughness and accuracy of students' responses, including the amount of prompting needed and the general fluency of the response. Assess the degree to which each student has comprehended the story, including personal references or affective comments.

system. In some cases, the portfolio is passed from teacher to teacher as a cumulative record of children's emergent literacy growth.

Several kinds of portfolios document literacy growth, differing in terms of their purpose and contents. If the purpose is to assist the classroom teacher in making decisions about students and reporting to parents, the contents should be rich and varied but not necessarily standardized. Students should have considerable choice in what goes into the portfolio so long as teachers are collecting enough information to guide their instruc-

Table 3.3, *continued*

4. If the story was read to the whole class, work with only four or five students because young learners will quickly forget what they have heard. Repeat the procedure on the next available day with another book, calling another small group of students from their activities.

5. If the story was read to a small group, gather retellings from those children and then repeat with subsequent small groups as needed.

Slightly More Advanced Students

1. Read one of the books to the whole class or to small groups.

2. Give students the option of drawing and dictating or drawing and writing about the beginning, middle, and end of the story they have heard. Folding a large piece of paper into thirds and labeling them for the story parts is often helpful for this activity.

3. Prompt students whose drawings/writings are not detailed enough with brief questions to jog memories; take dictation as needed.

4. Again evaluate for thoroughness, accuracy, fluency, and connections to self and affective comments.

Advanced Readers

1. Guide students who can read on their own toward the selection of books at a challenging but not frustrating level.

2. Have students write their retellings, still using story parts (beginning, middle, and end) as their guides. Encourage them to elaborate as much as they want.

3. Evaluate students for signs of thorough comprehension and extensions of the story to their own lives or to other stories they know.

Points to Look and Listen For

1. Accuracy of retelling

2. Elaboration with personal references or reference to other stories

3. Basic story elements, including setting, main characters, problem to be resolved, conclusion

4. Accurate sequencing of events

5. Identification of elements and events ("what the story is about"); this indicates sophisticated comprehension and may not be present in many retellings.

tional decisions and to inform parents. This kind of portfolio in all probability will go home with students at the end of the school year.

Another kind of portfolio is designed to showcase students' "best work." Teachers designate categories of work to be included and allow almost complete student choice in what is included. This form of portfolio is used most successfully with older children who have learned some level of objectivity in selecting work and who can reflect on why pieces are indeed their "best."

A third kind of portfolio is kept for school and district accountability purposes. Students and teachers have some latitude in selecting contents,

Much of children's daily work provides excellent, reliable assessment data. When classwork requires students to use their literacy skills in other content areas, teachers gain even richer understanding of students' learning. Written work completed in math, science, or social studies is often appropriate for a literacy portfolio.

but specific material must be included for each child to allow comparisons among students. This kind of portfolio often replaces a cumulative record folder and may even be used instead of test scores in making decisions about student placement. The development and use of an evaluation portfolio are discussed later in the chapter.

Teachers' decisions to keep portfolios of their students' work indicate certain assumptions. First, teachers know the difference between work folders and assessment portfolios; they know that criteria must be established and exercised in selecting what will go into portfolios. Next, teachers make clear statements that they have confidence in their own ability to evaluate their students' work and that they want to gather specific kinds of information to inform that process. Teachers also assert that they want to take the time to analyze and make sense of the varied artifacts of student work that can find their way into portfolios. Finally, when teachers pass portfolios on from grade to grade, they affirm that literacy acquisition is developmental—students' literacy growth can best be understood from an accumulation of data collected over time.

The South Brunswick Literacy Portfolio

Early childhood teachers in the South Brunswick, New Jersey, School District have developed an early literacy portfolio that travels with students from kindergarten through grade two. The development and introduction of the early literacy portfolio illustrate how teachers and administrators can work together to develop a common understanding of literacy acquisition and a common vision of how children should be assessed. The cover sheet of the actual portfolio, an accordion-pleated folder, is shown in Figure 3.1. Here are explanations of the contents of the portfolio:

1. Self Portraits—not analyzed in any way
2. Interview with Child—to gather perceptions about reading and writing and preferences for books

PORTFOLIO CONTENTS

Student's Name_____ School_____

Teacher's Name_____ Date of Entrance_____

	Pre K	Beg K	Mid K	End K	Beg 1	Mid 1	End 1	Beg 2	Mid 2	End 2
1. Self Portraits	*	*		*	*		*	*		*
2. Interview with Child		*			*			*		
3. Interview with the Parent	*	*			*			*		
4. Concept about Print Test		*		*						
5. Word Awareness Writing Activity (WAWA)			*	*	*	*	*		*	*
6. Sight Word List				*	*	*	*		*	*
7. Reading Sample				*	*	*		*	*	*
8. Writing Sample		*		*	*	*	*	*	*	*
9. Class Record			*			*			*	
10. Story Retelling	*	*	*	*	*	*	*	*	*	*
11. Optional Forms										
12. Higher Order Comprehension								*	*	*

* Asterisk indicates approximate time to enter an item in the portfolio.
  Teachers are expected to enter items when they need the data.
  Items should reflect current levels of literacy.

Figure 3.1
Cover Sheet for South Brunswick Portfolio Showing Collection Times

3. Interview with the Parent—to gather background information
4. Concepts about Print Test—see Clay (1979); see also earlier discussion of this test
5. Word Awareness Writing Activity (WAWA)—developed by teachers to assess extent to which children can apply knowledge of letter–sound correspondences in spelling thirteen regularly spelled words; see Gentry (1981)
6. Sight Word List—graduated according to grade level
7. Reading Sample—running record; see Table 3.2
8. Writing Sample—analyzed holistically
9. Class Record—summary comparison sheet
10. Story Retelling—see Table 3.3
11. Optional Forms—to record detailed extra data when children seem not to be progressing adequately; developed by teachers
12. Higher Order Comprehension—to assess more advanced comprehension than measured by retelling; developed by teachers

Specific benchmarks in the process of creating a portfolio are highlighted in Table 3.4 and will be discussed here.

Getting Started.   Deciding what will go into a portfolio can be perplexing, although the purpose of the portfolio will somewhat dictate the content. For example, if the portfolio will take the place of a cumulative record folder, as it does in South Brunswick, and is passed along to subsequent teachers, the required contents should be carefully determined so that the information communicates adequately about each student's literacy growth. Teachers will want to include specific kinds of information to supplement work samples and to provide a level of standardization for comparisons among students in a given class and indeed across schools that are using the portfolio for evaluation. In South Brunswick, the running records, retellings, writing samples, and some "testlike" evidence such as the Word Awareness Writing Activity provide this standardization and deepen the portrait of each student. In many classes in South Brunswick, teachers encourage students to add further work samples to show more of what they have been learning.

Guiding factors for determining what to include should be *breadth* and *clarity*. Breadth refers to the range of evidence presented in the portfolio. There should be a wide enough range to provide a thorough picture of students' development. The purpose of individual work samples should be clear so that anyone who reads the portfolio can easily identify the skills, concepts, or competencies students grappled with. If contents are ambiguous, assessments will not be as meaningful as they should be. This is especially important if, as will be discussed later, portfolios are going to be evaluated by someone other than the students' own teacher. If, of course, a

Table 3.4
Creating Portfolios

Generic Steps	South Brunswick
Getting Started	1. Teachers decide to develop a portfolio assessment.
1. Decide what evidence of student accomplishment you want to see.	
• Make a first guess about the information that would be useful for making the kinds of decisions you need to make about students.	• Teachers met in study groups to plan the portfolio assessment.
• Determine whether portfolios will be used to evaluate the class as a whole, individual students, or both.	• The first portfolio was field tested in several classes and refined for use in all kindergartens. Children carried their kindergarten portfolios on to first and second grades.
• Help students understand that their work will be collected into a portfolio so that they can begin to take part in the assessment process.	• Each subsequent kindergarten class began the process anew.
• Plan a field test or trial run of the procedures.	• Teachers developed, tested, and refined a scale for evaluating the portfolios.
Collecting Evidence	2. The portfolio is put in place in all K–2 classes.
2. Schedule a selection day or period.	
• Because students have been keeping work folders, they should have ample supplies of work from which to select.	• Work for the portfolio is collected at designated times throughout the school year.
• Exert as much structure on the selection process as seems appropriate for the maturity level of the students and your evaluation purposes; this means that if the portfolio is primarily to be used for school accountability purposes, teachers must determine most of the materials that will be included.	• Teachers collect individual pieces such as running records and administer group tasks to whole class; teachers devise management strategies to give them time to do this.
• Let the students make selections of what they think best shows what they are able to do or what they think supports the requirements of the portfolio.	
• If students are preparing a "best works" portfolio, have them write comments about each piece, either in a letter to the reader of the portfolio or on Post-it notes.	

continued

57

Table 3.4, *continued*

Generic Steps	South Brunswick
Evaluating Portfolio 3. Read the portfolios. • Read through a sample of the portfolios to evaluate contents, noting especially the following: • The range of reading and writing behaviors demonstrated by the evidence that the teacher has insisted be included and by the work the students have selected themselves • The adequacy of the evidence to give a full picture of students' achievement; that is, does the evidence on the whole show what each student really knows and is able to do? • The kinds of work samples students themselves selected and their contribution to the value of the portfolio to give clear pictures of each student. • Compare this list with the list generated in Step 1 to determine the kinds of information actually available for evaluating students' progress; this list becomes the first checklist for portfolio evaluation. *Assigning Scores* 4. Tally work samples and/or evidence of reading and writing behavior. • Use this tally to evaluate the effectiveness of the first selection day as a measure of students' progress. • If the information does not seem adequate to evaluate students' growth, restructure the selection process so that more specific kinds of work samples are included.	3. Portfolios are evaluated. • Teachers evaluate their students' portfolios and assign a score that matches the descriptors in the 6-point scale in Appendix B. 4. Portfolios are evaluated districtwide. • A sample of portfolios from each kindergarten to grade-two class is sent to a "moderation meeting" where a different teacher, unfamiliar with the students, evaluates the portfolios a second time. • Congruence between the two scores is calculated to ensure that the scale is being used consistently. • Scores are reported to the district as part of students' school records.

student or teacher decides to include something that is not totally clear, an annotation giving some background can easily be affixed with a Post-it note.

Whatever the purpose of the portfolio, it is wise for teachers to prepare a list of the basic categories of evidence to be included in each students' portfolio. Such a list is not inconsistent with student choice because it delineates what data the teacher will collect and what samples students may themselves select. Table 3.5 lists other forms of documentation that can find

Table 3.5

Possible Entries in an Early Literacy Portfolio and Entries from the South Brunswick Portfolio

General Categories	Required Entries in the South Brunswick Portfolio
Responses to Literature:	
• Reports on reading in any format: oral retellings transcribed or recorded by the teacher; written summaries; drawings	• Retelling • Higher Order Comprehension Task
Writing Samples	
• Writing done in class in response to assignments	• Assigned or Spontaneous Writing • Photocopies of Journal Entries
• Freewriting (e.g., entries in journals or logs)	
• Selections that students wish to include	
• Dictation in lieu of authoring	
• Examples of students' efforts to revise writing	
Examples of Writing in Content Areas	
• Any writing sample to demonstrate content learning	
• Graphic organizers	
Artwork	
• Pictures about what students have read	• Self Portraits
• Pictures about what students have written	
• Pictures about which students have written explanations or analyses	
• Self-portraits	
Tape Recordings:	
• Students reading what they have written	
• Oral reading samples	

continued

Table 3.5, *continued*

General Categories	Required Entries in the South Brunswick Portfolio
Data About Reading	
• Voluntary reading log	• Running Records
• Running record or other record of oral fluency (see Tables 3.3 and 3.4)	• Reading Samples
	• Sight Word List
• Nonstandard responses to reading, such as scripts for or photographs of plays or readers' theater	• Higher Level Comprehension Task
• Standardized reading test scores, if appropriate	
• Student–teacher summaries of reading conferences	
Other Data	
• Standardized measures such as test scores or results	• Word Awareness Writing Activity (WAWA)
• Summaries of interviews with parents or students	• Recording forms kept by teacher
• Relevant notes from the student to the teacher	• Interviews with parents
• Records kept by the teachers, such as anecdotal records, checklists, etc.	• Concepts about Print Test
Self-analysis and Reflection	
• Letter to teacher about oneself as a reader/writer/ learner (at beginning and end of school)	• Child interviews
• List of personal literacy goals	• Forms on which each child lists "What I Have Learned" and "What I Need to Do Better" in math, reading, writing (optional)
• Personal profiles, outlining students' sense of themselves as literacy users	
• Cover letter to portfolio reader, explaining what pieces show and why they were selected	
Wild Cards	
• Any example of students' literacy learning that they want to include in the portfolio	• Student-selected work

their way into an early childhood portfolio, cross-referenced to the contents of the South Brunswick Early Literacy Portfolio. Given the breadth of this list, it is easy to see how teachers can specify the contents of a portfolio to suit their own assessment needs and still provide ample student selection.

Teachers must be flexible as they develop a portfolio assessment system. They may discover that they have made too extensive or too scanty a list of evidence to collect. The process will be iterative, with many changes along the way to create the most efficient and meaningful portfolio. Many teachers in South Brunswick stress that constant review and revision are necessary to keep their portfolio assessment responsive to refinements in their curriculum (Salinger & Chittenden, 1994).

Collecting Evidence.   The actual compilation of work for a portfolio should take place several times a year, depending on when contents must be summarized for report cards, conferences with students or parents, or other reports of student progress. This process will not be a mad dash to find things to include if students or teachers have kept ongoing, cumulative work folders. In South Brunswick, teachers use many strategies to prepare portfolios (Salinger & Chittenden, 1994). Most teachers keep work folders from which they and the students can select writing samples to supplement the running records and other documents that the teachers themselves have been collecting. Some teachers photocopy journal entries that they think are especially good indicators of student growth. Because the contents of the portfolio are constrained by the portfolio's purpose as an account-ability instrument, teachers must be certain that all necessary documents are included; however, they must still allow considerable student selection of work to supplement the basic, required pieces.

If students are going to select entries for their portfolios, it is often helpful for them to work in pairs, discussing, comparing, critiquing, and possibly defending their individual choices. Students' choices, especially those of young learners, are often idiosyncratic; that is, their choice of their "best" paper or the one that shows the "most effective use of revision" may differ markedly from what the teacher would select. This does not mean that the selection is wrong or that the student does not understand stan-dards of quality; it means only that the student's evaluation of his or her work has been individualistic. Because knowing how and why the student has made the selections illuminates important thought processes, students are sometimes asked to write a letter to the reader of the portfolio or to annotate individual pieces with Post-it notes explaining the selection process. Initially, these letters or notes may be quite superficial (e.g., "This is my best paper because it's about going fishing with my brother"). But, gradually, students reflect more deeply about their work and feel more com-fortable expressing their own evaluations.

If teachers want students to be aware of their processes for construct-ing meaning and to become reflective, they must be willing to discuss with students their observations about strengths and weaknesses and buttress these discussions with concrete suggestions for improvement. This can be done in individual student–teacher conferences. By conducting such discus-sions, teachers invite students into the assessment process, giving them insight into learning and passing some of the responsibility for learning to the learners themselves. Conducted in a patient and supportive way, with-out judgment or criticism, these discussions can empower even young learners with new levels of independence. Students have support as they evaluate their work, come to understand standards for accomplishment, and learn appropriate language for talking about their work. Teachers may also discuss criteria for excellence during mini lessons or during language experience sessions (see subsequent chapters).

Evaluating Portfolios.   For practical purposes, teachers must have some way to describe the information in a portfolio so that individual efforts can be interpreted quickly and so that portfolios of different classes can be contrasted. Narratives and other recording sheets are the most efficient ways to summarize evidence contained in a portfolio—they allow teachers to make quick notes about what they see. These notes can be used as a reference in conferences with parents and others as a reminder of what students know and can do. Still, these do not really distill information in a readily usable form.

Teachers might also work collaboratively to create a developmental scale against which portfolios can be compared. In South Brunswick, teachers, administrators, and consultants studied many existing scales that described in behavioral terms what students did and how their products and academic performance looked at various stages of emergent literacy. They also studied evidence collected in many student portfolios and began to develop their own six-point scale. They wrote detailed behavioral descriptors of what students know and can do at the six developmental levels and tried to use the scale to rank students' portfolios. The goal was to provide a picture of how students "look" and perform as they move from preliteracy to more competent stages of ability. They fine-tuned their descriptors by making their language richer and more evocative of the developmental phases of emergent literacy until finally, after six drafts, they found that their "anchors," or descriptions of each level, were indeed aligned with what students actually did at as they progressed toward literacy. Independent of each other, two or more teachers could look at the same students' portfolios, compare the work with the scale, and place the students on the scale with high levels of agreement. This process, starting with a question of how to evaluate the portfolios efficiently, is an excellent example of real teacher research. The scale is presented in appendix B.

Assigning Scores.   One of the major differences between portfolios and work folders is that scores can be assigned to portfolios as an indicator of students' overall levels of achievement. These scores reflect holistic evaluation of the entire portfolio, not the sum of discrete grades. To arrive at such a holistic score, at least one reader goes through each entire portfolio relatively quickly to gain an overall, general impression of its contents, often in comparison with a developmental scale. Ideally, there should be two readers—students' own classroom teacher and one other teacher—so that two scores can be compared to ensure a level of objectivity.

As readers evaluate portfolios, they refer to a scale such as that described earlier. Readers consider all the evidence in the portfolio to determine where on the scale to place each child; that is, they balance all the evidence and determine which descriptive point on the scale is most closely matched to the evidence of student performance shown in work samples. In doing so, teachers draw upon their knowledge of how students behave at various stages of literacy development and can recognize evidence of those stages in the portfolio contents.

If the two readers disagree on the score that should be assigned, they must discuss their reasons and refer back to the work itself to resolve their differences. Ultimately, a numerical score is assigned to each portfolio, and this score serves as one criterion among others that the classroom teacher will use in evaluating a child for a marking term or longer period. It is especially important to remember that a developmental scale reflects normal progress from novice to more experienced levels of achievement and that not all children will reach the top of the scale at the same time. The individual scale points do not equate to letter grades but instead indicate stages of development.

In South Brunswick, teachers compare the contents of students' portfolios against the scale at the beginning, middle, and end of the school year. In the middle of the year, each teacher sends a sample of his or her portfolios, with the scale scores, to a moderation meeting. At this meeting, a second teacher evaluates the portfolio contents to double check for accuracy. When there is disagreement, a third reader checks the contents and arbitrates differences. If a teacher's ratings consistently differ from the second reader's ratings, all portfolios from a given class may be checked. This procedure ensures that the scoring process is reliable and that scores are valid for use at the district level.

GRADING IN A CLASSROOM-BASED ASSESSMENT APPROACH

The process of documenting student growth changes dramatically when reading and writing are perceived as integrated processes, when concerns in the literacy curriculum meld into each other, and when teachers invest in establishing portfolio assessment and in keeping written records of students' progress. The diversity, intensity, and quality of data that teachers gather validate teachers' accuracy in assessing students. Thus, if teachers who have adopted this approach to instruction and assessment should be questioned on their criteria for evaluating students, they can readily invite questioners to view their sources, to share their insights, and to realize how contextualized data far outweigh isolated test scores as a means of documenting progress.

Still, grading remains an ever-present reality. In many schools, even early childhood teachers must assign a letter or numerical grade to students' work at predetermined intervals. More and more early childhood educators are recognizing that letter grades and even designations such as "average" or "needs improvement" do not communicate meaningfully about children's progress. Narrative reports can be one alternative, but because these often require teachers to write extensive amounts of information about students, they are impractical except with small classes.

A good compromise between the extensiveness of narratives and the brevity of most report cards is a reporting format that offers a standardized and developmentally appropriate explanation of the *range* of achievement appropriate for any level and a brief teacher-written summary of each child's progress in terms of that standard. The explanation should be in straightforward language that all parents will understand and that will help to make sense of the teacher's comments. For example, a reporting form might explain the development of spelling competency, from beginning invented spelling to mastery of traditional spelling strategies; teachers would then state where on this continuum each child can be placed.

It is often beneficial to supplement a reporting form with a "parent portfolio" designed to highlight students' progress and also point out any weaknesses that must be addressed. Teachers may use "parent portfolios" as a central focus of parent–teacher conferences or may even send·them home for parent responses. The portfolio provides work samples as concrete examples of the literacy behaviors students are mastering. One primary-grade teacher reported successful use of such an approach (Marriott, 1993). She had her students, aged five to eight, keep writing folders, from which the teacher and students selected one sample per month to assess. After both teacher and student commented on the writing, it was sent home for parental assessment. The teacher cited assessments of a child's story about a trip to Sea World that read: *I Like Dolfins Alot becuse I like to see tham jup vray vray HIGH.* The teacher and child commented positively about the story, and the parent's response genuinely affirms what the child knew and did:

> I enjoyed the picture very much, I know what this would be about before I even read it. I like the action marks and the splash of the water! I also like how she wrote HIGH. You can truly get the point she is making and how much the show impressed her at Sea World. (p. 3)

The creation of such a reporting system is discussed in greater detail in the next chapter.

SUMMARY

Along with much of the redesign of literacy curricula has come a fortunate rethinking of assessment. The responsibility for assessment is being placed again where it belongs—in the hands of teachers and students. Teacher-made assessment devices that gather the kinds of information needed to make decisions about the curriculum and about individual students supplement and in some instances even replace externally imposed, commercial testing methods. Students' actual work samples—both oral and written records of what they can do—are being valued as sources of valid, reliable information about literacy growth. As teachers gain more control of the assessment process and as students become participants in the process, classroom instruction and student learning are bound to improve.

QUESTIONS AND TASKS FOR INDEPENDENT OR COLLABORATIVE WORK

1. Be sure that you can define each of these terms:

   * testing
   * assessment
   * classroom-based assessment
   * keeping track
   * checking up
   * finding out
   * interviews
   * conferences
   * running records
   * story retellings
   * portfolios

2. State in your own words the difference between assessment and testing. Compare your statement with those of other students. Which ideas are consistent and which are different?

3. Many researchers and teachers refer to informal, classroom-based assessment as "authentic assessment." This implies that more traditional testing may be unauthentic. What do you think this means? Do you agree or disagree?

4. List as many advantages as you can for classroom-based assessment methods for students, teachers, administrators, and parents. What disadvantages would you anticipate?

5. Select several books for young learners and try out the running record and story retelling procedures. Don't worry about "scoring" children's work but get a feel for the techniques involved in listening carefully for signs of reading strengths and weaknesses. Ask yourself whether the selection of books seemed appropriate and whether you obtained information that would be useful in planning instruction.

6. If possible, interview teachers who keep portfolios on their students. What are the advantages and disadvantages of the approach to assessment? How have they handled classroom management issues to allow them to implement this approach?

CHAPTER 4

Fostering the Home–School Connection

Most teachers of young children recognize the importance of strong links between children's home and school. They want to encourage the kind of home environment that will enhance the positive experiences children encounter at school, and they know that home support for school's intellectual and affective goals strengthens children's overall learning. The ideal situation is one in which there is mutual respect among parents,[1] teachers, and other school personnel and recognition of common concern for their "shared" children.

Still, many teachers do not receive training or advice on how best to establish connections between home and school, and they often feel that without formalized school programs to establish links, they themselves are ill equipped to make more than cursory overtures to students' caregivers (Fredericks & Rasinski, 1989, 1990b). Reasons cited include teachers' lack of understanding about how to involve parents, their fear that parents won't be able to give enough time to make a difference, mistrust of parents' intentions or abilities, or past failures to involve parents or other caregivers meaningfully. Such factors often produce indifference to the whole idea of establishing a supportive home–school relationship.

At the same time, parents themselves are often reluctant to seek involvement in schools, frequently because they also fear that too much time will be required or that they won't know what to do. For some parents, school had been an unpleasant experience and they distrust the system and what it represents.

BUILDING HOME–SCHOOL LINKS

There is no single correct way for teachers to establish a **home–school connection** and no single correct way for family members to support their children's learning. What is accepted practice in middle-class suburban schools may be viewed as inappropriate in other schools. Many variables, including cultural and language differences, can inhibit communication between school and home, just as these differences can inhibit real communication between teachers and students. As will be discussed in the next chapter, clashes of cultures can constrain teachers' and parents' best intentions.

As teachers seek to establish ties with their students' homes, they must recognize that school populations are changing rapidly; they must be sensitive to the very real demands placed on many of today's parents and families. Indeed, the very concepts of parent, family, and home have been redefined in recent years. Children's nurturing may be provided by single

---

[1] Throughout this chapter, the word *parent* is frequently used as a generic term for any adults who take care of children in the home environment.

parents, grandparents, or other relatives; and the parents of children in early childhood classes are often themselves just teenagers. Statistics on demographic shifts illustrate important trends but do not personalize the range of diversity in terms of home life, academic preparation, language, and expectations that can be found in one elementary classroom.

Poverty represents one cluster of variables that have deeply altered the fabric of life in the United States. The Children's Defense Fund has estimated that more than twelve million children live in poverty, often in neighborhoods where violence, drugs, and indifference have vastly redefined the very idea of childhood (see Kotlowitz, 1991, for a vivid illustration of this redefinition process). Among these children are many who have no homes at all; over half the total population of children who are homeless are five years old or younger, which means that hundreds of thousands of children come to school without the benefits of stable, responsive, orderly home environments during their most formative years. Teachers in early childhood classes need to be especially aware of the affective, nutritional, physical, and psychological influences poverty can have on young lives. These aspects of child development are rarely presented in teacher training programs, and beginning teachers may be totally unprepared to confront the emotional and physical needs of students whose early lives have ill prepared them for the risk taking and challenges of learning to read and write.

Teachers also have to recognize that they are often the "outsiders" in the communities in which they teach, and they must guard against the destructive tendency to stereotype groups of people, especially people from different societal groups. Stereotyping contributes to a set of expectations for background experiences, attitudes, abilities, inclinations, and behaviors that nongroup members cannot personally verify but that they may come to accept as truth. Stereotyping depersonalizes group members so that their idiosyncratic, individual characteristics are not readily perceived by nongroup members, whose expectations and attitudes have been shaped by what "they have heard" or what "research shows." This blindness may result in prejudging or misjudging both children and caregivers and always blocks genuine communication. Only by acknowledging the stereotypical ideas that they may hold about the students and the expectations that accompany those ideas can teachers begin to prepare the way for meaningful communication between the home and school.

Additionally, parents may have their own set of stereotypes and expectations for teachers because of economic, educational, ethnic, political, and even age differences. Parents may filter their interactions with teachers and their expectations through their predetermined set of stereotypes, thus increasing the obstacles to communication.

Binding teachers and parents together and motivating them to overcome potential difficulty is a desire for their "shared" children to be successful, especially as they begin to read and write. Parental manifestation of this desire can differ widely, and constraints of time, energy, and money often truly mitigate against traditional forms of home support. Teachers—and schools in general—need to find workable models that will make parents and caregivers feel that they are truly valuable partners in their children's learning. Researchers have found that "meeting parents where they are" is an important factor in improving the home–school connection. "The success of any one parent involvement strategy depends on how well it matches up with an individual parent's needs. The secret [to establishing a strong home–school connection] is to know who your parents are and to have in a school's repertoire as many options for involvement as possible. Doing so will ensure an appropriate match between a parent's level of commitment and willingness *and ability* to be involved" (Vandergrift & Greene, 1992, p. 59). Open communication is also cited as an important factor in building ties between home and school.

Many organizations today specialize in helping to bring about positive home–school connections (Fredericks & Rasinski, 1990b). Some provide training on how to establish links between homes and schools, and others publish newsletters and informational brochures. Additionally, many states have developed statewide networks of educators and parents to encourage home–school connections, and there are national initiatives such as those sponsored by the Barbara Bush Foundation for Family Literacy and RIF (Reading Is Fundamental) that provide information to parents and schools. A list of several national organizations is presented in appendix C.

In some communities, school districts establish programs to involve parents. These programs may be relatively simple, perhaps including a hotline for parents to call for help with homework or a newsletter listing local activities for children. In other districts, programs may be more ambitious. For example, Norfolk, Virginia, has developed a variety of programs to strengthen the home–school connection, especially for low-income families (France, 1992; France & Hager, 1993). The overall goal for the programs is to prevent reading difficulties before they begin. Secondary goals include helping parents to improve their own literacy skills and to increase their confidence in their ability to work with their children at home. The Norfolk programs target families with preschool and kindergarten students; their major features are activity packets (to be completed at home) and parent workshops, as described here:

1. The *Intergenerational Reading Project* includes a series of six hour-long workshops designed for two purposes: to improve the reading skills of participating parents and to help them learn strategies to strengthen the prereading and beginning reading skills of their youngsters. Its intended audience consists of parents with minimal literacy skills—those who lack confidence in their ability to read aloud with their children and to help them with schoolwork. During the workshop sessions, parents are taught different read-aloud techniques: echo reading, choral reading,

paired reading, storytelling, readers' theater, and chanting. Parents are also given books to take home to share with their children.

2. *Activity packets* are designed for parents to complete with their children. Some are designed to foster language development in kindergarten students; others include activities to strengthen reading, vocabulary, storytelling, handwriting, math, science, and social studies. Two series of packets focus on nursery rhymes. The kindergarten series is intended to foster thinking skills, and the preschool series is designed to encourage meaningful interaction between preschoolers and parents, thereby establishing the habit of talking about schoolwork.

Other features of the Norfolk program include certificates for parents who complete the workshop and parent logs for recording interactions between parents and children. The Norfolk public television station has run programs in support of the school district's efforts to increase parent–child interaction concerning literacy issues, and publications such as the *American School Board Journal* and the *Executive Educator* journal have recognized Norfolk's efforts as outstanding curriculum programs.

BUILDING THE HOME–SCHOOL CONNECTION

As school personnel in Norfolk, Virginia, found, achieving a successful home–school connection is a difficult task that requires open communication, patience, tact, and time. Teachers and other school personnel must be nonjudgmental and open, must accept what parents bring to the partnership, and must guard against cultural and class arrogance. The best possible programs are those that encompass all early childhood classes and may even extend downward to the preschool, day care, and Head Start programs that send children on to kindergarten. A commentary in *Education Week* (Rioux & Berk, 1994, p. 31) offered good advice on bringing about home—school cooperation:

> Don't start by putting the parents in a box. The box is the mind-set that the parents/families have things wrong with them that have to be fixed. Start, instead, from the base that the parents and families want the best for their children, are motivated to try and have strengths to build on.

Ideally, parents and caregivers join teachers and administrators in all aspects of school, from program planning to implementation, so that the level of commitment, involvement, and sophistication of parents steadily increases (Fredericks & Rasinski, 1989). Parents and teachers come to know and trust each other more as they negotiate long-term plans, attend workshops, and even socialize together.

Initial Communication with Parents

Communication between home and school is tremendously important, right from the start. The initial communication between school and home should set a tone of openness and cooperation that makes parents want to take part in their children's school experiences. Some schools prepare a general brochure about their early childhood program. In addition to telling parents how to register their children, such material can serve a real "public relations" role in making families feel welcome.

For example, the South Brunswick school system, mentioned in chapter 3, provides a brochure about its early childhood program. The cover shows children holding a banner proclaiming:

All I really need to know I learned in kindergarten.

The brochure also presents the mission statement of this early childhood education program:

The South Brunswick early childhood program is a joint venture of staff and parents. Its aim is to assure that children between the ages of 4 and 7 experience:
No Failing!
No Boredom!
No Fear of Mistakes!

The guide includes many pictures of children in school settings annotated by first-person statements, such as this one:

After summer's over, I will go to kindergarten. I will meet about 20 other children who will be in my class. Some of the children will walk to school. Some will ride a bus. We will all be new at this school, but we will make friends very quickly. . . .

My teacher will help me write my own stories. I will tell her stories and she will write them down. I will draw pictures to go with my stories. My teacher doesn't care if I make mistakes. She says that's the only way to learn. What a relief!

Finally, information provided for parents tells them about these elements of the program:

- The literacy portfolio (discussed in chapter 3)
- School health services
- School health regulations
- Registration and attendance, including the "school call up program," which checks on students who do not report to school on time
- Program goals and strategies

- Suggestions for acclimating children to their new experience
- Strategies for helping children at home and supporting what goes on in school

Here is what the guide tells South Brunswick parents about their involvement:

> Children bring to kindergarten a good deal of skill and knowledge. During the five years from birth to kindergarten entrance, children learn the meaning of thousands of words, master the art of speaking in full sentences, find out how hundreds of things work (including their own bodies) and discover how to get more information when they need it. The South Brunswick kindergarten program builds on work you have done in helping your children become young learners.

Alternatively, schools might distribute brochures such as those published in English and Spanish by the International Reading Association (see appendix C) or materials from other sources. For example, one organization publishes an "Owner's Manual for the 5-Year Old Model: School and Home Use." The title is catchy (if somewhat disturbing), but the information is good. Sections such as the "Limited Warranty" would catch parents' attention; it ends with, "In all cases, when treated with care, respect, and love, Five[s] will perform beautifully" (Grant & Azen, 1987, p. 8).

In addition to using materials developed by the school district, early childhood teachers should send an introductory letter home immediately after school starts. This initial communication can provide a brief introduction to the curriculum students will encounter and the goals and objectives for the year. Such a letter, models of which are presented in appendix C, must be written without jargon and in a friendly, informal tone. If a class includes children with home languages other than English, the letter should be translated. Most school systems can provide translating services for such purposes. Because young children often lose materials on the way home or in after-school care locations, teachers may want to pin the letter to bookbags or children's clothing or provide a tear-off slip that parents must sign and return.

Welcoming Parents and Caregivers

As family members begin to come forward with questions and concerns or with offers to help, they must be made to feel welcome, valued, and competent. Teachers at a particular grade level may want to host brief after-school meetings. Parents may be receptive to suggestions of readings from journals like *Young Children* and *The Reading Teacher* (see appendix A). Two short books, *Reading Begins at Home* (Butler & Clay, 1979) and *Writing Begins at Home* (Butler & Clay, 1988), clearly explain emergent literacy; parents can readily see how they can support their children's growth. Parents who cannot get to the school during the day may send notes to the teacher, and these should be attended to quickly and respectfully, with suggestions that parents call the teacher at a designated time to discuss concerns further.

Sometimes, parents need time to observe the children in action before deciding whether they want to volunteer to work in the class. Inviting parents to visit and observe is a good welcoming gesture; but teachers should time the visits so that the classroom does not become too crowded with adults as children are themselves becoming acclimated to school routines.

Offering Explanations

The next stage in the process of involving parents entails careful explanations of the policies, organizational procedures, routines, and expectations of the classroom. Explanations help parents realize how the teacher's decisions and plans are designed to foster children's literacy growth; understanding classroom organization and the underlying rationale helps potential classroom volunteers better see the place they can occupy there. A detailed newsletter, individual parent conferences, and discussions on parents' night can all serve to communicate this information.

After observing a bit, talking to the teacher, and reading materials about the educational program in their children's classroom, parents and caregivers have information to help them decide the level of involvement and participation they want to undertake. If they volunteer to become a regular part of the class, they must realize that their first assignment will be to undergo some training and orientation to prepare them for their new role. Preparation of training tapes for volunteers is an excellent project for a Parent–Teacher Association to support.

FINDING THE RIGHT LEVEL: SUPPORT, INVOLVEMENT, AND PARTICIPATION

A strong home–school connection can exist on several levels, ranging from **support** for children's growth and for goals espoused by their children's schools to long-term **participation** as a regular part of classroom activities. The middle ground between these two points can be thought of as **classroom involvement**—less frequent but definitely meaningful commitments of time spent in classroom activities. These three levels are discussed next.

Support

Ideally, all parents and caregivers of young learners will want to support their children's teachers, but many do not know how to accomplish this goal. On the one hand, some parents may "push" their children too fast;

other parents may simply not realize how to interact with their youngsters in effective ways. Parents demonstrate their support by encouraging children, talking and reading to them, and in general being advocates for the goals of the schools their children attend. Support does not necessitate expensive educational toys or trips; it is not dependent on the extent to which parents can become actively involved in their children's life at school. Support for children's development requires mainly time and respect for children as growing, learning individuals. Parents need to understand this difference.

In some cases, teachers must educate parents about the rich opportunities that exist for them to offer real support to their children; they can send newsletters, hold parent–teacher meetings, and conduct individual parent conferences. It is important, of course, that these suggestions do not appear to be judgmental or value laden but rather affirm what might be called the "curriculum of the home." Included in this curriculum are the many "literacy events" that abound in most home environments. Table 4.1 lists activities that teachers can suggest to parents. By letting those at home know that the school expects—and respects—certain kinds of interaction with children, teachers communicate important messages to parents.

At a more specific level, parents can support the emergent literacy curriculum in their children's classes—*if they understand the principles that underlie it.* Teachers and schools have the responsibility to explain the curriculum in terms that parents understand so that home and school activities are not at cross purposes in their support of emergent literacy (Morrow & Paratore, 1993). The very idea of a curriculum in which children read and write a lot instead of doing extensive skill activities may be totally bewildering to parents; papers with invented spelling and grammatical "errors" may be alarming. The level of independence and choice children demonstrate may falsely suggest a lack of formal teaching to parents accustomed to a more traditional approach. Careful explanations of goals, objectives, methodology, and routines, presented in plain language, are necessary in gaining parents' support. As will be discussed later, assigned homework is an important vehicle for encouraging parents to support what children do in school.

Whether or not parents are regular participants in the classroom, frequent, informal, but informative communication between school and home can offer explanations of what students are doing and provide concrete ideas for supporting children's learning. Inherent in this is teachers' understanding that literate behavior differs from home to home and that their best stance is to encourage parents to find ways to model and share literacy with their children that are appropriate within each individual family structure.

Involvement

Parents and caregivers who cannot participate regularly in class can still be meaningfully involved by devoting a morning or day to the class on an infre-

Table 4.1
Home Activities for Parents and Children

- Talk to children about what they have done in school during the day; listen carefully and respond with interest.
- Look at work that children have brought home and have children explain what they have done.
- Talk to children about what you (parents) have done during the day or are doing around the house.
- Discuss what children do around the house, including books they are reading, movies and television programs they have seen, and hobbies they engage in.
- Model behaviors such as reading for pleasure, reading the newspaper, consulting reference materials (*TV Guide*, cookbooks, how-to books, etc.), writing letters, paying bills, and so forth.
- Communicate with children through simple messages, possibly posted on the refrigerator or bulletin board.
- Read to children.
  - Select a wide range of books and stories in many different genres.
  - Ask thoughtful questions about the stories, not ones that require "yes/no" responses.
  - Ask children to retell the stories.
  - Give children a chance to select stories to listen to (even if they are repeated often), but also suggest listening to stories that you remember from your own childhoods.
- Give books as presents; encourage other family members to do the same.
- Get a library card and take the child to the library often.
- Label some objects around the house and let children label objects in their own rooms.
- Write letters with the children to family and friends; share letters received; encourage children to write letters to friends and to send thank you letters (see Figure 4.1).
- Encourage children to write their own letters, poems, and stories; offer help and correction when requested but do not overcorrect and criticize emerging skills.
- Suggest that children dictate stories if they want; read the transcriptions together.
- If possible, set aside a quiet corner for children to read and write and to do homework; provide pencils, pens, paper, perhaps a diary, and storage and display space.
- Support children's efforts to read and write; resist the temptation to "play teacher" or to focus on errors or details of spelling or handwriting; emphasize the content of what children write and their enjoyment of what they read.

quent basis. Their tasks may include reading to the class or to small groups, sharing some skill at which they are proficient, attending class trips, or participating in special events such as holiday celebrations.

How to make the best use of parents who can be part of the classroom only on an infrequent basis is indeed a challenge. It is important that volunteers' time be well spent in terms of the needs of the class; it is also important that volunteers view their visits as enjoyable and productive. These parents and caregivers will not have the continual interaction with the children that can establish their "authority" and roles as resource persons; they will also

Figure 4.1
Sample Thank You Letters   Note especially features such as the word *resubscription* for "magazine renewal"; note also the use of quotations around *Ranger Rick,* the two exclamation marks, and the grown-up cursive signature. In the letter from David (not the same child mentioned in chapter 1), note the factual information gleaned from what were actually children's versions of *field* guides.

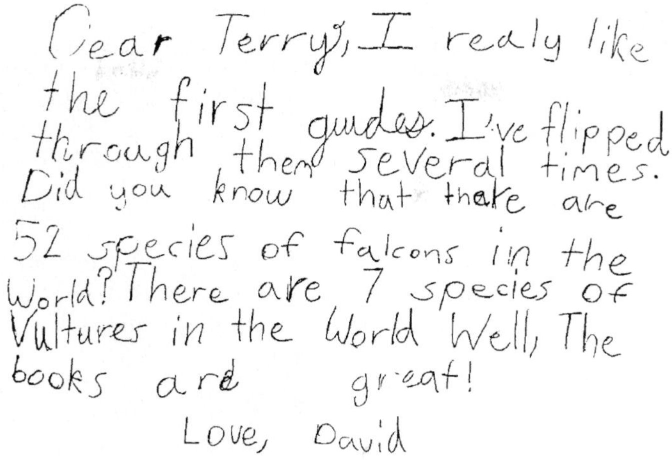

Dear Terry, I realy like the first guides. I've flipped through them several times. Did you know that there are 52 species of falcons in the World? There are 7 species of Vultures in the World Well, The books are great!

Love, David

Sample 1

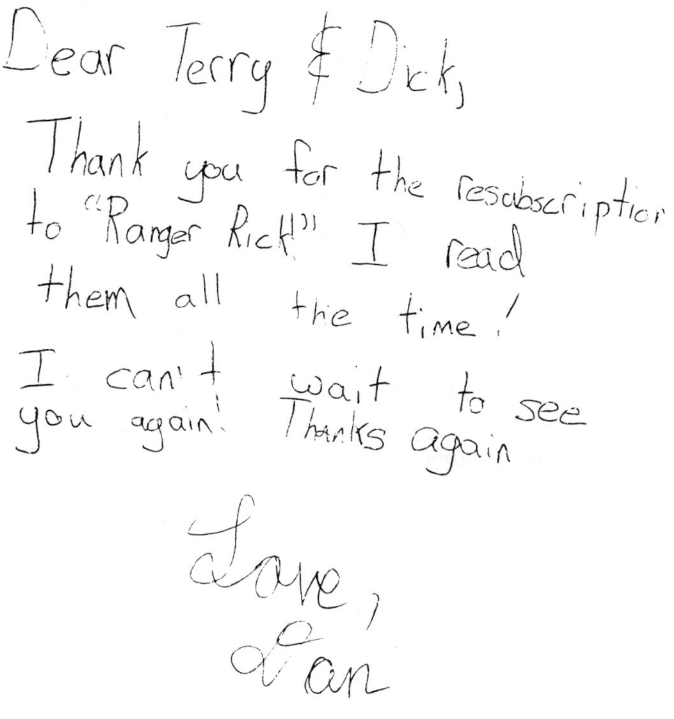

Dear Terry & Dick,

Thank you for the resubscription to "Ranger Rick!" I read them all the time! I can't wait to see you again! Thanks again

Love,
Dan

Sample 2

An important task for parent volunteers is reading quietly with one or two children.

lack the insight into the rhythms and routines of the class that would enable them to "pitch in" as readily as more frequent visitors. Additionally, they may not be able to participate in any "training" teachers provide for volunteers and will feel insecure about taking on substantive tasks with the children. If volunteer training tapes are available in the school, parents might like to borrow them in advance of their visits. On their own, early childhood teachers can easily develop expectations of what infrequent volunteers should know about their participation. Samples of activities and tasks are listed in Table 4.2.

If teachers know that some parents, grandparents, or other caregivers can be available on an infrequent basis, they can set aside for them specific, discrete tasks that are not essential to the daily routines of the literacy curriculum but that can be enriching and meaningful for both adults and children. Reading to or with individual children is one example; taking dictation is another important task. Also, teachers might survey this group of parents to determine interests or skills they might be able to share with small groups or with the whole class. For example, the mother of one of my first-grade students was a professional weaver; she volunteered several days a month for a whole year to teach interested students basic weaving procedures on looms made for the class by another parent.

Participation

Large commitments of time and energy are necessary for regular participation in children's classrooms. Those who can devote one or more days per week to

Table 4.2
Samples of What Parents Can Do in the Classroom

Parents who participate on a regular basis can do the following:

- Read to and with individuals.
- Read to and with small groups.
- Listen to children read.
- Transcribe children's dictation.
- Supervise art activities.
- Participate in ongoing projects.
- Share their own skills and talents in ongoing projects, such as sewing, weaving, bookbinding, woodworking, poetry writing, and so forth.
- Take students to the school library.

With training from the teacher, parents can do these activities:

- Lead "author's chair" or literary conversation groups (see chapter 9 for details).
- Conduct small group instruction on an ongoing basis.
- Offer remedial or enrichment work to individuals.

Parents who participate infrequently can do the following:

- Read to and with individuals and small groups.
- Listen to children read.
- Play learning games with students.
- Talk to and with students about their work or topics of interest.
- Share their skills in special, short-term projects.
- Go on class trips.
- Judge contests.

Parents who visit only on rare occasions can do these:

- Be a "celebrity reader" with small groups.
- Share special skills, talents, or interests.
- Judge contests.
- Go on trips.
- Listen to children read.

The individual schedules, talents, and inclinations of parents, coupled with the needs and characteristics of individual classrooms, will dictate the extent to which parents can play active roles in their children's education in school.

working in the school can become real partners in the learning process, assuming specific responsibilities and serving as aides, tutors, or resource persons without necessarily taking on academic roles. (See Table 4.2.)

By being in the classroom often, parents observe children interacting with peers; forming, testing, and rejecting hypotheses; learning, struggling, and wasting time; becoming frustrated but trying again. They also see the teacher offering comfort, support, information, and occasional "nudges" when children need to be encouraged to stretch their minds to meet new challenges. From these observations, parents come to appreciate issues of classroom management, lesson planning, and group dynamics—the general rhythms of classroom life. Further, children begin to accept the authority of adults other than their teacher (and their own parents) and to turn to visiting adults as learning resources. Adults who come to know a class in this way can help teachers personalize the literacy curriculum at a time in children's lives when one-on-one attention and adult modeling can be the vital elements that make instruction and practice "click" for young learners.

If teachers want parent participation on a regular basis, they must be willing to spend time nurturing, encouraging, and training these volunteers. Many of the agencies listed in appendix C have printed and videotaped material for training volunteers, but these can only supplement personal attention from teachers. Expecting too much too soon is perhaps the biggest mistake teachers can make in working with volunteers. Parents' skills and abilities will vary widely, as will their understanding of the literacy curriculum with which they will assist. A gradual, sensitive, and supportive introduction to the class is necessary if parents are to become successful classroom participants.

COMMUNICATING WITH THE HOME

As has been emphasized, communication between home and school should be ongoing, two-way, and respectful. Official letters and brochures written during the course of the school year should be supplemented by informal letters that keep family members apprised of the activities that individuals are doing or in which the whole class is participating. Frequent communication helps teachers demonstrate their concern and lends authority to suggestions for activities family members can undertake with their children. If letters are sent home only when a student encounters a problem, the relationship between home and school can become quite strained. Always, letters should be free of educational jargon and whenever possible written in children's home languages.

When letters are being sent to all students' homes, they should be shared with the class. This sharing can serve several purposes. First, it helps students understand why it is important that letters get home safely.

Second, children see that writing is an important, valued method of communication between the most important people in their lives—their caregivers and their teachers. Further, letters written home can play a subtle role in the literacy curriculum. Children love to look at "adult things," and by following along as the teacher reads what is being sent home, young learners are sharing in adults' communication. Beginning readers may pick up or affirm some sight words and will start to understand the structure of this form of written discourse. Leaving space at the bottom of a letter for each child to personalize the message brings children further into the communicative process. From a practical perspective, requesting that a signed tear-off slip from a letter be returned emphasizes teachers' seriousness and provides a means for presenting comments or questions from the home.

HOMEWORK

A more subtle form of communication is the kind of homework teachers assign. Homework should reflect the work that students do in the classroom and extend learning begun during the school day. Parents ought not to feel that they, instead of the teachers, are providing instruction. Teachers can encourage home support by making homework assignments clear, challenging, and unambiguous. This is especially important for parents who do not spend time in the classroom itself.

The best assignments for young learners will often elicit parent involvement. Teachers should remember, though, that many parents work and that homework assignments in which parents must participate should not make their time with their children stressful. If parents have to tutor children, puzzle over an ambiguous worksheet, or gather materials for a complex art project, the homework assignment may intrude on time that should be spent in pleasant conversation or simply sharing a book. Yet, clear, worthwhile assignments provide a window into their children's school life and offer a topic for discussion.

Homework, if given, should be developmentally appropriate, meaning that it should be easy enough for children to do relatively independently and should not be too time-consuming. Complex assignments, often arts and crafts projects, do little to reinforce school work. These projects may in some cases stimulate parent–child collaboration, but this is not always the case. If parents can't or won't help children, or if materials and resources are simply unavailable, children may not be able to complete the task adequately. Equally, some parents may do more than their share of the work. Either scenario is counterproductive to the real purpose of homework and creates an unhealthy tone of competition among children in a class.

The only homework some early childhood teachers assign is nightly reading, either to or with parents or siblings. This approach, as will be discussed next, is absolutely fine. Other teachers may make more diverse assignments, balancing written work with activities to reinforce skills instruction. Whatever the assignments, the teacher should ensure that there is a *written* notation about what students are to do. This notation may take the form of a weekly "contract," a daily assignment sheet, or an entry that students have copied into their notebooks (and that teachers have checked for accuracy). Communicating the nature of homework with parents in this way establishes good patterns of behavior: children know that they should bring the assignment home and parents know that they should check for it. Additionally, written notations about what has been assigned can avoid the confusion that may occur when children depend only on their memories for what they have to do. It goes without saying that students in early childhood classes, no matter how diligent, have much more important things to think about than what they have been assigned to do at home!

READING AND WRITING WITH CHILDREN

Among the best homework assignments is sharing a book with the folks at home. Prereaders may simply listen to a story that someone reads; beginning readers may read easy books to a parent or sibling and snuggle as someone reads to them. Setting up a regular classroom lending library can encourage parents to read with and to their children regularly. Children look forward to taking their book home each day and sharing it with others the next day (often teachers send books home in plastic bags to keep them clean). Steps for formalizing such a lending library appear in appendix C.

Even with a lending library, parents and older siblings may not know how to make the best use of the time they spend reading with youngsters. Suggestions from teachers can encourage the folks at home to recognize the importance of what Holdaway (1979) called the "bedtime storybook learning cycle." Time spent sharing books should be a special, quiet period during which a child snuggles next to the person reading. Especially with prereaders, the child should have a "line of sight" view of the text and pictures so that he or she gains familiarity with their orientation on the page. From time to time, the reader should stop and ask simple questions to enhance the child's enjoyment and engagement. Questioning is appropriate for older children, too, whether they are reading themselves or listening. Teachers often need to help parents understand that the most appropriate questions seek predictions, opinions, or expansions, not literal facts or superficial reactions to what has been read.

Writing with children is also an excellent at-home activity that may or may not count as formal "homework." Parents and children may keep journals of what goes on at home, at school, and at work; they may record special events, vacations, wishes and dreams. They make entries whenever they feel like it, not necessarily on a daily basis, with parents taking dictation for young children and encouraging older ones to write themselves.

When parents share books with their children at home, they actively support the goals of an early child-hood literacy program. Story time should be plea-surable—a time for reading and talking about the sto-ries that are shared.

REPORTING ON PROGRESS

Communication about the literacy curriculum, student activities, or strategies for home support is easy in comparison with the task of reporting on students' progress. Filling in grades on a report card and writing a brief sentence about each child has always been a time-consuming task but one that was relatively noncommittal compared with the in-depth reporting that best suits the approaches to literacy instruction advocated in this book. The richness of the experiences students encounter cannot be captured in single grades and certainly is not reflected in a standardized test score. Nor can a few statements made at a parent–teacher conference convey students' overall progress.

Although teachers of young children frequently see parents or other caregivers before or after school, parent conferences may be the only opportunities for sustained discussion of students' progress. Organizing an agenda, gathering materials, and making notes about each child can make conferences more beneficial for all concerned. Teachers should present the child's strengths and weaknesses; comment on academic achievement, emotional growth, and behavior; and suggest ways to support the child's learning at home. As mentioned in chapter 3, centering the discussion on actual work samples helps parents understand the developmental nature of literacy acquisition and specific concepts such as invented spelling and story retelling. Such explanations are essential for parents who might not understand the cognitive underpinnings and purpose of the work their children pull from their bookbags each day or are asked to do as homework.

Early childhood teachers need to present as full a picture as possible of students' progress. When portfolios are kept for assessment, teachers have a ready-made supply of work samples to share with parents. Flood and Lapp (1989) have also suggested a "comparison report," which can be thought of as a parent equivalent of the student portfolios discussed in chapter 3; it would contain work samples collected by the teacher and students at various points in time to represent progress throughout the year. One of the most valuable aspects of a parent portfolio is that it provides real examples of what students know and can do successfully. As much as possible, students themselves should be involved so that "a portfolio becomes a joint project for the teacher and the student—[and] there will be two voices capable of and willing to explain progress" (Flood & Lapp, 1989, p. 514). Parent portfolios can be sent home immediately before conference time so that parents can study the contents and perhaps, as suggested in chapter 3, comment in writing on their child's work. Alternatively, after using portfolios in parent conferences, they can be sent home to accompany a narrative report on students' progress. Such a portfolio is not evaluated to become part of students' cumulative records. If children keep portfolios as part of the regular assessment system, they can also be used during parent conferences. Indeed, teachers in South Brunswick, New Jersey, often cite this use of the portfolios as their most valuable attribute.

If teachers decide that children may take their portfolios home as a record of growth during the early childhood years, this can be considered a right of passage of sorts from one period of school to another. In South Brunswick, children in kindergarten through grade two keep portfolios that are passed on to each successive teacher. At the end of second grade, the portfolios are sent home.

In one school in the South Brunswick district, sharing the portfolios was one aspect of an important ceremony. Children began reviewing their portfolios two weeks or so prior to this important assembly, and each child wrote an essay entitled "On Becoming Eight: Learning to Read and Write." At an assembly attended by second- and third-grade teachers and students, each child read one sentence from his or her essay. Some children commented on what they had *not* been able to do in kindergarten and first grade; some highlighted primarily second-grade accomplishments. Then the children listened to three third graders read essays about the differences to be encountered as students left the "lower school." At the end of the presentations, the second graders, who had been anxiously searching the audience all the while, found their way to a parent, grandparent, sibling, or other adult with whom to share the three years' worth of work collected in their portfolios. Every child had some significant adult with whom to share this moment, for children whose caregivers could not attend spent the time with a former teacher. As the children proudly displayed their work, the third graders quietly passed around the auditorium handing out carnations and stating, "Welcome to third grade." This assembly represented a true bringing together of children's home and school experiences.

Many school systems do not require formal report cards in the early childhood years. The rationale is often that children's learning during this time span is so fluid that more harm than good is done by categorizing progress, even with scales using terms such as *outstanding, satisfactory,* and *needs improvement.* Some school systems have recently experimented with report card formats that can better explain what students are actually doing and learning. Such report cards attempt to blend the time-consuming qualities of descriptive inventories with clear descriptions of the many strategies and skills that constitute literacy behaviors. Thus, a report card may have explanations of behaviors such as learning to spell or developing strategic behaviors for reading; these descriptions give parents a sense of the developmental contin-uum inherent in learning these complex behaviors. Teachers accompany these descriptions with brief, written assessments of students' progress on each dimension of learning and perhaps refer parents to specific work samples that illustrate students' developmental levels. The value of this approach is that parents gain some understanding of how multifaceted early literacy learning actually is and perhaps can even "see" where their children are on the learning continuum. It is essential, of course, that explanations be short and concise if they are to be meaningful to parents unaccustomed to educational terminology.

SUMMARY

Parents and other caregivers can be valuable partners in young children's acquisition of literacy. Their efforts can enrich children's classroom experi-ences and support literacy learning at home. However, there are no easy ways to establish links between the home and school. It is often up to teach-ers to initiate these links, to make the contacts that let family members know that, even if they cannot become regular classroom volunteers, their support and involvement are welcome.

QUESTIONS AND TASKS FOR INDEPENDENT OR COLLABORATIVE WORK

1. Be sure that you can define each of these terms:

    -   home–school connection
    -   support, participation, and classroom involvement (from the home)

2. If you are a parent, keep a week-long log of the interactions you have with your children that you think might benefit their literacy develop-ment. How many of them were planned attempts to help them academ-

ically? How many were not planned but would be helpful anyway? Which kind seemed to be more enjoyable for both you and your children? Compare your log with that of other parents and report your findings to fellow students who do not have children.

3. What are your feelings about homework for young students? Try to find typical assignments in grades one through three. Which seem worthwhile? Discuss this issue with others in your class.

4. Interview a prekindergarten or day care teacher, a kindergarten teacher, and a teacher in first, second, or third grade. With each, discuss their feelings about parent involvement. Find out whether they view it positively and what they do to encourage it. Compare the results of your interviews and cite specific differences you find. How can you explain the differences?

CHAPTER 5

Culturally Sensitive Instruction

T he population of children entering school is changing, and the task of schools to be ready for all new entrants has become even more complex than it has been in the past. James A. Banks, an authority on multicultural education, urges educators to face certain realities. He has written (1991/1992), "The growing number of people of color in our society and schools constitutes a demographic imperative educators must hear and respond to" (p. 33). Demographic changes, discussed in detail in this chapter, include the increasing number of children who do not speak English by the time they enter school, those whose early experiences leave them unprepared emotionally and intellectually for school, and those who experience some sort of cultural discontinuity in their transition from home to school settings.

Early childhood educators must be especially ready to tackle this demographic imperative, for they are usually the first contact students have with formal schooling. They help acclimate students to school and spur them on the path of academic learning, regardless of students' early experiences.

THE DEMOGRAPHIC IMPERATIVE

One of the realities inherent in the demographic imperative is that teachers can no longer assume that most of their students will be more or less "the same." Children in any one class may differ across linguistic, cultural, and social dimensions. It is also safe to assume that teachers and students often come from very different backgrounds that have shaped their individual expectations for school in diverse ways. Finally, teachers would be foolhardy to assume that schools will be able to offer all the services needed to accommodate the needs of students from diverse backgrounds. Teachers themselves must find ways to meet students' individual needs, maintain accord in their classrooms, and help each child achieve to the best of her or his potential.

Linguistic Factors

Recent immigration from Mexico, Puerto Rico, and Central and South America has filled classes with children whose first (and often only) language is Spanish. Additionally, many native-born children grow up in communities where radio, television, religious services, newspapers, billboards and other signs, and the conversations they hear around them are primarily in Spanish. For many of these children, bilingual education programs are available to help them make a smooth transition from early learning in Spanish to instruction in English.

But Spanish is by no means the only non-English language heard in U.S. classrooms. A recent study reported that the number of U.S. residents who speak a language other than English at home had reached an all-time high of 12 percent (National Center for Education Statistics, 1993). Many of these individuals were born in the United States but live in communities where Chinese, Vietnamese, Farsi, Russian, Lao, or any other of the twenty-six languages mentioned in the report are heard in homes, on the streets, and in the media. For many of these children, there are no bilingual education programs to help them in their transition to formal schooling.

Added to these populations of children who do not speak English are the many children who "code switch" between two languages, as is common along the Mexico–United States border and in certain parts of Louisiana where Creole (a mixture of French and English) is often the home language. In these cases, children's speech is a mixture of their first language and English, with English words, phrases, and expressions interspersed in highly rule-governed ways. Lara (1989) cites an example of young children's code switching. Upon opening to a story in a reader, a Mexican-American child said, "*Mira, los* bears *están* dancing." Another child quipped, "*Y los* bears *tienen* hats *y hay* baby bear *y están en el* circus" (p. 278).

Individuals code switch between languages for a variety of reasons, including lack of the needed word in the dominant language, emphasis, humor, consideration of the listener's dominant language, and expression of cultural identity (Lara, 1989). Teachers need to be careful that they do not misinterpret code switching. Some children who code switch readily between their home and school languages may appear to be more fluent in English than they actually are. Their knowledge of syntax and their vocabularies are firmly rooted in their home language.

Many children also enter school speaking *dialects* of English, the most common of which is frequently referred to as *Black English* (Smitherman, 1977). Dialects differ from more standard versions of English in their grammar (syntax), pronunciation, and vocabularies (semantics); they are strongly rule governed and systematic, with an underlying linguistic logic that allows for clear communication between speakers of the same dialect. Dialects also frequently engender debate. Gilyard wrote (1991): "The idea of Black English is still controversial despite research dating back three decades, which documents that it is a legitimate linguistic system and not merely a collection of verbal aberrations arrived at by the reckless violation of the rules of a so-called superior variety of English" (p. 27).

Children who learn a dialect as their first language may also learn to code switch between their home speech and more standard English. To cite Gilyard again: "My mother was a bidialectal speaker, capable of producing Black English and Standard English as well. And . . . even in my preschool years my own move toward bidialectalism was well underway, made possible no doubt by my awareness of my mother's verbal maneuvering. I had seen how she could speak to a grocer, a salesman, a doctor, or a stranger in one manner (Standard), and then turn around, watch me carelessly knock a bowl of cereal on the floor, and exclaim, 'Now look what you done did!'" (pp. 30–31). If they have not learned to code switch—to be bidialectal—by the time they enter school, young dialect speakers who sense acceptance for their speech patterns quickly learn to understand their teachers' "different" ways of talking and soon move toward use of more standard speech patterns.[1]

Dialects are also strongly marked by regional language differences that can be confusing even when one is discussing everyday events. Talking about bringing a "bag lunch" for a picnic provides a social context for children used to referring to bags as "sacks" or "pokes"; but if a storybook introduces the term without context, children may be thoroughly confused. Equally, a child who states that he forgot his "poke" may draw blank stares from a teacher.

Strategies for meeting the needs of children who speak languages other than English and for helping these children to move toward fluency in English are presented in this and the next chapter. The most important points to remember in working with these children is that their home languages and their native competency are to be respected and honored. Language is a part of who each person is; no language is intrinsically better than any other language, and grammar and stylistic elements of language are social artifacts, not representations of cognitive ability.

Cultural Factors

Differences in racial, ethnic, and cultural backgrounds can cause tension among even the most well-intentioned teachers, school personnel, and parents. Children can encounter conflicts as well, especially when their own culturally determined sense of what school should be differs from the actual culture of the school they attend.

The idea of **school culture** is an important and often overlooked concept. Teachers' attitudes, expectations, and actions contribute to the culture of an individual classroom, but the factors that determine the culture of an entire school are far broader. A school's culture is influenced by stated or unstated beliefs about competition, risk taking, independence, and motiva-

---

[1] What kind of language should teachers speak? For a long time, English speech that followed precise grammatical rules was referred to as "Standard American English," and dialect variations were called "nonstandard English." Linguists, people of color, educators, and others soon noticed that the distinction between "standard" and "nonstandard" English belittled any language variation that deviated from textbook-perfect grammar.

No totally satisfactory term has yet been offered to replace "standard English." Some suggest "global English," a relatively vague term; others suggest "English of commerce" to reflect the importance of "good" grammar in the workplace. Delpit (1990, p. 251) refers to the "politically popular dialect form in this country," stressing that those who do not have access to this form of speech "are less likely to succeed economically than their peers who do" (p. 251).

tion. Whether the school espouses a teacher-centered or child-centered approach to classroom management and lesson planning is also a factor, as is the extent to which the school is able to provide students an environment where they feel safe and nurtured. Increasingly, this last factor has become a cause for serious concern. When children—and sometimes even teachers themselves—fear for their safety not only on the way to and from school but inside the school building itself, learning cannot thrive.

Children's homes and broader cultural environments shape their expectations for school and determine much about how they learn. If the culture of their school places expectations upon them that they simply cannot fulfill, youngsters' early school experiences will be confusing, disheartening, and indeed threatening to their very sense of themselves. A common example is children from backgrounds where cooperation is valued more than competition. For these children, a classroom where independence and individual achievement are rewarded can quickly dampen their otherwise enthusiastic expectations for school. They won't know how to respond, and in their confusion they may slip into patterns of passivity or hostility, both of which can be equally destructive.

Teachers, too, must be alert for cultural conflict. As stated in chapter 4, their expectations for individual students may be tainted by beliefs in racial, ethnic, or cultural stereotypes. Teachers may misinterpret the behavior of a child from a different cultural group and inadvertently underestimate the child's academic potential (Hilliard, 1989; Prothero & Barsdate, 1991). Routines for turn taking and answering questions provide two examples of how this may happen.

Children are not born knowing how to take turns during discussions and conversations; they must learn this routine. If their families do not encourage verbal turn taking, this behavior, so highly prized in school, will simply not make sense. Not understanding what to do, children may call out at random, seemingly in violation of established protocols. Consider also how teachers frequently ask questions that require a show of academic knowledge. If students come from backgrounds where questions directed toward youngsters usually require only factual information about what has been directly experienced, then content-based questions (whose essential purpose is to help review what has just been taught) seem very strange. Children may resist answering such questions because they know that the teacher already knows the answer.

Now contemplate the false assessment teachers might make from these two examples. The child who seems to ignore verbal turn-taking rules might be deemed a behavior problem, whereas the child who stumbles over an answer or fails to answer questions at all might be classified as a slow learner. Both assessments could be extremely wrong; and they could easily lead to tracking, referral, labeling, or the overall perception of deficiencies that the children might never overcome. In reality, the two behaviors stemmed from conflicts between the home and school cultures, conflicts that teachers should recognize and help to iron out.

Social Factors

Many children live in homes where money is tight, where making do and keeping food on the table and shoes on children's feet are difficult tasks. Perhaps the child is being raised by a single parent, often a mother; perhaps one or another parent has been laid off or cannot find work. The stress these circumstances place on families can be immeasurable.

Additionally, more than twelve million children live in families whose yearly income falls below the poverty level, and increasing numbers of very young children have no stable homes at all. Often they live surrounded by violence, drugs, and indifference; their mothers may be mere children themselves, totally unprepared for the responsibilities of supporting and sustaining children. Spending the formative early years in such surroundings does little to prepare children emotionally and intellectually for school—their lives are chaotic, often without routines. Not only have they lacked bedtime stories, trips to the zoo, and other experiences, they have done without the warmth and nurturing that build self-esteem, confidence, and willingness to take risks, all of which are essential for early school success. Often their teacher—if they stay in one class long enough—is the most stable adult figure in their lives.

Teachers need to avoid the assumption that because children come from low-income or nontraditional homes they have had no preschool experiences with literacy. Still, the ways children see literacy used as part of everyday life can differ widely and is often influenced by social and economic factors. Finding out how literacy is used in different kinds of homes is important because such information can help teachers and administrators make their schools ready for all children.

Two researchers, Taylor and Dorsey-Gaines (1988), conducted extensive studies on low-income families in a large northeastern urban area. They spent long hours with the families they studied, and what they found defied the stereotypes of such homes as places where school is suspect, books are absent, children are neglected, and literacy is devalued. Because the homes they studied were often stressful, "the parents' provisions of a literate environment and support of their children's education [were] somewhat balanced (however precariously) with the strong need for the children to become independent survivors in a sometimes hostile world" (p. 15). Still, the researchers observed that the "families spent time together, that there was a rhythm to their lives, and that they enjoyed each other's company. Friends visited. Children played. People helped one another. Sometimes there was sadness and grief, at other times there was anger and resentment, but there was always a quiet determination in the way in which they approached the difficulties that confronted them" (pp. 191–192).

Additionally, parents in this study made many efforts to get children ready for school and supported what the schools offered. Indeed, the researchers contended that the parents were "taking the necessary steps to enable the children to succeed at the tasks that were set for them. The children learned their lessons well, and [there were] at least some indications that school literacy was meaningful" (p. 95). Equally important, Taylor and Dorsey-Gaines observed many instances of parents using literacy independently and sharing reading and writing with their children. In these homes, literacy was clearly valued as a functional tool in the parents' lives; they paid bills, read newspapers, used certain reference materials. In some homes, adults also turned to reading as a source of relaxation. Children might not have had as deep and rich preschool literacy experiences as children in more affluent homes, but they did see that their family members valued and used reading and writing in purposeful ways.

Studies such as that of Taylor and Dorsey-Gaines emphasize that literacy means different things in different environments and that support for literacy takes many forms. It is up to early childhood teachers to discern what reading and writing have meant to children prior to school and to build on that base of knowledge when children have not had ample experiences with bedtime stories, trips to the library, and parents and siblings discussing their own reading and writing tasks.

RESPONDING TO DIVERSITY WITH SENSITIVITY AND CELEBRATION

The increase in the number of school entrants from diverse backgrounds has important implications for early childhood education. The classroom climate, instructional methods, and materials must all be sensitive to children's backgrounds. A school environment that denies children's home culture and language cannot support their emerging self-concept, self-esteem, and confidence as learners. Further, cultural and linguistic diversity must be valued as attributes that enrich the entire school population (Vasquez, 1990).

The basic principles of culturally sensitive instruction are presented here.[2] They are simple, straightforward, and equally applicable to children in classrooms in urban, rural, and suburban areas:

---

[2] The terms *culturally sensitive* and *culturally responsive* education are used more or less interchangeably in current professional literature. These terms imply that the classroom environment is of primary importance and is designed to recognize, accommodate, and celebrate differences. Within such an atmosphere, teachers also present information that expands students' understandings about their own and their peers' cultural backgrounds.

1. All students are considered to have the inherent resources and abilities necessary for them to achieve academic success.
2. It is the responsibility of the schools to ensure that conflicts between home and school cultures do not inhibit students from achieving to their full potential.
3. There is no single best method for teaching all students; therefore, teachers try to find diverse pathways to meet individual students' needs.
4. Teachers do not need to duplicate the home environment of their students in the classrooms; instead the classroom environment should motivate mutual respect and encourage students and teachers to strive for mutual accommodation.
5. High standards and high expectations are maintained for all students; rather than lowering standards or creating double standards, teachers find ways to help all students achieve.
6. Diversity is considered a strength within the classroom, in children's communities, and in the nation as a whole.
7. Students' home cultures and languages are considered their foundation for learning; in no way are students asked or forced to reject their heritage.

There are two core components to this approach: respect for all people and an awareness of language.

FIRST CORE COMPONENT: RESPECT

Respect as a core component of culturally sensitive instruction is evidenced in several different ways. First, teachers should show respect for the different groups represented in the classroom—this respect comes from substantive knowledge and understanding and real information about diverse groups of people (Boute, LaPoint, & Davis, 1993; McCracken, 1993). In their response to the demographic imperative, teachers have the responsibility to become informed about their students' cultural backgrounds.

Teachers also need to identify, confront, and then strive to modify their own biases about the groups represented in their classes, especially if many different groups are represented. McCracken (1993) bids her readers to engage in heady self-analysis, and this may involve hard work. For example, she suggests teachers ask themselves whether they think stay-at-home mothers provide better nurturing for youngsters than mothers who work outside the home. Having answered that, teachers should push the question to include mothers who do not work outside the home but are young, poor, uneducated, unmarried, and on welfare. Does the answer change?

Respect is also shown in the expectations placed upon children by the school and by their individual teachers. Ideally, there should be a schoolwide commitment to high expectations and standards for all children. All teachers have respect for children's innate abilities to be academically successful when they are given appropriate **opportunities to learn**. This means that teachers and schools need to accept the responsibility for finding diverse pathways to learning so that linguistic, cultural, and social differences do not become obstacles to student success (Prothero & Barsdate, 1991).

The Kamehameha Early Education Program (KEEP) developed in Hawaii is an excellent example of how a school and its teachers were determined to give minority students real opportunities to learn. The program was established in 1971 to serve native Hawaiian children (Au & Jordan, 1980; Jordan, 1985). Researchers and teachers developed a plan to modify the school environment to minimize students' sense of cultural conflict—that is, to make the school culture harmonious with the culture of students' homes. Among the innovations was the introduction of a "talk-story" approach in reading instruction. The children were already accustomed to collaborative storytelling in their families: one person, usually an adult, begins a story and others add pieces until a total story is constructed. By being allowed to use similar story construction strategies as they discussed what they had read—rather than adhering to turn-taking routines—students made gains in their abilities to comprehend text.

The classroom environment must engender respect among teachers and students—respect that includes openness and honesty about racial, ethnic, and cultural differences. Consider these three related quotations.

> Young children note race [and ethnic identity] as another factual aspect of an individual (in the same way they notice gender). . . . When we fail to acknowledge differences in individuals, we may send a message that differences are not appreciated or that they are negative. Additionally, when we ignore or negate racial differences we fail to individualize and meet children's needs—the needs of the child of color and the needs of the child *inquiring* about differences of color and, perhaps, of culture. (Boute, LaPoint, & Davis, 1993, p. 22)

> Anything a child feels is different about himself which cannot be referred to spontaneously, causally, naturally, and uncritically by the teacher can become a cause for anxiety and an obstacle to learning. (Paley, 1979/1989, p. xv)

> We can continue to view diversity as a problem, attempting to force all differences into standardized boxes. Or we can recognize that diversity of thought, language, and worldview in our classrooms can not only provide an exciting educational setting, but can also prepare our children for the richness of living in an increasingly diverse national community. . . . [Teachers must] celebrate, not merely tolerate, diversity in [their] classrooms. (Delpit, 1990, p. 264)

What these educators are recommending is markedly different from the long-held view that teachers should help students concentrate on the similarities among their peers and minimize differences. Yet, diversity exists—in languages, skin colors, and background experiences—and young children can be helped to recognize diversity not just as a fact of life but as a source of learning, excitement, and enrichment. Achieving this kind of classroom environment is not easy. Two specific categories of teacher behaviors emerge from the writings of educators such as those cited.

First, teachers must be willing to talk openly about issues that are heavily value laden and to confront head-on children's questions and concerns about the diversity evidenced in their classrooms. Some educators suggest that teachers must do more than answer learners' questions—they must encourage their students to discuss and study the diversity they see around them (Delpit, 1990; Paley, 1979/1989). For beginning teachers, the recommended level of openness and honesty may be hard to achieve. Teacher educators Boute, LaPoint, and Davis (1993), all of whom are African-American, write of the care they take to help the white student teachers whom they supervise feel at ease with such discussions. In such situations, providing factual information about the diverse groups represented in a classroom can be a start toward teaching others to be comfortable with diversity.

Structured methods of talking about diversity with students can also help. Teachers often need models for what they are learning to do. Talking openly about issues of values, trust, and respect may be new for them. Table 5.1 highlights one very successful approach, Naomi Drew's *Learning the Skills of Peacemaking* (1987/1994). Drew is a classroom teacher whose curriculum development work grew from her commitment to share her ideas about peace and respect with her young students. As she implements her program, she is always sensitive to students' developmental needs and to the attitudes they bring from home. Her weekly lessons, outlined in her book, infuse themselves into the fabric of her classroom, where even environmental print reminds children of appropriate ideals.

In Naomi Drew's kindergarten class, a chart dictated by the children reinforces lessons on peacemaking. The title of the chart is "A Peacemaker Is Someone Who . . ."

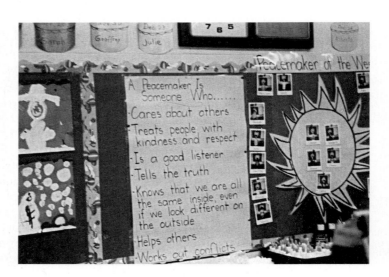

Table 5.1
Brief Summary of Methodology for Teaching Peace

In her book *Learning the Skills of Peacemaking,* Drew (1987/1994) suggests ways that teachers can help even very young learners understand

- The responsibility each person must assume for bringing about a peaceful world,
- The interconnectedness of all people, and
- The importance of each person's unique attributes, styles, and visions.

These clearly constitute the foundation of culturally sensitive teaching and of a classroom where respect for each other flourishes among students.

Drew begins with the contention that "Peace begins with me" and bids children to talk, write, and draw about the process of creating a peaceful classroom. This base of discussion is both very concrete (most children would prefer a peaceful classroom) and very abstract. Children are encouraged to think about their own ideas, to question, and at their own level to analyze situations that cause conflict among their peers. As they write in "peacemaking journals" (p. 67) or help select a "Peacemaker of the Week" (p. 71), they are investigating important ideas about cultural sensitivity and responsiveness. By becoming familiar with the bulletin board ideas "Roots Feed the Tree of Life" (see Figure 5.1) and the "Ladder of Peacemaking" (see Figure 5.2), students begin to understand what it means to be responsible citizens of a multicultural/multilingual world.

The second set of behaviors concerns the choices teachers make for teaching methods, instructional activities, and classroom materials, all of which should reflect and celebrate diversity. This does not mean that teachers provide a "hit or miss, tourist curriculum that offers occasional superfluous glimpses" of different cultures (McCracken, 1993, p. 14; see also Banks, 1989, 1991/1992). Such a superficial approach, often presenting primarily the "foods, feasts, and festivals" of different groups, trivializes cultural groups and the individuals who represent them. Further, this approach can misrepresent American ethnic groups, peoples whose cultural perspective incorporates aspects of their original homeland with attributes developed in response to life in the United States. For example, second- or third-generation Mexican-Americans living in El Paso, Texas, have very different lives from those of family members who are still living in rural areas in the state of Chihuahua, Mexico.

In contrast to a trivializing "foods, feasts, and festivals" approach, teachers can help young children develop concrete understanding about similarities and differences among other members of their class. Without reducing lessons or activities to trivial, one-shot experiences, teachers can acknowledge and celebrate the cultural heritages represented in the class. Activities that use the arts—music, movement, dance, storytelling, painting, drawing, weaving—and that spring from children's literature can contribute substantially to discussions of diversity and cultural heritage. These experiences have their own representations in diverse cultures, and these repre-

Figure 5.1
Roots Feed the Tree of Life This idea for a bulletin board allows children to see the countries from which their classmates' families have come.

Reprinted from Learning the Skills of Peacemaking, by Naomi Drew (1987/1994) (B. L. Winch & Associates/Jalmar Press). Used with permission from B. L. Winch & Associates/Jalmar Press.

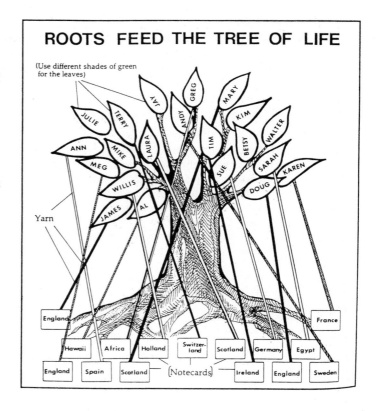

sentations can be studied and enjoyed. Additionally, children can readily participate in these activities in meaningful ways (see Epeneter & Chang, 1992; Green, 1993; McCracken, 1993; Neugebauer, 1992). However, teachers must be ever vigilant that no piece of music, finger play, rhyme, or book introduced to children communicates racial or ethnic stereotypes.

Teachers can also introduce factual material about the cultural heritage of students. Again, good children's books can be invaluable. Parents and community members are excellent resources as well. Guidelines for selecting books are presented in chapter 11.

SECOND CORE COMPONENT: AWARENESS OF LANGUAGE

Awareness of the importance of language is the second important component of culturally sensitive instruction. The languages children bring from home are part of their very being, part of what defines them as individuals and as members of a cultural group. The instructional value of teachers who speak the children's language cannot be overestimated. They provide links with home, often share children's cultural background, become role models, and can communicate easily with parents. But, as stated before, matches in teacher–child language are not always available. It is incumbent upon early childhood teachers, therefore, to be both sensitive to language differences and knowledgeable about methods to accommodate differences within their classrooms.

A common goal of early childhood programs is students' sense of themselves as competent language users. Another goal, when bilingual programs are not available, should be to help students reach toward mastery of English, their language of instruction. It is essential, though, that children's home language not be minimized or denigrated. To achieve this second goal, teachers can provide non-English-speaking students with the kind of language-rich environment that marks strong early childhood programs. In fact, many of the characteristics of child- and language-centered early childhood programs can be as nurturing of second-language learners as they are of children who have learned English as their main language (see chapters in Spangenberg-Urbschat & Pritchard, 1994, to substantiate this point).

For second-language learners, activities and people provide scaffolds for acquiring English. Interesting activities give children a context from which to draw information. Peer teaching begins almost immediately and is

Figure 5.2
The Ladder of Peacemaking This bulletin board idea can be used to develop concepts of global peace and responsibility. Each section of the ladder should be discussed carefully to ensure that students understand how the component parts fit together and where they, as children, figure into the grand scheme of peacemaking.

Reprinted from Learning the Skills of Peacemaking, by Naomi Drew (1987/1994) (B. L. Winch & Associates/Jalmar Press). Used with permission from B. L. Winch & Associates/Jalmar Press.

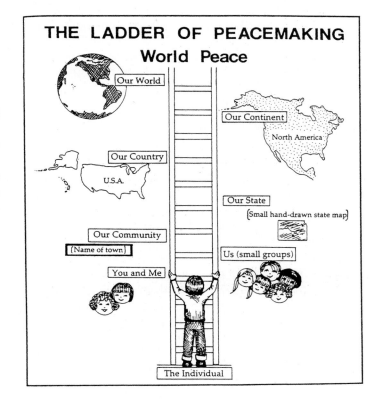

a powerful tool. Second-language learners see what is going on and what is being used; they hear labels, names, and descriptions; they listen for extended conversations and verbal formulas that draw the activities together. Gradually, they begin to learn English while English is being used purposefully and naturally. The routines of the classroom—such as snack time, use of centers, and dismissal time—also provide scaffolding and should be kept as consistent and dependable as possible. English learners can perceive the structure of the classroom, understand and participate in many activities, assimilate vocabulary, and grasp intuitively the communicative nature of many interactions.

In such an environment, teachers' acceptance of the communicative efforts of all children affirms young learners' natural approach to language learning; it encourages children learning English to experiment with their new language in purposeful ways. The language richness of classroom life includes the conversations that children have among themselves. Teachers need to provide opportunities for children to play and work together, to create their own language communities in which English learners perceive a need to communicate and feel comfortable doing so. Block areas and other centers, collaborative projects, and playtime are all excellent venues for peer-to-peer communication and teaching.

Even if principles of strong early childhood programs are equally supportive of the growth of all children, teachers must also be attuned to specific needs of children from differing linguistic backgrounds. The transition to school is simply easier and smoother when the language of school and home are the same. Teachers can accommodate students' needs as they learn to listen and speak, read, and write in English, but they must first assess what children know.

Assessing What Children Know

Standardized tests are repeatedly criticized for providing limited measures of young children's language skills. This criticism is especially valid for second-language learners and nonstandard dialect speakers. Teachers themselves are better able to gather background information and assess concept development, language skills, and levels of socialization. If teachers understand children's language, they can converse with them directly or eavesdrop as children interact with others or talk to themselves. Such informal oral language assessments provide accurate measures of children's language strengths and needs. Samples of children's attempts to use English reveal traces of the syntax and vocabulary of their home languages and give teachers indications of the extent to which young learners are becoming proficient in English.

Teachers also must assess how much information children can extract from regular classroom situations (e.g., clean-up time, lining up for lunch) and from nonverbal behavior (e.g., scowls, frowns, smiles). Receptive language skills develop first, and children who choose not to communicate orally in English may still understand what is being said around them. Children's physical responses are important indicators of comprehension, as are children's general demeanor and sense of comfort in an environment where their home language is not used.

Parents can sometimes provide information, especially about previous school or child-care experiences or language use in the home. Parents can also help teachers understand whether shyness is a personality trait or represents real fear of the new situation. Language differences can exaggerate insecurities, but young children's natural curiosity and interest in language should, in time, contribute to socialization.

Learning to Communicate

It goes without saying that the transition from home to school is easiest when the language or dialect of home and the language of school are the same. When the languages of children's two important worlds are different, young learners may need special help in adjusting to their new environment. Essentially, they must learn to "translate" into standard English the words for concepts, procedures, wishes, and demands that they know perfectly well in their first language. Some children must strive for bilingualism; others, as the previous citation from Gilyard suggested, strive to become bidialectal.

Additionally, the *patterns of verbal interaction* children have experienced at home may be very different from what is expected in school, so even if children understand all their teacher's words, they may not understand his or her intent. To illustrate, Delpit (1988) suggests that children accustomed to hearing direct orders at home are often confused by the "veiled commands" teachers often use. For example, a child might not recognize a teacher's question "Is that where this book belongs?" as equivalent to his mother saying, "Put that book away!" As suggested earlier, children need to learn protocols for verbal behaviors so that their particular verbal styles are not misinterpreted as disruptive or disrespectful behavior or as a lack of learning.

Two other points are important for teachers to remember. First, learning a new language or learning to function in a second dialect takes work, and children can easily become exhausted by the energy they must expend. They may know answers to questions and have comments to make and simply not have the energy to search for the needed English words to communicate. Freeman and Freeman (1993) caution that "listening in a second language is more tiring than listening to one's native language. Second language learners may appear to have shorter attention spans than native speakers, but in reality, those students may be suffering from the fatigue of trying to make sense out of their new language" (p. 19). Reluctance to respond or initiate conversations does not mean that children are not learning; receptive language (listening and learning vocabulary and language structure) precedes fluent oral production, and often a smile or nod of understanding is sufficient indication of progress toward English competence.

The second point concerns the importance of teachers' constant monitoring for children's understanding of what goes on in the classroom. Many bilingual programs teach young learners the basic concepts of all academic subjects in their home languages to ensure a strong educational foundation. When such instruction is unavailable, children can easily fall behind. Failing to understand even a few words of a lesson can cause children confusion or misunderstanding (Freeman and Freeman, 1993). These cautionary words are true for children who speak dialects of English as well. Although they may ostensibly know all the words teachers are using, dialect speakers may not know certain key technical terms or may have trouble because of the teacher's intonation patterns or regional accent.

Teachers need to present information in many ways—offering support with pictures, concrete objects, and manipulatives, gently checking up on children's understanding and providing many opportunities for review and reteaching. Of course, this is basic, good teaching, but teachers must be wary of appearing condescending or "talking down" to young learners as they attempt to support efforts to learn English.

Collaborative learning groups and peer projects that couple native speakers with English learners can reinforce learning in positive ways. Other activities—such as cooking, making puppets, doing art work, or presenting dramatizations—offer contexts on which teachers and students may comment and from which children can draw language. If English speakers are participants in group activities, they will probably provide verbal accompaniments to the project and will contribute to teachers' discussions. Teachers can sit in on such groups and fill in information and terminology that is needed to support learning.

Language play in English with nursery rhymes, songs, and poems is also helpful. Giving children many opportunities to talk and to question increases their chances of learning content information and increasing their English communicative skills as well. The best activities are those that not only provide many language opportunities but also encourage—almost nudge—children to use language in a variety of ways. Nudging is not the same as demanding use of the target language and in no way carries judgment. The important point for teachers to remember is that immersion in language and motivation to use emerging skills will help young learners acquire their new language in as natural and purposeful a way as possible.

LEARNING TO READ

A tenet of bilingual education is that if children learn to read in their home language, they will be able to make a smooth and rapid transition to reading in English; one learns the mechanics of reading only once (Freeman & Freeman, 1993). However, when children with limited English proficiency are learning to read English, teachers must help them understand and make use of the interrelatedness of their emerging oral skills and the challenges presented by reading English. Teacher transcriptions of children's dictated stories (the language experience approach), often full of words in English and the home language, can provide beginning material to help young learners get the "feel" of reading. (This approach is discussed in detail in subsequent chapters because it is an important component of the early literacy curriculum.) When children's literature is used for instruction, teachers must take time to assess learners' background knowledge and build requisite understanding about what they will read.

Teachers' reading of good children's literature is also valuable. It familiarizes learners with the intonations of standard English, the sounds and

Holidays are a vital part of each person's heritage, and children's literature can be part of classroom celebrations. But teachers should never assume that all students celebrate the same holidays or in the same way. Affirming that there are different holiday celebrations helps children understand and appreciate cultural diversity. Teachers can familiarize students with Santa Claus hats, menorahs, dreidels, Chinese New Year dragons, and symbols of other holidays. Books describing different holiday celebrations are easy to find as well.

patterns of stories, and concepts of print, such as the relationships between illustrations and text. Books with repetitive patterns and predictable stories are especially good, as are big-book versions of these stories (see chapters 8 and 11). Children can identify the connection between teacher and student verbalization and the illustrations in the book. Predictable refrains and repetitive sentence patterns encourage second-language learners to join in. Again, the material and the situation provide the scaffolding.

Stories about children's heritage can provide excellent links between home and school and can stimulate good discussion. Some books, such as *My Day/Mi Dia* (Emberley, 1994), are written in two languages; *My Day/Mi Dia* depicts a day's activities at home and at school with appropriate terminology offered in English and Spanish. *Let's Go/Vamos* (Emberley, 1994) shows places children enjoy visiting, such as the zoo and the circus, and again uses labels and simple text in both languages.

Principles discussed in subsequent chapters provide more detail about learning to read in supportive classroom settings. It is important for teachers to remember that learning to read is a complex cognitive task and that students learning both to speak and to read in English need to be given time to make sense of their new tasks. Children who come to school speaking dialects of.English should have no trouble learning to read—so long as teachers provide them with ample experiences to become familiar with books, print concepts, and story structures. Teacher transcription of personal stories can be helpful here, too.

As children who are learning English as a second language and who speak dialects actually begin to read, teachers need to be especially careful to focus their attention on what might be called "big aspects" of reading (Fitzgerald, 1993). Table 5.2 lists several of these aspects.

Additionally, teachers must be tolerant of what may seem to be errors—insertion of words or grammatical structures from their home language or dialect, code switching, heavily accented pronunciation, or omission of words children cannot orally decode. So long as children seem to be reading with comprehension, teachers should ignore such deviations from text. Signs of comprehension evidenced by enjoyment of the story, apparent comfort with the act of reading, or answers to questions are better indicators that students are learning to read than perfect matches between oral utterances and text. Too much correction interrupts the important activity of getting meaning from text and obscures the fact that reading is for constructing meaning. Delpit (1990) cautioned teachers not to "confuse dialect [or English language] intervention with reading instruction. To do so will only confuse the child, leading her away from the intuitive understandings about language that will promote reading development, and [pushing her] toward a school career of resistance and a lifetime of avoiding reading" (p. 258).

Teachers may not see results of instruction and practice immediately; children gradually piece together all that they are observing and learning. So long as teachers continue to support growth and to provide enriching language

Table 5.2
"Big Aspects" of Reading and Writing

Rather than focus on small details or on the correction of errors, teachers of children learning to speak English as their second language and learning to read and write in this new language should help them understand these concepts:

1. Reading and writing are **communicative processes that involve sending and receiving messages** through print.
2. When one reads, one should try to **get the gist of the text**—that is, the main idea or theme that the author of the piece is trying to transmit.
3. Try to **make the most important inferences** from text and to begin to **understand the different text structures** represented in stories, informational pieces, and other texts.
4. When one writes, one should **identify and communicate to a particular audience** and write in a way that will **enable that audience to understand** the message being communicated.
5. Learn that there are particular structures for writing **for different purposes and to different audiences**.
6. **Think about one's reading and writing and monitor one's success** by using metacognitive strategies; students may not at first be able to express their strategies in English, but they should be encouraged to try to develop an awareness of what they are doing as they read and write.

experiences, children can be expected to progress. Individualized help from a trained aide, parent volunteer, or older tutor who speaks a child's home language but will encourage the use of English can be especially beneficial.

LEARNING TO WRITE

No matter what language children bring with them to school, they should be encouraged to write as soon as they themselves feel ready to commit words to paper—in whatever language seems most comfortable for them. Children who are allowed to take risks with language use and who know that they will not be punished for mistakes construct their own rules as they use written language.

Allowing children to begin to write in their home language or dialect encourages them to experiment with and sort out the letter–sound correspondences, sentence patterns, and grammatical rules; it allows them to express ideas that they consider important. Writing in English follows as children gain confidence in their ability to express ideas in the language of the classroom. Writing in "standard" grammar ensues with practice and feedback on beginning efforts.

Children will benefit more from "real" writing than from sentence and grammar drills. As with reading, assistance from someone who speaks children's language can be very helpful. The "writing assistant" can help children translate ideas from one language to another and can transcribe stories written in both languages.

As children begin to write, teachers need to focus on the "big aspects" of their beginning efforts to encourage their communicative competence and confidence (again see Table 5.2). Recognizing that beginning efforts will reflect nonstandard syntactic patterns and word choices, teachers should encourage second-language learners to participate as soon as possible in classroom writing activities. Their writing efforts can then support and reinforce beginning efforts to communicate and read in English.

REALISTIC EXPECTATIONS FOR THE EARLY CHILDHOOD YEARS

The process of learning a new language or dialect is hard work; it is often slow, with initial periods of silent observation and reflection. The process of adjusting to a new culture—the culture of English-speaking schools—is also slow. Teachers need to recognize that children will progress at different rates, often showing no outward progress as they think their way through their new situation, learn their new language, and gradually adjust. As with first-language learners, receptive language will develop first. Children will be able to understand teachers and peers before they themselves begin to verbalize. Listening and doing as asked, responding nonverbally or with smiles, or responding with a simple utterance are all signs of progress in language mastery and should be warmly welcomed.

Finally, children who are adjusting to a new culture, learning a new language, and simultaneously trying to learn the many school-related routines, facts, skills, and strategies may seem overwhelmed with their task. Teachers may perceive them as overly quiet and reticent and possibly infer that they are not learning. This might be a totally incorrect inference. Teachers need to give children as many varied opportunities as possible to demonstrate emerging academic competence and must also guard against prematurely judging learners' academic potential. It is essential that children never be made to question their skills, intelligence, and worth as they are confronting the tremendous task of finding their place and identity in school.

SUMMARY

Teachers do not have to learn a whole new way of teaching when students from diverse cultural, linguistic, and social backgrounds enter their classrooms. They must, however, work hard to provide a classroom where diversity is considered a strength, a powerful force for enriching the curriculum and the lives of students and teachers alike. Instruction that is responsive to cultural diversity is based on high expectations for all students and respect for linguistic and cultural differences. Language-rich, child-centered early classrooms can be welcoming places for children from diverse backgrounds and can provide them with the intellectual and emotional support they need to adjust and to thrive in what may at first seem an alien environment.

QUESTIONS AND TASKS FOR INDEPENDENT OR COLLABORATIVE WORK

1. Be sure that you can define each of these terms:

    • school culture
    • opportunities to learn

2. The chapter suggested that teachers can provide activities to "nudge" children to use language in a variety of ways. Think of as many instructional and social activities as you can that would nudge children who are learning English as a second language to use English in productive ways. Compare your list with others and evaluate the benefits of your ideas.

3. Interview three or four people of any age for whom English was not their first language. How did they learn English? If they learned it in school, was their instruction sensitive to their needs? How did they learn to read and write English? Compare your interview data with those of others in your class.

4. In small groups, discuss apprehensions and anxieties you and your fellow students may have about teaching in situations where the children are from different cultural backgrounds and speak languages other than the one(s) you speak. Can you identify biases, fears, and stereotypes that may inhibit your abilities to interact easily with your students and with their parents?

CHAPTER 6

Making Progress with Communication Skills

Don Holdaway (1979) summarized how young children control their own learning. "To put the matter very simply," he wrote, "the child's own system acts as an amazingly sensitive teaching machine" (p. 23). This teaching machine functions in different ways throughout children's development but is probably never more active than as children learn to use language to communicate with others.

A BRIEF DISCUSSION OF LANGUAGE ACQUISITION

Children exhibit a wide range of differences in language development. Some speak early, some later; some speak a lot, some are quieter. No matter how many or what kind of languages they hear around them, children pass through definite stages of cooing, babbling, and experimenting with speech sounds and begin to use oral language at roughly the same age. Babies seem to have an innate neurological/biological/intellectual potential for learning language; they attempt to communicate with those around them long before they can actually speak, and their oral language emerges without direct instruction from parents and caregivers. Even before it can be readily understood, children's emerging oral language reflects the sounds, sentence structure, vocabulary, and social use of the languages they hear around them.

Preverbal communication can be thought of as a "placeholder" for what children actually mean. The term *placeholder of meaning* refers to the nonstandard strategies children develop to express themselves. In this case, pseudocommunication through gestures, babbling, and other speech-like sounds "holds the place" of actual speech and expresses the meanings children want to communicate.

Playing with Language

Throughout their transition from infancy to the toddler stage and beyond, young children learn primarily through play and manipulation of their environment. Children play quite naturally with elements of language—such as word order and meaning, expressive noises, pitch, intonation, and rhyme—to test ideas about how language works. Alone, they use **language play** to amuse themselves or to practice what they are discovering about oral skills. With other people, children may try to amuse, question concepts, test the power of language, and check their assumptions about communication. The examples in Table 6.1 illustrate how children test the limits of language through play.

Table 6.1
Examples of Children Playing with Language

Example 1
A three-year-old boy demonstrated language play as he sat with his six-year-old sister, Nina, and me. His aunt had moved in with the family shortly before my visit, and he was uncertain about my place in the family structure. He chanted "Auntie Jane" several times in reference to his aunt and was told she was not at home. Turning to his sister, he questioned, "Auntie Nina?" and laughed. I represented a challenge: "Auntie Terry?" As his sister and I tried to explain, his mother entered, and he was able to turn his confusion into a joke. Laughing loudly and confidently, he yelled, "I know! I know! Auntie Mommie!"

Example 2
I overheard a child of two years, eight months break off his fluent conversation with his mother to give the following monologue during the landing process at a large metropolitan airport: "We're at the *air*port. We're *at* the airport. We're at the air*port*. We're at *the* airport. We're *on the ground.* We're at the *airport.*" The child tested more than twenty variations in sound before tapering off and resuming his conversation with his mother about changing planes and continuing their trip home.

Example 3
Language play can also be a means for children to express hostile, resentful, or outrageous ideas without incurring parents' or caregivers' anger. Play, after all, is play and not to be taken seriously. Garvey (1977, pp. 39–40) reported a conversation that illustrates this behavior well. It will sound familiar to anyone who has spent time eavesdropping on young children:

Conversation	
Female (five years, seven months)	Female (five years, one month), on play telephone
1. Mommy, mommy, I got new friends called Dool, Sol, Ta.	
	2. Dool, Sue, and Ta?
(Both laugh)	
3. Those are funny names, aren't they?	
	4. No, It's Poopoo, Daigi, and Dia . . . Diarrhea.
(Both laugh)	

The laughter in conversations such as these marks the interactions as play. Ritual insults, mock threats, and outrageous comparisons are other examples of this kind of linguistic play.

Thinking about Language

Young learners exert tremendous cognitive energy as they puzzle over the way language sounds and how it is put together. They also try to discover what different words mean and how language is used socially. Children seem to try to manipulate situations so that they can get information about sounds, intonation, voice patterns, gestures, and facial expressions. Watching and listening provide the "raw materials" from which young children actively construct a sense of how communication works.

LEARNING ABOUT CONCEPTS

Children's language provides insight into their concept learning. In his classic and highly readable book *From Two to Five*, Chukovsky (1963) referred to children as "linguistic geniuses" because of the ways they explore, test, and reach conclusions about the concepts they experience in the world. He recorded many children's statements about their thinking and their efforts to make sense of their world. The statements reflect children's efforts to connect intellectually what they know and the new experiences they encounter. Consider these brief statements cited by Chukovsky:

- Walking along a beach, a child saw a ship in the distance and said, *Mommie, Mommie, the locomotive is taking a bath* (p. 1).
- *The sea has one shore but the river has two* (p. 21).
- *I like garlic, it smells like sausage* (p. 21).
- *Why do they put the pit in every cherry? We have to throw the pit away anyway* (p. 21).
- *They bury old people—that is, they plant them in the ground and from them grow little children, like flowers* (p. 48).

These statements illustrate how "fuzzy" children's initial concepts may be. Caregivers must be alert to the naive, poorly formed, and incomplete nature of many beginning concepts to ensure that they and their young students communicate clearly with each other. Helping children clarify fuzzy concepts without implying that the concepts are wrong takes tact and skill but is an important part of early childhood teaching.

Children come to understand concepts through three kinds of experiences. The first kind is *direct interaction* with concrete objects or personal experiences. Children learn about dogs by seeing dogs, about books by handling books, about singing by singing. The best preschool environments are those in which children *do* many things, handle many different familiar and unfamiliar objects, and engage in conversations about what they see and do.

Thinking about concepts such as "same and different" increases children's understanding of abstractions and their ability to talk about such concepts.

The second level of experience is *interaction with pictorial representations* of objects and experiences. Photographs, drawings, cartoons, and other representations are more abstract than concrete objects, even though children can hold them and trace around outlines of what they see. Because pictures are more abstract, it is harder for young children to extract information from them; learning to do so takes maturation and experience. Still, pictures can be valuable learning aids. As they introduce pictures to children to help them develop concepts and vocabulary, early childhood teachers should provide as many back-up concrete experiences as possible. A unit on plants, for example, should start with a demonstration of real plants so that children can see, feel, and smell leaves, stems, and soil. Real seeds should be planted, ideally in a transparent container so that roots will be visible. Houseplants, garden plants, flowers, vegetables, bushes, and trees can all be experienced in one form or another. Then, to expand the concept, children may examine pictures of strange and exotic plants that do not grow in their area.

Being able to extract information from pictorial material is a necessary skill for learning from books. A child of two might look at an early childhood science book and enjoy the pictures, but a somewhat older child will often study the same pictures and surprise those around him by commenting on how the "bush in the yard has leaves just like the ones I saw in a book." Even without reading skills as such, the child has learned to gain information from a printed source.

Experience with abstractions represents the final and most sophisticated means by which young children learn about concrete objects. In early childhood classes, abstract representations of information frequently take the form of "teacher talk" or teachers' oral reading. Children listen to the teacher, try to understand, and attempt to gain information without concrete referents. They must think about something they cannot directly experience. For example, a discussion or book about the desert will make little sense to children in inner-city Detroit or rural Vermont. Unless children have had appropriate background experiences, they will either not understand what the teacher is saying or will misunderstand as they try to tie the new information to something they already know.

Teachers can build children's background knowledge by providing as many direct experiences and good illustrations as possible. For example, bringing cactus plants to class and sharing well-illustrated books can help children begin to understand what deserts are, especially if teachers tie learning about cacti and lizards to what children know about other plants and animals.

ENCOURAGING LANGUAGE GROWTH

Teachers can help children expand vocabularies, strengthen concepts, and clarify abstractions by their own modeling, expansion, and questioning. *Modeling* is the caregiver's own use of correct terminology, clear statements, and verbal expansions. If a child refers to his yellow slicker with the word *purple*, the caregiver could model appropriate use by replying, "No, your slicker is yellow, like the counter by the sink." If another child called her dark blue sweater purple, the caregiver might reply, "No, it's blue. Blue and purple sometimes look almost alike. Let's find something purple so you can see the difference." Here, the caregiver is using *expansion* to clarify vocabulary and concepts; that is, the caregiver accepts the child's statement without judgment, corrects it as necessary, and adds new information to clarify a faulty concept. The child feels that he has learned something rather than that he has been corrected.

Questioning is a trickier procedure, one that is difficult for teachers to use successfully. As Routman (1989, 1991) pointed out, there is no handy guide to help teachers learn to ask effective, developmentally appropriate, challenging questions. Often teachers ask questions designed, however unconsciously, as a quiz or follow-up to what has just been taught, rather than as a way to exchange information with a child. Chapter 5 cited research suggesting that some children find such questions bewildering because they know that the teacher already knows the answer. Questions should be used to elicit children's opinions and ideas, their feelings, and their analyses and evaluations. Such questions probe for real information and genuine thought and show respect for even the youngest learner as a capable, thinking person. They allow children to display the depth and breadth, as well as the inaccuracies, of their knowledge base. Teachers gain insight into what children really know and understand and what else needs to be taught or clarified.

Learning English as a Second Language

As stated in the previous chapter, no matter what language children learn as their first language, they engage in dynamic, playful experimentation to gather information about how language works. They build up a storehouse of conceptual knowledge reflective of their cultural and experiential backgrounds and understand the "rules" of their first language. They come to school enthusiastic and ready to learn.

Children who have first learned a language other than English use the language of their home as their reference point for grammar, vocabulary, and concepts. Teachers must help children connect learning in their first language to their new learning opportunities in English. Experiences that expand background knowledge, frequent checks on understanding, and teaching strategies geared to individuals' diverse learning pathways enable children to make sense of instruction offered in their new language.

PRAGMATICS

In addition to learning how to speak and listen, young children also learn about the structure and conventions of their social world and about the relationship between language and those conventions. These relationships, referred to as **pragmatics,** include the socially and cognitively determined decisions that speakers make about style, vocabulary, tone, register, and so forth as they use language to attain specific goals. Examples include giving directions, making requests, telling jokes and stories, making up songs, offering explanations and evaluations, assuming new roles through voice changes, passing judgment, and initiating, maintaining, and ending conversations (Cazden, 1983, 1988).

Children learn about pragmatics directly from adults and through their own observations, practice, and play. Traditionally, children have learned about language conventions in the home; however, as more children are entrusted to preschool programs, the task of helping youngsters learn the complex functions of language will be shared by teachers. Table 6.2 summarizes what children learn about pragmatics.

The social conventions of language that children bring to school reflect the values and customs of their homes and communities. Children who curse or use socially inappropriate terms do not, in all probability, realize

Table 6.2
What Children Learn about Pragmatics

Names
- Children learn that people and things have specific names.
- They also learn that names can be changed arbitrarily and playfully, and that making such changes can be an effective way to gain attention. Forming rhymes with names is a common way to experiment with names (e.g., Lenny/Benny/henny/menny/nenny, etc.).

Directives and Requests
- Preverbal infants point, gesture, slap, smile, scowl, squeal, cry, and use other noises to indicate choices, requests, and directives.
- In beginning speech, use of words like *want, more,* and *allgone* express desires and needs.
- Use of the imperative verb form (e.g., "Give me a cookie," with the subject *you* understood) appears at about age three, sometimes accompanied by the "magic word" *please*; children seem to know the power of the word *please* and differentiate its use depending on audience and intent. Many children are more inclined to use *please* in school than at home.

Stories
- Adults' comments on children's actions are the initial models for sequenced "stories," and, by eighteen months, children begin to recite their own commentaries on what they do (e.g., "Climb the stairs, put my foot up, other foot up," etc.).
- By age three, children can create story characters verbally and describe their actions.
- By age four, they can attribute motives and feelings to their creations.
- As they get older, especially if they have had models, children may tell highly elaborate stories, complete with ghosts, devils, make believe, ritual insults, and quotations with appropriate changes in voice. Two or more children may collaborate and tell a joint story with well-orchestrated turn taking.
- Movies and television, as well as children's books, provide many models of storytelling (and pragmatics in general) for young learners.

Common Expressions
- Children learn individual expressions and patterns of speech from the media and use them often without a totally developed understanding of the meaning they convey.
- Even young children may use expressions that are crude, offensive, stereotypical, or inappropriate because of "models" they do not understand. The models may be family, the media, or older children. Teachers need to respond to inappropriate expressions firmly but nonjudgmentally to help children understand appropriate "school language."
- Teachers may need to alert parents to children's use of "inappropriate" language so that they, the parents, can help children become aware of language differences between home and school.

that they may be offending the teacher. Some classmates may not understand that the language is unacceptable, whereas others may even be amused and titillated to hear these words coming from a peer; others may be deeply offended (without really knowing why) and can be cruel in rejecting the speaker. Teachers who hear children using inappropriate language must be firm but not judgmental in their insistence that "We don't use that term in school," with the goal of broadening children's vocabulary choices and knowledge about language use. A different tack, firmer and more insistent, must, of course, be taken with children who knowingly use offensive language for effect. Because these children have learned the pragmatic reality that certain words elicit certain responses, their behavior is deliberate and should be treated like any other discipline problem.

Contextualized and Decontextualized Language

As children learn about pragmatics, they learn that language may be either contextualized or decontextualized. **Contextualized language** consists of verbal interactions based on the shared knowledge and experiences of speaker and listener, such as discussion about people or things in the immediate environment or about topics of common interest and mutual familiarity. Children's ability to produce and comprehend contextualized language develops over time from participation in the routines and rituals of their environment.

Decontextualized language, on the other hand, is more abstract. Meaning comes from the words themselves, with relative independence from any specific context or concrete referent. Stories in a book are good examples of decontextualized language because the characters and settings exist only in written, two-dimensional form. The discussion of learning about the desert mentioned earlier also illustrates decontextualized language for those children who have not experienced a desert firsthand.

School language in general, both oral and written, is also decontextualized because teachers and students do not necessarily share mutual assumptions and experiences. Content and topics are relatively abstract and not directly present. What teachers say may not make sense to a young child who is unfamiliar with the "jargon" of school. Try to imagine what a five-year-old thinks the "middle sound in 'cat'" or "a silent letter" actually means. Additionally, what books have to say to beginning readers may seem equally meaningless unless children enter school with some concept of decontextualized language from which to develop school-related "scripts" or patterns of communication.

Learning the Language of School

Just as they begin to learn that many school situations involve decontextualized content, children learn that there is a special "language" that they must be able to understand and produce if they are going to participate fully in school activities. This language includes many verbal patterns for direct and indirect questioning, requests, and instructive lectures; for discussing abstractions or people and objects that are not present or are imaginary; and for discovering sequential and causal relationships in what they hear and read. Children must also understand the special language used in books.

Teachers of children in preschool, kindergarten, and early primary grades can help children master this language. As mentioned in previous chapters, teachers provide children with helpful "scaffolds." In this case, teachers may scaffold entire instructional situations. Remember that scaffolds are interchanges in which adults at first utter entire "scripts" and gradually allow children to fill in parts of those scripts as they master necessary skills. For example, as teachers read to very young learners, they may stop and ask questions about the story. They then refer to the story as they provide answers to their own questions; this is a scaffold to inform children what is expected in this kind of interchange. With time, teachers expect the children to answer questions themselves, although teachers may fill in information to complete youngsters' responses. From these experiences, learners generalize what is expected and can readily answer more and more questions on their own. They have learned an overarching script for this kind of classroom interaction.

As teachers gradually "open up" lessons to allow children more challenge, they must remember that children want very much to please. Without understanding the true nature or purpose of a lesson, they will often "fake" behavior or imitate what they see others doing to gain approval and affection. Children in early childhood classes may not necessarily know that what they do is supposed to make sense. In nonjudgmental ways, teachers need to ask students whether they understand school-related activities; they must observe young learners for signs of confusion or misdirection. Asking children to repeat procedures or content "in their own words" is also a good method for checking on their understanding. Teachers need to remember that children accustomed to hearing discussions about school in their own homes will more readily understand this kind of school dialogue (Heath, 1982; Taylor, 1983).

Finally, teachers should ensure that children feel comfortable enough to ask for clarification if they do not understand what is going on. Learning how to ask for help is part of learning the scripts of school language.

INSTRUCTIONAL ACTIVITIES FOR LISTENING AND SPEAKING

Although oral language development during the early childhood years seems to move forward according to its own momentum, direct instruction in specific kinds of speaking belongs in a well-formulated early childhood language arts curriculum. By their very nature, exercises that refine oral language skills also develop listening skills. Here are some factors that contribute to children's listening abilities:

* *Maturation.*
* *Motivation* (do children believe that the process of listening is worthwhile and that what they hear is interesting?).
* *Specific instruction* in how to listen attentively.
* *Modality,* especially preference for an auditory modality—that is, from birth, some individuals seem to prefer to receive information by hearing and are more attentive than others to auditory cues. Children who are "auditory learners" develop and display strong, dependable listening skills early in life. They would rather hear a story than look at a book, they like to sit very close to a record player, and they may seem to be day dreaming as the teacher speaks but later show that they had been listening very attentively.
* *Auditory memory* capabilities—the amount of auditory information that a person can store mentally and retrieve for later use, as well as the ease with which they can do this; young children who learn all the words of a song the first time it is sung or recite poems along with the teacher display strong auditory memory abilities, which can be strengthened with practice.
* *Auditory perception*—the ability to distinguish one sound from another, blend sounds together, and sequence and repeat sound; this is an essential component of learning to spell and read.
* *Auditory acuity*—the ability to distinguish between sounds on the basis of pitch, tone, and loudness; teachers must remember, however, that individuals hear sounds differently depending on the speech community from which they come. A common test of auditory acuity is to ask children to distinguish between "minimal pairs"—such as *pen* and *pin*—which differ only in one sound (in some dialects, however, the short *e* and short *i* are voiced in the same way, as though the words were homophones).

Activities to foster growth in listening and speaking should allow children to use all their senses; touching, tasting, and smelling give children something to talk about. Activities should encourage children to move, and, whenever possible, children should see a written copy of what they are hearing, memorizing, or reciting. Even if they are not yet able to read, seeing the graphic image connects what is heard and said with the written symbols of language. Naturally, activities should include as many opportunities as possible for play and should encourage thinking and problem solving.

Listening and speaking activities can be frustrating if children do not know what is expected of them or if tasks are beyond their cognitive abilities. If, contrary to what would be developmentally appropriate, teachers ask children to hold in their memories more complex auditory patterns or longer strings of words than they could possibly remember, the goal of increasing listening and speaking skills will be thwarted. Beginning any instruction with discussion of expected behaviors increases children's understanding. Children may also need clear instructions in "good listening manners" and verbal turn-taking behaviors. Repeating the rules and expectations before each lesson keeps children alert to the special behaviors required of them.

Successful listening and speaking instruction involves two-way responsibility. Children have to understand that their tasks involve listening to any auditory stimulus, organizing it mentally, and responding to it in some way. Their response may be oral or physical—speaking, answering, clapping, or following directions. At the same time, adults need to remember the importance of treating what the child has to say as worthy of attention and of trying hard to understand the child's meaning. The child's meaning should be the basis for the adults' next comment, and adults should always try to gauge the child's understanding of what has been said. This is especially true when children are learning English or are unfamiliar with school instructional scripts or routines.

Rhymes, Poems, Jingles, and Finger Plays

Nursery rhymes, counting rhymes, poems, jingles, songs, and chants from games can all build listening and oral language skills. Children's natural playfulness embraces the words and sounds, and the funnier they are, the better. The words become even more effective learning material when children are invited to manipulate the sounds by imitating teachers' exaggerated readings or devising their own funny voices to personify a familiar chant or poem. Children should be encouraged to make up and present their own jingles, rhymes, and poems. Children who speak more than one language should use their dominant language with teacher translations provided for the rest of the class. The self-confidence and knowledge about language that these activities encourage are invaluable.

Finger plays are fun, too, and encourage auditory memory and clear speaking skills. Finger plays require that children coordinate words, often in rhymes, with actions. The most basic finger plays have children moving their fingers—clapping, moving fingers up and down their arms, wiggling fingers, hammering, sewing, and so forth. With more complicated finger plays, children move their faces, arms, or whole bodies. Children can participate even before they have learned the actual verses by merely following along with the movements. Early childhood teachers can use finger plays to develop vocabulary and concepts (for example, "Itsy Bitsy Spider" reinforces directional awareness) and to help children release pent-up energy.

Appendix A lists books that contain finger plays and other activities. Teachers are reminded to be aware of stereotypes presented in many of the traditional rhymes and finger plays and to avoid their use.

Conversations and Discussions

Structured oral interchanges in the form of conversations and discussions help all children learn strong listening and speaking skills and are especially beneficial for children who may not have learned the conventions of verbal turn taking and carrying on conversations in their homes. Knowledge of scripts for conversations and discussions expand children's understanding of the pragmatics of school language.

Teachers often use "rug time" or "sharing time" to hold short conversations or discussion. A focused topic—for example, What We Did on Our Trip to the Farm—works well to help children learn to listen to each other, not repeat what they have heard, and stick to a specific topic. If the conversation is about an object or animal present in the room, children should be allowed to handle it. The goals for these activities are to keep children on task, involve as many children as possible, and expand language and concepts. While accepting anything that is said, teachers maintain momentum by restating, clarifying, and commenting on what is presented. Thus, for example, a teacher leading a discussion with four-year-old children might say, "Yes, Steven, Lois told us about the cows we saw on our trip, too, but you told us their color. You said they were black and white. We've also talked about the pigs we saw; Jimmy said they were big, and Rachel said they were cute. Can anyone tell us something else? I remember that the farm had ducks. Who remembers seeing them? Oh, lots of you saw them. Ana, would you tell us what you thought about the ducks?" Discussions can lead naturally into teacher transcription and the language experience approach to creating beginning reading material. (See chapters 8 and 9.)

Older children benefit from longer, more open-ended discussions and can actively participate in group problem-solving sessions in which they think through practical problems and evaluate solutions. Brainstorming is a good procedure to use for problem solving. In brainstorming sessions, children can offer any kind of comment or suggestion because all ideas are accepted and recorded. Children's imaginations and creative abilities come to the fore when there are no unacceptable answers. For example, children might suggest ways to decorate their classroom for a holiday, improve the storage system in the painting area, or make presents for Mother's Day. Even if none of the suggestions proves practical ("No, we can't paint the room orange for Halloween"), the process of brainstorming together is beneficial. Writing activities can easily follow such brainstorming sessions to round out the experience.

Experiences with Books and Other Graphic Stimuli

Children benefit from many different kinds of experiences with printed materials—making up their own stories, describing what they see, listening to someone read to them, browsing through books, and reading on their own. Wordless picture books and individual pictures that tell a story can encourage children to interpret visual material, sequence and express their ideas, and make up extended stories. As individuals tell what they have seen in a picture or compose a narrative for a wordless picture book, their peers listen, evaluate, comment, and add their own ideas. Children's words can be combined to form a dictated chart story to further enhance emerging reading skills. Questions about what was dictated strengthen listening comprehension. Open-ended books or pictures are best because they encourage children to draw upon their imaginations and past experiences to compose creative, meaningful oral language. Numerous wordless picture books are listed in appendix A.

It is not that important who reads to young children or tells them stories, so long as someone reads to them *at least once a day*. Aides, volunteers, children from an upper grade, and student interns can all be trained to be effective readers for young children. Parents and community members who are gifted storytellers often enjoy spending time in preschool or early childhood classrooms because audiences there are so receptive. A very positive experience for children learning English as a second language is to have someone read to them in books written in their home language; this is an excellent task for parents, community volunteers, and bilingual students from upper grades.

I witnessed a kindergarten class in which one of the children frequently read to his classmates. The boy was an excellent and enthusiastic reader and seemed completely unaware of how advanced his skills were. Having watched his teacher read to the class, he knew how to turn the book to show the pictures and even had a sense of how to pace his words. The teacher had introduced this boy's reading to the class as an exciting and different activity—"Today we have a real treat. I have asked Jimmy to read to you and I'll just listen"—and the children received their classmate's accomplishment with appreciation and support. Throughout the year, Jimmy read to the whole class at least once a week and often read to small groups as well. He gained a strong sense of himself and was able to introduce many children to favorite books and to his love of reading.

Directed Listening–Thinking Activity

Reading to children is most profitable when teachers adopt an approach often called a **directed listening–thinking activity,** or **DLTA**. With this approach, teachers read, question, and encourage children's thinking about the stories being presented. The basic lesson, which is as applicable to a discussion or instructional sequence as to storytelling or reading, has five parts: establishing background, setting purposes for listening, active listening (without interrupting the speaker), following up on what has been presented, and extending the ideas to relate the story, topic, or skills. Table 6.3 outlines these steps more fully. Although teachers should not dilute children's enjoyment of storytime by turning the experience into a didactic session of quizzing for right answers, careful, thought-provoking questioning before, after, and during reading can help children learn to listen attentively, purposefully, and critically. Because it is modeled on principles of sharing literature in a comfortable, low-risk setting, the DLTA is a strong complement to children's small group reading instruction.

Questioning in a DLTA can also serve a diagnostic purpose. Because of diversity in language and experiential backgrounds, children will differ in

Table 6.3
Instructions for a Directed Listening–Thinking Activity (DLTA)

Objective: To encourage children to listen attentively and to interact thoughtfully with stories presented orally.

Assumption: Teacher has selected the story to be shared carefully and has prepared to read the book with expression.

Procedures:
1. Call children to circle for story.
2. Show the cover of the book and read the title.

   "I'm going to read this book to you today. It's called *Rich Cat, Poor Cat* and it's by Bernard Waber*. What do you see on the cover? What do you think the book will be about?"
   [Elicits that there is a plump, bejeweled cat and a thin one slinking by a garbage can; wants children to suggest that the book may compare their lives.]

3. Read a few pages (depending on amount of text per page). Show the pictures for each page, allowing children enough time to see them clearly.
4. Ask children to make predictions based on what has been read. Summarize or request summaries if needed to maintain story line.
   [Reads description of rich cats and of Scat, a street cat.]

   "Who can tell me what we've heard so far? What kind of pillow does it say Scat has? Would that be nice? Why not? Why do people call her Scat? Do you think she likes that name? What's going to happen?"
   [Elicits that rich and poor cats have been compared, that Scat has been described, and that Scat sleeps on cobblestones. Clarify term *cobblestones* for those who do not know it. Discuss name "Scat" and entertain all guesses about the rest of the story.]

---

continued

Table 6.3, *continued*

5. Stop again and repeat procedure after several pages.

    "Who can tell me about those rich cats? Did you hear what I read last? 'There isn't anything very special in Scat's life?' How does that make you feel?"

6. Continue process through significant sections of book, stopping to summarize and elicit predictions.

    "Well, what do we know about rich cats? Poor Scat, the book says that she is nobody's cat! Do you think that will be forever? What could happen to change it? Look at that picture of Scat; how does she look?"

    [Summarize and elicit guesses about Scat's life; allow children to suggest that she could get run over, could be taken to the pound, or could, ideally, be adopted; do not give away ending by overly responding to any possibility.]

7. Complete book with questions about how children liked it and which parts they liked best.

    "How many of you thought that would happen to Scat? How does she feel now? What do you think made the little girl and her mother take Scat home? How do you think Scat likes her new name?"

    [Elicit that Scat was adopted, that she probably feels happy, that the people were nice, and that Scat, now Gwendolyn, is finally a "rich cat." If no one notices, point out that the bejeweled Gwendolyn on the last page is the same as the picture on the cover. Let children respond to the book's content and make relevant comments about their own cats, neighborhood cats, pets in general.]

*Waber B. (1963). *Rich cat, poor cat.* Englewood Cliffs, NJ: Scholastic.

their abilities to understand what is read to them. Some may show that they are not comprehending by fidgeting during storytime, whereas others may never indicate their lack of understanding. By questioning the children, teachers can discover those who might not fully comprehend what they are hearing and thus can help to make future experiences more meaningful. Questions should be general and open-ended, eliciting summaries, opinions, or reactions to stories; they should not focus on trivial details.

Using a technique called *guided imagery* as part of a DLTA provides children with opportunities to listen appreciatively to stories, to exercise their imaginations, and to learn visualization skills. The traditional guided imagery experience is a sequential story of ten minutes or so that the teacher reads as children listen, usually sitting in a relaxed posture with their eyes closed. Children are encouraged to fantasize to the evocative words and to practice visualizing the scenes that they hear. Teachers may also play music while they read or while children just relax, draw, or paint.

Movement Activities, Dramatics, and Improvisation

Movement activities, dramatics, and improvisation are highly motivating because they capitalize on young children's need to move and be active. *Movement activities* begin with children's natural sense of rhythm and enjoyment of motions such as swinging, stretching, or tumbling. Children may engage in movement activities by themselves or in coordination with others. If the class terrarium had a snail in it, for example, children should be encouraged to watch it carefully before trying to pantomime how it moves. They may even talk together about how the motion should be imitated, with the teacher helping to develop new vocabulary by interjecting terms such as *slither*.

Music can also be used to encourage children's movement. Sometimes, music can stimulate spontaneous dancing, as children listen and translate what they hear into movement. This happened in one of my first-grade classes. The children were listening to "The Nutcracker Suite" and drawing.

Activities that involve looking, listening, and moving are important aspects of an early childhood literacy curriculum.

At the "Dance of the Sugar Plum Fairies," a little boy stopped drawing, rose from his seat, and without saying a word bid his classmates to follow him dancing around the room. I watched, totally fascinated, and obliged when the self-appointed sugar plum fairies asked me to play the music again. "The Flight of the Bumblebee," "Peter and the Wolf," and "Pictures at an Exhibition" are also excellent choices for use with children, as are many pieces of jazz.

Directed-movement activities are harder than they appear because children must receive a directive for how to move and interpret its meaning, often by coordinating an action word (*wriggle*) with a qualifier (*quickly*) and a locator (*across the floor*). Next, they must draw from memory how to perform these actions physically and then actually perform them, ideally in a way that will not make them feel too foolish. Because these behaviors involve linguistic, cognitive, psychomotor, and social functioning, they are valuable parts of an early childhood program, but they lose their effectiveness when perfection is required. They must remain fun—little bodies and minds stretching together—and never take on a testlike aspect.

Spontaneous *dramatic play* often occurs in the housekeeping or block area as a natural part of early childhood activities. Providing different props encourages children's imaginations. Through such play, children learn about many pragmatic functions of language. They try out different roles and behaviors, pose and solve problems, and stretch their imaginations. When books and paper supplies are available, children often incorporate them into their dramatic play. For example, a piece of paper can be used to take phone messages, as a menu in a restaurant, or as a letter from a friend or family member.

Improvisation and dramatics as planned activities also strengthen understanding of social uses of language and are excellent means for demonstrating the need for good speaking and listening skills. Improvisation is a good starting point for introducing dramatics to children. As they improvise, children experience focused role playing. Often they can release emotion, express humor, and gain insight into conflicts or distressing situations by "trying" different roles and appropriate voices, movements, and characteristics without the effort of producing an actual play. Improvisation as a follow-up to story reading reinforces appreciative and interpretive listening skills and gives teachers a view of how well children have comprehended what they have heard. As in their spontaneous dramatic play, children also enjoy improvising characters from television or movies.

Using dramatics is hard work (see Sebasta, 1993). When teachers decide for the first time to produce a play with young children, they frequently do not realize what a complicated project they are about to undertake. Coordinating all aspects of a production requires time and patience, as shown by the experience of one of my former students. During an internship in a second-grade class, she decided to write and produce a play for parents' night. The children were all Mexican-American, and their classroom instruction was conducted in both English and Spanish. The intern decided to use both languages in her play. The steps for developing a dramatic production are presented in Table 6.4 and illustrated with entries from the intern's journal about her experiences.

INSTRUCTIONAL IMPLICATIONS: GRAMMAR AND SENTENCE STRUCTURE

As stated in the previous chapter, regardless of the language or dialect children learn first, they exert tremendous cognitive energy toward its acquisition. Understanding this places teachers in the strongest position to help all young learners begin their progress toward mastery of standard usage without sacrificing use of their home language.[1] Children do not have to give up their own way of speaking or their home language when they enter school; they should be strongly encouraged to draw upon their oral language skills in all communication and as a base for beginning writing.

Yet, children do need to reach toward competence with language as used by teachers and as encountered in books so that they can benefit from instruction and participate fully in class. Many educators support this contention. Delpit (1988) has stated that implying to students "that it doesn't matter how [they] talk or write is to ensure their ultimate failure" (p. 292). This goal does not have to be incompatible with the culturally responsive instruction discussed in chapter 5.

Appropriate Strategies

Young children often use novel sentence structure or word choice, sometimes because of their developmental level in language learning and sometimes because of confusion with dialects or second languages. Many teachers wonder about the effectiveness of correcting young children's nonstandard expressions. Correction, in and of itself, is usually not productive, especially if laced with impatient judgment. Children need to be developmentally ready to understand and produce some particular grammatical or structural feature of oral language before they can even understand that they are being corrected. Restating children's comments in standard usage, helping them to hear differences between the registers of home and school, and verbally expanding children's statements to more standard forms are far more effective behaviors than making corrections. Their effectiveness

---

[1] The term *standard* here refers to language that conforms to widely recognized grammatical rules and conventions. It is the language of commerce and broadcast journalism, without the idiosyncratic ethnic, regional, or personal usage that children bring with them to school.

Table 6.4
Producing a Play

Step 1:
Develop an Idea for a Play
Journal Entry: The classroom teacher prompted the idea of using sections of the Mexican culture, as the students could more readily relate to the theme....I began an outline and elaborated on a script so that I could present it to the children for feedback....I introduced the idea of a play as an oral speaking/listening lesson; discussed what is meant by "performing a play"; discussed various types of plays; and brainstormed about any specific type of play they would like to perform.

Step 2:
Build Interest and Background Knowledge
Journal Entry: Conducted another oral speaking/listening lesson in English (English as a Second Language). The theme was the concepts of bilingual/bicultural identity, ancestry, and family origin—how they relate. One student brought up the fact that he has been told of his Aztec ancestry. What more could I ask for? Naturally—what is a person to do? Capitalize! A play was born!

Step 3:
Assign Parts
With young children, the most capable speakers and actors should be given major parts, with alternative parts or jobs devised for less capable, shy, or unwilling children. All children should be involved in some way, but no child should be forced to assume a role against his or her will.
Journal Entry: Children took turns speaking about their respective backgrounds, origins, grandparents, parents, and some traditions they practiced, while I took note of their speaking abilities. I needed two main speakers for the play. I admit this was a little sneaky, but effective for my purposes.

Step 4:
Plan for Sets, Costumes, and So Forth
Teachers must plan costumes, sets, music, and children's stage movements, often with children who do not want speaking parts participating in these tasks.

Step 5
Rehearsals
Children's ability to memorize will vary, as will their stamina for repeated practice. Children must understand the importance of their cooperation but not feel stressed or overly anxious. Clear explanations of expectations and ample teacher support are essential. Teachers must realize that it will take a long time to learn parts and to coordinate actions and that, even then, some children may go blank at the time of actual dress rehearsals or performances.
Journal Entry: Dress rehearsal! We worked on reciting loudly and distinctly and pronouncing properly. We practiced several times until they were able to do their parts on their own without my assistance. The students were a little nervous but excited.

Step 6:
Production
The processes that everyone has shared are the important aspects of producing a play: the planning, cooperation, coordination, problem solving, and specific language skills practiced for this new kind of speaking. The end results may be a bit disappointing, given all the work; but they may also be wonderful.
Journal Entry: Show Time! Relaxed and enjoyed the presentation. The kids were great! The parents seemed to enjoy it, too.

---

lies in their similarity to one of the ways children learn oral language in the first place—by attending to the language models they hear around them.

The best way for teachers to help children gain competency is for teachers themselves to be good models—to use language in grammatically correct yet creative ways. Too many early childhood teachers oversimplify their oral language; their speech is correct but dull, artificial, and condescending. Children, better than anyone else, know that language is dynamic; and teachers need to model interesting, varied ways of stating ideas, wishes, commands, questions, and statements.

Instruction in the fine points of grammar and sentence structure can be offered to the whole class during short mini lessons, to small groups during work periods, and to individuals during conferences. Instruction will be most effective if it is offered in context—that is, as part of real work students are doing (Calkins, 1981). For example, teaching rules for comma use in isolation from students reading or writing will be far less productive than pointing out commas in texts students are reading, discussing commas inserted into a dictated story, and helping children associate the use of commas with the pauses they make when they read orally or speak.

Children's literature can also provide language models, especially if teachers' oral reading demonstrates enjoyment and appreciation for the flow and cadence of the written texts. Selecting books carefully and preparing oral reading adequately allow teachers to use children's literature as another means of enhancing children's grasp of oral language.

SUMMARY

During the early childhood period, children discover the power of language for communication with those around them. They also discover the intricacies of their language structure as they experiment with word choice and sentence structure and learn the rules of their language community. By the time they enter school, they will have mastered most of the structural conventions of the speech of the language community in which they have been living.

Skills for listening and speaking are a standard part of early childhood curricula, but they remain just subjects to be taught unless teachers place them within the larger context of what children are learning about: the social uses of language. Movement, dancing, dramatics, and verse are central to children's mastery of language skills during these years and must be included in activities designed to strengthen listening and speaking skills. One goal for all instruction is effective communication among students and teachers and among students themselves. A language-rich environment where children enjoy conversing and find speaking and listening purposeful activities is also the ideal setting for children who are just learning English to practice their emerging skills.

QUESTIONS AND TASKS FOR INDEPENDENT OR COLLABORATIVE WORK

1. Be sure that you can define each of these terms:

   - language play
   - pragmatics
   - contextualized language
   - decontextualized language
   - directed listening–thinking activity (DLTA)

2. Children's beginning understanding of concepts is often referred to as fuzzy. What do you think *fuzzy* means in this context? What kinds of problems can arise between children and early childhood caregivers because of children's fuzzy conceptualizations? Discuss with other students a situation to illustrate this point.

3. Visit a preschool or day care center and spend time talking to children. Do you have any difficulty understanding them? Do they understand you easily? Observe the teacher carefully. What special language skills does he or she have? What skills does the teacher seem to be lacking? What are the strengths and weaknesses of the "language environment"? Does it seem to support children's language learning? If not, how could it be better?

4. The social uses of language (pragmatics) vary according to social groups. Why must early childhood teachers be aware of this? What can caregivers and teachers do to help children whose sense of pragmatics differs from that of most of the children in a class? Pragmatic linguistic play may be offensive to teachers and to some children, but it is a natural part of learning about social uses of language. Suggest ways teachers should respond to this kind of play, citing any real situations you may know of.

5. Learn several finger plays and use them with young children. How easily do the children learn the finger plays? Do they like them? Do they learn all the words? What do they do for words they do not know? What kinds of finger plays seem most popular?

6. Observe several early childhood teachers reading to children. Do they use a directed listening–thinking approach? Try the approach yourself with children ages three, four, five, and six. How does it work? What, if any, adjustments did you need to make for each age group?

CHAPTER 7

Awareness of Print

By the time they enter school, children have acquired an abundance of information about reading and writing. This early learning has been motivated by their own curiosity and by explorations of the print that bombards them every day. Adults and other literacy users provide youngsters with literacy events that strengthen their emerging knowledge. Ferreiro (1986) reminds us, however, that even when young learners have ample support,

> To grow into literacy is not a restful traveling from one stage to another. Many ups and downs are found on the way, the precise meanings of which need to be understood. As any other growing in cognitive domains, it is an exciting adventure, full of unknowns, with many turning points where anxiety is difficult to keep under control. (p. 48)

This chapter discusses how children develop an initial awareness of the functions and purposes of print; it also discusses the means by which children reveal their emerging sense that written language is an important and useful means of communication. Children learn a unified whole—many interrelated pieces of information, facts, skills, and procedures prepare them for later literacy growth. Several categories of learning will be presented here: learning about print production (handwriting and spelling), learning about reading, and learning about talking and thinking about literacy.

WHAT CHILDREN LEARN ABOUT PRINT PRODUCTION

By observing other people reading and writing and by asking questions, children become aware that print, like oral language, is a means of communication. After having used gestures, babbling, and beginning speech as placeholders for their first efforts at communication, children begin to realize that the mysterious squiggly marks of print are **intentional placeholders** of some other kind of meaning. Understanding that print makes sense to those who can unlock its code is an important foundation for children's ultimate understanding of literacy. Young children also realize that print can be used for several distinct purposes. Cochran-Smith (1984), who studied the day-to-day lives of children in a preschool, suggested that prereaders knew "a great deal about contexts in which print could be used, purposes for which print could be used, strategies for interpreting print in various contexts, and relationships between oral and printed language" (p. 77). She discussed eight specific uses for print that the children knew and understood within their preschool environment:

1. Substitutes for spoken utterances, such as messages between teacher and parents
2. Sources of information, such as signs

3. Social messages, such as labels or logos on clothing (e.g., Oshkosh overalls), team names on baseball caps, and messages in greeting cards
4. Memory supports, such as the name tags a teacher often has children wear the first days of school until names are learned
5. Means of self-expression, such as teacher transcription of a child's feelings or emotions, either informally or in a formal instructional session
6. Presentation of information in an efficient manner, in activities such as making lists, graphing, or otherwise recording relevant classroom information in chart form
7. Acquisition of new knowledge, from books and other print materials, often as a support for more contextualized experiences
8. Classification of status, as in children's names written on labels in their clothing and pictures or signs that indicate different learning centers in the classroom

Over time, children also develop a rudimentary understanding of how print is actually produced. This learning is developmental, progressing from curious observation to experimentation and naive feelings of competence. One researcher, Marcia Baghban (1984), kept a three-year comprehensive diary of her daughter Giti's oral language, reading, and writing development. Initially, Giti observed her parents writing but at no time was she specifically taught to write herself. She saw her parents write frequently in their professional roles and as part of routine household tasks. Curious about their activities, Giti "made a connection between the movement of the pen and the traces on paper and [once] she was assured that these effects could be repeated, she fell in love with the production . . . she was determined to write" (pp. 89–90). Her development was as follows:

- 17 months: scribbling on sheets of paper
- 19 months: controlling the amount of dots, circles, and wavy lines on each page
- 21 months: writing on any 4th-class mail her parents gave her
- 23 months: writing for as long as ten minutes
- 24 months: beginning to babble over her work as if reading a story

Soon Giti made an important realization. "The day she looked at the *KMart* logo on a card, pointing to the *m* and saying, 'Onalds,' she attempted *m* in her writing. After completing a row of peaks, she began another row and said 'Marce,' associating *m* with [her mother's first] name as well" (pp. 52, 54). Having received a puzzle with her name for her second birthday, Giti soon began to practice *G*s in isolation.

- 27 months: requesting dictation from her parents, especially names of family members and favorite places; beginning to spell her name orally—

iti—and to singsong *baba,* probably in response to the frequent requests for spelling her name and the family name

Giti also continued to write, especially on junk mail and catalogues, "always on the side that had lines which needed to be completed. Rather than writing on the written language, she started to aim for the spaces between the lines for her own writing" (p. 60).

- 29 months: could dictate for thirty minutes and then intoned and practiced the words herself; *G* seemed to be her favorite letter, and she frequently wrote *Giti* and *Grandma.* She also liked to write *McDonalds.*
- 30 months: approximated her name independently; letter forms became more sprawled and looser, closer to drawing
- 31 months: began to say "I draw"
- 32 months: could distinguish her drawings from her writings; began to play school (where the subject was writing) but was beginning to take more interest in others outside of the home; wrote letters and put them in envelopes, which she "mailed" by taping them to her door; could fill in forms neatly, sticking to the allowed spaces
- 34 months: stabilized her orientation in writing from left to right; also learned to underline

Baghban's record of Giti's writing growth illustrates how one child learned about print. Was Giti Baghban advanced, gifted, precocious? Not necessarily. Her parents and others supported her efforts and talked to her during and about her writing. She had models, materials, and encouragement in her attempts to figure out the principles that govern print production.

Principles of Print Production

In 1976, Marie Clay, a New Zealand educator, proposed that children's writing experimentation leads them to discover important principles of print production. Figure 7.1 shows examples of young children's experiments with print.

The first principle that children discover is the **intentionality of print**—that is, that squiggly marks of print communicate meaning. Children demonstrate this principle when they "read" their scribbled messages or insist that someone else read them. Children's drawings offer other demonstrations. Often children will point to one mass of scribbles as a "picture" and to another mass as the "name of the picture," meaning that one is drawn and one is written. Recall that Giti Baghban did this at thirty-two months. Some youngsters will use only pens and pencils for writing and only crayons or markers for drawing because each method of marking on paper has its own set of tools. Gradually, the "writing" scribbles approximate real letters.

Sample 1. Child drew lines to make paper look more "school-like."

Sample 2. This writer is still discovering how letters are oriented on the paper. She also used decorations.

Sample 3. The smiling star was used for decoration in this example of self-initiated exploration.

Figure 7.1 *continued*

Young children discover the principles of print production through experimentation and play. Their writing shows many repetitions of basic shapes and is often decorated with drawings and lines. Youngsters also benefit from "real" writing experiences, such as "signing in" each day as they arrive at day care.

SIGN IN/SIGN OUT

DATE _____			
Child's Name	Parent's Signature	Time In	Time Out
Valerie			↙VᴬLᴇRIᴇ
LEAH			L Ɛ A Ƚⱼ
Christine			CʰrⁱˢｭIᵛ E
Victor			VⁱCㅜOᴿ
Lucas			L U.CAꙅ
Elizabeth			EⁱiZɑ₍₎ᴅᴼᵼɦ
Virginia			Vⁱⁱⁱᶜiʰiɑ
Jennifer			ᐅᴧ ᴊODO ᵇᵎ
michael			MᴷɦʲＬᵎ
Anita			A M ㅜ A
uzo			ᑫᒻᴧꓳ
Christal			COⁿ’Tⁱ
Nicholas			⊝ ᒻᒻ ⁱ ᴧ
Von			
Jeremy			ᵠ /ᴬ

Sample 4.   Each morning as they arrived at their daycare center, 3-, 4-, and 5-year old children signed in. This was part of their daily routine. Notice the variety in signatures. (From LBJ Day Care Center, El Paso, TX. Used with permission.)

Figure 7.1, *concluded*

From observation of environmental print, children also learn that the production of individual letters is achieved by using relatively few strokes of the pen or pencil—they discover the **recurring principle**. Essentially, children realize that the "kinds of lines are not what allows us to distinguish between a drawing and a piece of writing. In fact, we produce both of them by using straight lines, curved lines, or dots. . . . The difference is the way the lines are organized" (Ferreiro, 1990, p. 15). These lines, often referred to in handwriting instruction as "circles and sticks," can be used over and over in varied ways to accomplish all written communication. With time, children also realize that the conventions of print production put limits on the ways the "circles and sticks" can be varied. For example, there are slight but very significant differences in the orientation of the strokes needed for the letters *b, d, p, q,* and at times *g;* depending on penmanship style, the same can be true for *m* and *w, n* and *u.*

In demonstrating their understanding of the recurring principle (see Figure 7.1), children first create pairs of letters or pseudoletters or use them for decorative purposes on drawings. They are exploring the limits within which letters may be varied and still retain their identity (Clay, 1976). As skills increase, children apply the recurring principle to words and create a distinct pattern of marks for one word and different patterns for other words until they have "written" a list, letter, or story, which they can "read" quite successfully. This writing does not reflect letter–sound correspondences yet is much more than random scribbling or drawing. The practice is spontaneous; children are investigating the limits within which they write and the ways they can vary the basic pattern of each letter or word and still maintain its identity as something they recognize as "writing."

Wider observations of print, spontaneous practice, feedback from those with whom they share their writing, and actual instruction give children control of letter formation and help them understand the **directionality principle**. Children figure out that print traditionally begins at a corner of a surface, moves across the surface in a line, makes a downward turn, and moves again from left to right in a parallel line. Actual left to right progression is a very advanced application of this principle. The child whose letters march from left to right across the bottom of the page understands directionality more than the child who scatters words at random; but neither is as advanced as the child who tries to write horizontal lines of print and spreads them diagonally from the top left to bottom right corner of the paper. This last child knows what to do but is impeded by immature visual–motor coordination. Gradually, such coordination improves, and left-to-right directionality becomes a habit.

As suggested previously, young children often distinguish between their drawing and writing efforts. Initially, this understanding refers to the production of these two forms of communication, but later the distinction becomes more complex. Children also discover that although a direct relationship exists between a drawing and the objects that the drawing represents, the corresponding written image—the squiggles on paper—holds no visible relationship to the object, person, or concept they stand for. To illustrate, the combination of letters *d-o-g* stands for *dog* and could be written as a label on a picture of either a beagle or a Great Dane as a sign that says *dog* to anyone who can read English. Of course, some children will take liberties with this **sign principle**, as shown in the writing presented in Figure 7.2.

Children must also understand that the graphic images used as a written sign for a word are predetermined, somewhat arbitrary, fixed, and only moderately changeable. For example, the only changes that can be made in the *d-o-g* combination of letters, if the word is to remain *dog*, are those that can be made because of what Clay called the **flexibility principle.** This refers to the range of variations (or flexible changes) possible within typesetting and manuscript printing (e.g., *Dog, dog, DOG*) and cursive script.

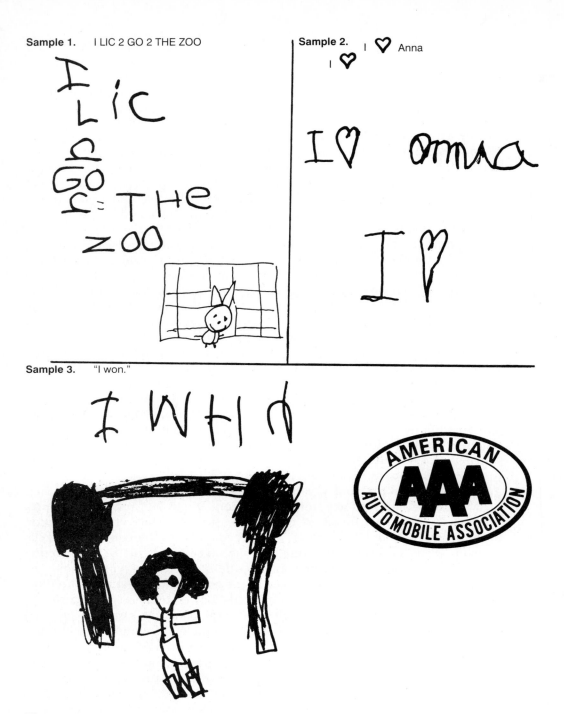

Sample 1.   I LIC 2 GO 2 THE ZOO

Sample 2.   I ♥ Anna

Sample 3.   "I won."

Figure 7.2

Young writers discover that words and pictures are different but still use "signs" to convey their messages. In sample 1, the child used a backwards *2* for *to;* sample 2 shows a heart standing for *love;* and sample 3 incorporates a sticker into the message "I won."

Practice Leads to Fluency

Many children practice handwriting skills spontaneously, often by making lists. Clay called this the **inventory principle.** Children first list letters or numbers, then letter combinations, words, and eventually phrases and sentences. They may copy examples of classroom environmental print, and eventually they structure inventories to pose challenges and suggest tasks. A child might write "I can write the ABCs" and then write the letters of the alphabet; another might write "Do you know my friends?" and then list their names. Writing "Numbers I can write" or "Words I know" are common variations. Figure 7.3 shows samples of children's inventories.

Part of this inventorying includes exploration of ways to vary height and width to make tall, short, fat, and skinny letters and ways to add curls, hearts, and other designs to letters or stories. Children also explore punctuation by dotting *i*s and *j*s elaborately and by inserting periods and commas throughout their text. These behaviors indicate that children are confident enough about their skills and curious enough about print that they will stretch the traditional boundaries of "proper" print. Figure 7.4 shows how several children experimented with their names.

Much of the understanding that children gain about print production develops without direct instruction or explanation from adults. Children gather information about how writing is produced, and the set of rudimentary principles evolves from this information. This kind of learning reflects how preschoolers construct ideas about other aspects of their worlds. Teachers need to assess what and how much children know about print production and use that knowledge base as a starting point for instruction.

As children share their knowledge about print with each other, each child gains in understanding and competence.

ABCDEFG#IJKLMNOPQR
STUVXYZ
TAMMYS
MOMMY

Sample 1.

MTV
Mary Dog
123456 78910
Marcie
egg red
for the a car

Sample 2.

The moon
It's big
it's pretty

it's fat

it's fall

it's in space-

Sample 3.

140

Figure 7.3
Writing out self-initiated inventories of numbers, letters, words, and sentences are valuable learning experiences for young language learners.

Albert

Pearl

Pearl

David

Crystal

Figure 7.4
Children who feel confident about their writing will often experiment. Albert added what he referred to as periods to his name for decoration. Pearl wrote her name in English and Spanish (Perla) and added decoration; she also wrote a multicolored version of her name and became so involved that she used a *B* instead of an *R*. David showed his emotions in a signature on a drawing. Crystal also used periods to decorate her name.

Children's Concepts of Words

Before children can learn to read and write successfully, they must understand what words are. Exposure to environmental and other print has taught them the beginnings of this *concept of words*—that a graphic representation stands for some oral utterance (Adams, 1990). Understanding the sign principle, discussed earlier, is a start, but children also must learn that there is a one-to-one match between print and speech and then must learn to attend to the *boundaries of print* they see in texts. Listening to children's speech gives some indication of why this concept is difficult. The child who says, "Momma, Iwanna glasamilk anacookie," may be a long way from understanding that the utterance is made of ten distinct words—Momma, I want a glass of milk and a cookie—and not four oral utterances. Beginning writing shows some print–speech awareness, but initial efforts may be so skeletal that it is difficult to know exactly how children have conceptualized the transfer from speech to print. Young writers may also run their words together with no "white space" to indicate word boundaries, or they may arrange their print vertically. Teachers can help children become more aware of words as distinct units of meaning in several ways. Transcribing children's early written efforts helps beginning writers, as does oral reading of what children write. As teachers or students read, the teacher should point to each word, lifting the finger at each word, to provide an auditory reinforcement of the concept of text as a composition of many distinct units.

Invented Spelling

Just as young children experiment with letter formation, they experiment with patterns for putting graphic images together to form messages. Like early speech and pseudoletters, **invented spelling** is a placeholder of children's meaning. It is also a powerful manifestation of early literacy play, as children invent "a writing system out of the alphabet . . . [in a] survival game to develop the sorcery to penetrate the secrecy [of printed communication]" (Moffett & Wagner, 1993, p. 33). Invented spelling develops from observation, incidental learning, and children's reasoning processes. Thus, learning to use invented spelling is similar to making other kinds of "discoveries" as preschoolers explore their world.

The Beginnings of Invented Spelling.   Beginning writers do not understood that in standard spelling the sounds of oral language—phonemes—are represented by specific letters and that consistency in letter–sound matching allows readers to interpret the messages presented in printed text. Thus the first stage of invented spelling, often called *deviant* *spelling,* consists of random letters and pseudoletters strung together to convey a message (Beers & Beers, 1981; Gentry, 1981). Because deviant spelling can be read only by the child who has written it, it is easy to overlook the importance of this stage in emerging literacy.

With experience, children progress from knowing "for sure" that they are actually writing "real" words to understanding that there is more to writing than they at first thought. This knowledge—that there must be some match between the letters they write and the phonemes they hear as they utter words—leads them to the second stage in invented spelling, *prephonemic,* or *early phonemic, spelling.* This spelling shows a primitive awareness of alphabetic principles with one-, two-, or three-letter strings to represent phonemes children hear in words they are trying to spell. Sometimes children stop after writing one or two phonemes of a word; they may use only those to placehold the entire word or may fill in the rest with a random string of letters. It is easy to understand the sparseness of the beginning spellers' output when we think about the total mental effort they must expend.

The third stage, called *phonetic,* or *letter-name, spelling,* demonstrates a nearly perfect correspondence between letters and phonemes. When they spell, children consciously break each word into its phonemes and try to match letters on the basis of the similarity between the phonemes they hear and the names of the letters. Children select primarily those consonants with a stable and predictable letter–name match or those that regularly represent only one phoneme. If they use vowels at all, they will use primarily long vowels, which "say their name." Many letter–name spellers are still prereaders in that they can read their own writing but can read at best only a few sight words in standard spelling. Figure 7.5 contrasts examples of early phonemic and letter–name spelling that accompanied drawings collected on the same day in a kindergarten class.

Up to this point, children may not actually have conceptualized the process of "spelling"; rather, they think of their behaviors as part of a dynamic process called "writing." Glenda Bissex (1980), who studied her son Paul with the same intensity that Marcia Baghban used to study her daughter Giti, offered a good description of invented spelling:

> Five-year-old Paul was in the house. I was outside on the deck reading. After he had tried unsatisfactorily to talk with me, he decided to get my attention a new way—to break through print with print. Selecting the rubber letter stamps he needed from his set, Paul printed and delivered this message: RUDF (Are you deaf?!) Of course, I put down my book. (p. 3)

Bissex further reported: "Paul himself described what he was doing as 'writing' rather than 'spelling' . . . [H]ad his main interest been in spelling *words,* he would have written word lists; what he wrote, however, were *messages*" (p. 35).

I LoᵬfR

1.   I learned about fire.

i B WZ. mᵀᵇ

2.   I broke the window with my table
     (per instructions given at fire station).

I ᵮgAgAt AFSF

3.   I finally got out of the fire station.

I LRND HOW TO DOᵌSᵀOOP DrP and ᵖOL

4.   I learned how to stop, drop, and roll.

I LR ND Hot STOPROP an ROW

5.   I learned how to stop, drop, and roll.

XeUbᵇᵈr Sopro parᵇr.

6.   You better stop, drop, and roll.

I lic to lrn a bdot flyr the flyr is dag rds

7.   I like to learn about fire
     The fire is dangerous.

I hrd haw to pit awt Safle.

8.   I learned how to get out safely.

Figure 7.5
After a visit to a fire station, kindergartners drew and wrote about what
they had learned. Part of the demonstration had been how to "stop, drop,
and roll" in case of a fire at home. Children in this class had been writing
for several months. Notice the variety of expression and invented spelling.

Progress in Invented Spelling.   Literacy progresses because of frequent opportunities for purposeful writing, observations of people writing,
and incidental and direct instruction. As children confirm the stability of
some letters and discover the irregularities of English spelling, they put the
pieces of the spelling system together and use their writing to externalize
what they are learning. Their spelling enters the *transitional stage.*

Transitional spelling looks very much like standard English. It contains vowels (including digraphs and diphthongs), consonant blends, and inflected endings, as well as many conventional spelling resulting from children's memory of sight words or accurate application of emerging spelling skills. Nonconventional spellings in this stage reflect young writers' attempts to make sense out of the spelling system—for example, spelling *boat* as *bote* because of a wrong choice of how to make the initial vowel long. Look closely at the stories presented in Figure 7.5 to see what these young writers were thinking about spelling; also try to infer what they know about punctuation and the mechanics of composition.

Correct or Conventional Spelling.   In the final stage of invented spelling, children demonstrate nearly correct spellings in most spontaneous and assigned writing activities. Some children achieve conventional spelling more or less on their own, whereas others need more direct instruction to help them toward competence. As will be discussed in chapters 8, 9, and 10, good spelling instruction recognizes the continuum of communication skills and stresses the connections among oral language, composition, and reading. Spelling is viewed as a skill to be mastered in order to make one's writing more efficient and effective; instruction builds upon what children have discovered for themselves about writing.

Timing.   Children's progress through invented spelling does not follow a precise timetable. Developmental in nature, spelling skills seem to evolve over time, as children use what they are discovering. Henderson (1985) has suggested the following rough outline of spelling development:

- Children aged one to four years experiment with writing while still unaware of letter–sound correspondences.
- Children aged four to six years are invented spellers who begin to attend to letter–sound matches and to discover spelling principles.
- Children aged five to eight years are competent spellers who bring reading instruction to bear on their writing efforts and make constant progress toward conventional spelling.

This progression is illustrated by different ways Bissex's son spelled the word *directions: DRAKTHENS* (five years, seven months), *DRAKSHINS* (five years, eight months), *DIREKSHONS* (seven years, five months), *DIRECTOINS* or *DIRECTIONS* (eight years, one month), and finally *DIRECTIONS* (eight years, seven months). Bissex (1980) wrote, "That particular word, or any word, could have been corrected earlier but might have stood as an isolated item to be memorized. When Paul finally mastered *directions*, he wrote lists of what he titled 'hard words,' including many ending with *-tion*. His spelling reflects the learning of a principle, not merely a word" (p. 88).

Children learn about print from books and classroom environmental print, such as charts and signs. They need to handle books, to explore how books are put together, and to investigate how books tell their stories.

It is, of course, important for teachers to remember that even within supportive, literate classrooms, children will progress at different rates. The best way to "teach" spelling is within a dynamic, purposeful writing program so that children see the value of competent spelling as they attempt to communicate their thoughts and ideas. Additionally, children learn strategies for monitoring their own spelling and figuring out unfamiliar words.

WHAT CHILDREN LEARN ABOUT READING

In addition to developing concepts about print production, young children also gain a strong sense of what reading is all about. They learn what books and other printed matter are and what they do (Clay, 1979; Cochran-Smith, 1984; Goodman, 1986). Additionally, many children "come to print with high expectations, not only that they will succeed in unlocking its mysteries, but also that the mysteries are *worth* unlocking" (Holdaway, 1979, p. 38). Teachers are responsible for helping children meet their expectations.

One of the most significant sources of children's knowledge about books and reading is the experience they have sharing books with parents and other caregivers.[1] During storybook reading, a child shares very spe-

---

[1] Sharing books with young children is the significant activity here. The person who shares books is often a parent, but other caregivers—including older siblings—are equally effective informal teachers in this important endeavor. It is important to remember that children who attend preschool programs in which teachers read to them gain many of the same advantages as children who hear stories each night at bedtime.

cial, quiet, and focused time with an important adult. What has been called the "bedtime storybook learning cycle" provides children with much of their beginning information about reading; as will be discussed in chapters 8 and 9, this is an important model for formal reading instruction in early childhood classes as well. Holdaway (1979) stated that book sharing "provides a stimulus for satisfying interaction between parent and child, different, richer and more wide-ranging than the mundane interactions of running the home. *The major purpose from the parent's point of view is to give pleasure, and the parent is sustained in this behavior by the ample bonuses provided* [by the child's enjoyment]" (p. 39; italics in original).

From book sharing experiences, children refine their understanding that print conveys meaning. If they share a wide variety of books, they realize that print can tell a story, make one laugh, provide information, or perform many other functions (as discussed earlier). They learn that the "subject matter" of print is varied and that some pleases them more than others. For example, some children love "scary" books, whereas others don't like them at all.

Children's vocabulary and control of sentence structure increase as they hear the different ways books convey their messages. Additionally, they realize that the vocabulary, syntax, and intonation patterns of "book language" differ from everyday speech. Purcell-Gates (1988, 1989) demonstrated this point by studying two groups of kindergartners—ones who had the experience of being read to before entering school and ones who had not been read to before entering school. Purcell-Gates asked children in each group to pretend to read a story from a wordless picture book to a doll and also to tell her about their last birthday party. She compared the language used by each group of children on each task and found that the children who had been well read to used markedly different language as they pretended to read: their stories sounded like the text of storybooks. Among the attributes children demonstrated were sound effects (*Ka-plash*—the stranger fell overboard), literary syntax and vocabulary (Down the road they went; The *villain* came in; The prince had to *battle* the dragon), and the use of dialogue ("Oh, oh. We're locked in here") (Purcell-Gates, 1989, p. 292).

By tracking the print that is being read, children also affirm much of what they are realizing about print production. They see that the print moves in a particular direction, especially if the adult moves his or her finger under the words; and they see the "white space" that marks boundaries between words. They observe the ways letters are formed with a limited number of strokes, and they identify letters and even words they have seen in other contexts. Watching and listening also reinforce children's understanding that print differs from illustrations and does not look like the messages it tells.

As children gain experience with books, they generalize information about how books are put together to communicate meaning. The important principles about books and other print media constitute the *Concepts about Print Test* mentioned in chapter 3 (Clay, 1979). Knowledge of these principles is essential for children to feel at ease with books and with the behaviors they must use as they actually begin to read. The following principles suggest the information that children must have to advance as readers (Clay, 1979; Cochran-Smith, 1984):

1. In books, signs, and other print media, meaning is conveyed by the print; it is often enhanced but rarely fully conveyed by accompanying illustrations.
2. Books usually begin at the front of the book and proceed to the end, with print in books usually beginning at the left-hand side of a page and proceeding to the right-hand side.
3. The order of words in a line of print is essential to conveying meaning.
4. Book reading and other print-related pursuits are appropriate for people of all ages and often are considered more important than other activities.
5. Book reading can be an entertaining, relaxing, and informative activity for children and adults to share as well as an appropriate solitary activity.
6. Children and adults can be either readers or listeners.
7. Situations and characters in books often reflect real life and can be helpful in solving real-life problems.
8. Stories from books are often translated into other media.
9. Children and adults can interrupt and ask questions or make comments during book reading; discussion of books is a positive activity.
10. Books are created by and for people of all ages; children can create their own books.
11. Books can be valued possessions; individual literary tastes, even among children, will differ.
12. Books can be a means of verifying or disputing hearsay or questionable ideas.

Children explore reading by picking up books and pretending to read; they may also retell or reenact a story they have heard. As in play writing, children try out a behavior they have observed and get the "feel" of a skill they want to master. Children's first demonstrations of this knowledge may be relatively silent. Only a smile or giggle will suggest that the child is reexperiencing the act of sharing the book with someone and is perhaps retelling the story silently to herself or himself. Children will also engage in oral storybook retellings, episodes in which they retell a story that has been read to them or tell a story based on the illustrations in an unfamiliar book (Holdaway, 1979; Sulzby, 1985a,b, 1986). As suggested in chapter 3, story retellings are an important assessment tool because they provide insight into children's emerging abilities. Children reveal strategies for making sense of print, their understanding of how print functions, and their initial sense of story structure. There seems to be a developmental pattern to story retelling. Researchers have classified such storybook retellings in three ways: descriptive comments governed by pictures but not telling a story, real storytelling governed by pictures, and real storytellings governed by print. These retelling styles exist on a developmental continuum that ranges from beginning understanding to quite sophisticated behaviors; they are explained in Table 7.1.

LEARNING ABOUT TALKING AND THINKING ABOUT LITERACY

As their skills grow, young children also begin to master the language needed to talk about writing, reading, and books (Goodman, 1986; Sulzby, 1985a,b, 1986). Part of what they learn is the necessary vocabulary, terms such as *let-*

Table 7.1
Behaviors Used During Storybook Reenactments

The value of storybook reenactments is that children can get support and help at an appropriate level and do not have to muddle through the beginnings of reading in frustrating aloneness. Here, indeed, is Vygotsky's idea of the child receiving help today in preparation for independence tomorrow.

Level 1: Descriptive Comments Governed by Pictures but Not Telling a Story

Children's behaviors:

- Commenting as though the action conveyed by the pictures was taking place here and now; labeling and commenting on the pictures
- Appearing to be commenting primarily to themselves
- Appearing to rely on memory rather than text or illustrations to construct a story to retell
- Skipping or recycling a story part; pausing as if trying to remember the story

Through this process, children are becoming familiar with book format and handling; they are attending to pictures closely enough to label and comment and, at low level, are translating "book language" into oral speech. Doing this in the intimacy of one-on-one interaction with an adult affirms children's guesses about how books "work" and makes book handling a pleasurable part of the school experience.

Level 2: Real Storytelling Governed by Pictures

Children's behaviors:

- Using "booklike" and/or "speechlike" language
- Citing phrases from the original story and common clauses like "Once upon a time..."
- Including story patterns that sound booklike but were not in the actual model
- Offering evidence that they recognize that language in books is different from regular speech
- Using story-reading intonation as evidence of their sense of themselves as "reading" the book to their audience

The content of children's reenactments may or may not match the content of the original story, and the total reenactment may or may not present a coherent whole.

continued

Table 7.1, *continued*

Level 3: Real Storytelling Governed by Print

Children's behaviors:

- Reading words they recognize at sight
- Laboriously sounding out some of the words
- Skipping other words rather than sounding them out or replacing them with appropriate synonyms
- Demonstrating that they are in fact beginning to read with comprehension by smiling or laughing at points in the story, changing voices, or commenting on plot, characters, or setting

Retellings at this level indicate clearly that children are beginning to figure out some aspects of reading and need encouragement and support in their effort. Acceptance of what they are doing, answers to their questions, and enthusiasm for their reading will provide momentum for more growth.

Level 4: Other Evidence

Children's behaviors:

- Providing an almost verbatim recitation of the story, coming primarily from memory, with little visual tracking of the printed page
- Refusing to "read" because "I can't read yet," even though there is strong indication that the child is progressing well toward literacy

These behaviors suggest understanding of the mechanics of reading (even if the child refuses to read) and a strong sense of story. Children who demonstrate these behaviors should be invited, but not forced, to read orally in a quiet, safe setting. Encouraging children to track words by running their finger under lines of print can also be helpful.

---

ter, word, book, and *page.* Children can often discuss how they have learned about literacy, and they explain how they have learned from other people, from school, or from their own efforts and experimentations (Sulzby, 1985b). They can discuss differences between drawing and writing and, as discussed earlier, distinguish between everyday speech and booklike language.

Most important, children begin to be able to talk about their own processes of constructing meaning from and with print. This behavior is important for several reasons. Children's talk about their processes communicates much about the strategies they use for reading and writing and about any misconceptions they have developed in their early stages as literacy users. Because children's vocabularies for talking about literacy will differ, teachers need to listen carefully to each individual and coordinate what children say with evidence that can be gained from story retelling and work samples. Cumulatively, these data help teachers determine levels at which to gear instruction.

Anne Haas Dyson (1988) has spent many hours listening to young children as they learn to write. The following excerpt from one of her studies illustrates the extent to which young learners can indeed comment on their own literacy activities.

> In the kindergarten, Maggie had often been silly with her texts (e.g., reading them in a falsetto voice), but her texts themselves had not been funny. Late in the first grade, though, she began to find them quite funny ("I can't believe what I'm writing. This is so funny").
>
> One funny text was a story about two friends, Alice and Lacey. Maggie orally elaborated upon her written characters: "Alice and Lacey are the real people. They're real names. Anyone could be them." These "anyones" had common experiences, particularly common for Maggie—they were consistently late to school: as she put it in her text, "as usual they Got a tarDy tag again." The "as usual" reflects the resigned but slightly amused stance Maggie herself often adopted. (pp. 375–376)

Dyson (1994a) has also found that children can use their writing as a "ticket" to social acceptance, as when they write adventure stories that they then invite their classmates to reenact on the playground or in class dramatics activities. These efforts to use writing in a deliberate way to manipulate social situations suggest that students are making conscious decisions about the texts they create so that their writing can "reach" a specific audience and serve a specific, nonliterary purpose.

Dyson (1994b) also points out that young boys seem to write mostly about adventures and action figures such as superheroes, whereas girls are more concerned with interpersonal issues and feelings. Although this differentiation may sound too pat and stereotypical at first, it really supports the concept of young writers as individuals engaged in serious cognitive work through which they puzzle out some of the issues that concern their emerging sense of who they are.

SUMMARY

Adults readily accept that children are strongly motivated to develop oral language skills, but, in truth, children's motivation extends to other forms of communication as well. Experimentations with print production, authoring skills, and reading parallel children's explorations with other aspects of their world in both their intensity and their purpose. Children engage in these activities to better understand what they see around them and to participate in activities that intrigue them. As with so many of childhood's endeavors, investigation leads from initial practice to increasing mastery of new skills and abilities. In reaching for mastery, young learners express who they are and who they want to become.

QUESTIONS AND TASKS FOR INDEPENDENT OR COLLABORATIVE WORK

1. Be sure that you can define each of these terms:

    - intentional placeholders
    - intentionality of print
    - recurring principle
    - directionality principle
    - sign principle
    - flexibility principle
    - inventory principle
    - invented spelling

2. The topic of formal handwriting instruction was not discussed in this chapter. Based on the information presented about children's discovery of principles of print production, what do you suppose would be the most effective way to encourage children to strive for legible handwriting skills? Discuss this question with others in your class. How many of the suggested methods seem to stem from adult memories of how handwriting has been traditionally taught?

3. Interview children between the ages of three and eight to see how many of the concepts about print and books they truly understand. What pattern of development in understanding can you detect? To what extent can children remember the sources of their information about print and books? Was it experiential or observational, or was it in response to their questions?

4. Many early childhood educators think that writing and reading centers have no place in preschool and kindergarten classrooms because they force "academic" subjects on students too early. How do you feel about this? What justification(s) can you offer for including these kinds of learning centers in classes for young children?

5. As a class, collect samples of writing from children aged three to eight; identify types of writing (story, letter, artifact of dramatic play, etc.) and types of content (what the writing is supposed to say). Tally the number of different kinds of writing represented across the age levels, and study the samples for trends in the development of attributes—such as sense of audience, coherence of message, variety of purpose, clarity and sophistication of presentation, "correctness" of conventions of print and spelling, and legibility of handwriting. In addition to differences that result from the developmental levels of the students, what, if any, differences do you notice between the work of boys and that of girls?

CHAPTER 8

The Beginnings of Literacy
(Preschool and Kindergarten)

T here is no single "preliteracy" curriculum, no set of activities guaranteed to present all the concepts and skills necessary to get children in preschool and kindergarten "ready" for reading and writing. What does help are a literate classroom environment, where teachers demonstrate the value of literacy, and an ongoing commitment to the idea that young children enter school already engaged in literacy explorations. Ideal preschool and kindergarten classrooms are places where children's emergent literacy is fostered and allowed to grow. This chapter discusses life in this kind of classroom. The term **emergent literacy** acknowledges the importance of children's attention to the various uses of print in the environment and emphasizes the continuum of language growth from oral language skills through mastery of reading and writing.

An underlying principle of an emergent literacy classroom is the idea of *support:* teachers endeavor to foster intellectual and emotional growth by providing verbal, instructional, and physical support for learners' explorations of literacy. Children do not suddenly and dramatically begin to read and write. Instead, they approximate reading and writing in their attempts to piece together the puzzle of how these behaviors function. The process is cumulative and developmental. Children's approximations, both in behaviors and in actual marks on paper, are placeholders of conventional literacy performance. By attending to what children are doing (i.e., by being kid-watchers), teachers can instruct at the appropriate teaching point, "nudging" children forward, reinforcing existing understanding, and helping children undo misunderstandings about reading and writing. Teachers act upon Vygotsky's (1962) statement, "What the child can do in cooperation today, he can do alone tomorrow" (pp. 103–104). Table 8.1 presents a kid-watching essay written by a kindergarten teacher.

Early childhood teachers understand that learning to read and write is a complex, difficult task that no child will accomplish without considerable struggle, work, and energy. Remember what Ferreiro (1986) said: "To grow into literacy is not a restful traveling" but "an exciting adventure, full of unknowns, with many turning points where anxiety is difficult to keep under control" (p. 48). Children need confidence in their abilities, stamina, and support for what they are doing. Experiences in preschool and kindergarten provide the foundation for this confidence. Knowledge of children and of specific supportive strategies for instruction are teachers' tools to enhance children's progress. Here are some realities of learning to read and write:

- Learning to read and write usually takes a long time, as children explore and process information and build their own models of how literacy works.
- Young learners may show no evidence of learning for long periods of time and then suddenly demonstrate that everything is "falling into place."
- Children who are just learning literacy behaviors need many experiences with oral and written language; they need to see and hear language used in different ways and for different purposes.

Table 8.1
If Only I'd Started Sooner . . .

Last year was the first year I asked my students to write their own sentences using words from the sight word list....About the middle of this year, I noticed some of my more advanced students writing on their own. I showed these pictures to another teacher and learned that the writing was a valuable learning experience for the children. I started to give the students papers and encouraged them to write. Some of the children claimed they simply could not do it. Little by little, they saw the other children doing their own writing and tried it themselves. It took constant reassurance before these children began to feel secure.

About this time, I read my first literature on invented spelling. I began to experiment with formats with which my children would be comfortable. I found they loved colored pens on white paper. They also liked to draw pictures with their stories. I found that they wanted to read their stories to me as soon as they finished. This presented a problem when the whole class wrote at once. Some of the less mature students forgot what they had written before they could read it back to me. If I were able to write down what they had written, in normal spelling, before they forgot, I could tell them if they then later forgot. I eventually began to have the children write in small groups on a rotating basis.

The form the children most often used was a picture with the story on the same page. The more advanced students started with the story, then the picture. Soon, all the class was using this method....Once, a child wrote a whole series of disjoined sight words and told me a sentence that neither made sense nor followed the sight words. I asked him what his picture was about. He told me. I then asked him to write it while I watched. He started to sound out and write his words. He was very nervous! After he finished, I read his sentence back to him, pointing to each word as I read. He was amazed that I could read his writing. He was thrilled when he saw he could read his writing. Here was a child that was "far below grade level" having his first major success in the game of reading, writing, and spelling. I truly felt like a teacher.

My only regret is not starting sooner. Next year I will start at the beginning of the year....

C. Kidder. End-term report, ECED 3553, University of Texas at El Paso, 1986. Excerpted and used by permission.

- Young learners need and benefit from repetition of experiences; this includes hearing and seeing the same book over and over and writing the same words and messages repetitively.
- Children learn best when they are listening to, reading about, or writing about things that interest them.
- When children's attention flags and they begin to lose interest, a literacy lesson or activity should stop.
- When teachers feel themselves becoming frustrated—when they begin to think, "This is so easy, why aren't the children getting it?"—it is time to give everyone a chance to rest.

HELPING CHILDREN REFINE THEIR EMERGING LITERACY SKILLS

When teachers recognize the concept of emerging literacy and accept the idea of the appropriate teaching point, they approach the task of helping children become literate in very specific ways. First, they make their classroom as rich in print and literacy experiences as they can. They adopt the workshop approach suggested in chapter 2, adapting procedures to meet the developmental needs of their young students. They recognize that literacy learning is a social activity and make provisions for children to interact with each other. Many opportunities during the day invite students to take part in literacy-related events. Children are not "pushed" but are encouraged to achieve to their individual potential.

Next, teachers determine the extent to which children have acquired the personal attributes, developmental skills, and conceptual understanding needed for initial stages of literacy instruction to make sense. See appendix B for questions you might ask about your students. Answers would generate a multifaceted profile of each student to enable you to make appropriate instructional decisions. Because the learning and development represented in these questions are not tied to age-determined benchmarks, the list should not be considered prescriptive; students will demonstrate these attributes and stages in individual ways and at individual times.

Teachers can provide three distinct learning experiences to support emerging literacy. Each provides information and assistance at appropriate teaching points and invites students to assume active roles in their learning. All take advantage of the social nature of literacy learning, and all approximate parent–child interaction with scaffolding and modeling. The three

The shared book experience—children and a teacher or other adult sharing a story—is an essential component of the early childhood literacy curriculum.

approaches are **shared literacy experiences,** the **language experience approach** to the teaching of reading, and **extensive writing.** These approaches, presented in increasingly challenging ways, are the core experiences of each childhood literacy instruction.

SHARED LITERACY EXPERIENCES

A literate classroom environment includes books, writing materials, environmental print, art supplies, comfortable places set aside for browsing through books, other early childhood equipment, furniture, and supplies—and even more books, some of which may have been made by the teacher or by the children themselves. Free access to books helps children link their beginning hypotheses about literacy with the "real thing." Through the close relationship among children, an adult, and books, children who have not had books in their lives learn that reading is enjoyable, meaningful, and important. They learn what a story is and how it is put together. Children whose home life has been enriched by books feel immediately comfortable and receptive to whatever "instruction" evolves from this familiar **shared literacy experience.**

Storybook Reading

The term *shared literacy experience* is central to beginning literacy instruction. The approach translates the closeness of parents and child sharing a book—what Holdaway called the "pre-school bedtime story learning cycle"—into a workable classroom approach (Holdaway, 1979). *Storybook reading* is the first stage in this approach and should be a regular part of every preschool and kindergarten class. Good storybook reading must be an active process that includes talking about pictures and text, making guesses about what will happen, comparing stories read on different days, and at times engaging in specific follow-up activities like drawing or role playing. Storybook reading as an instructional approach builds on the concept of the directed listening–thinking activity discussed in chapter 6. Discussion should be mutual, with teachers asking questions and encouraging listeners to do the same. Questions may elicit recall or inferences; they may seek to identify concepts, words, or ideas that children do not understand so that confusion can be clarified immediately; and they should always encourage thinking. Storybook reading teaches children that reading is enjoyable and that what is read should make sense. Children failing to gain this insight while they are still at the listening stage may encounter difficulties later when they themselves begin to read.

The best books for successful storybook reading with young children are those with relatively simple stories; good, related illustrations; and large, clear print. Topics should be appropriate for young learners—familiar enough to make sense but challenging enough intellectually to maintain children's interest. Wordless picture books work well, too, especially with small groups of children. Children "read" the pictures and construct the story themselves.

The traditional method for sharing stories finds the teacher seated, holding the book, surrounded by a circle of children sitting on the floor or on chairs. Although it is efficient, this method quickly loses the "visual intimacy" of the bedtime story setting. A storytime circle should be small and informal, with children snuggling as close as possible to the teacher so they can see the pictures and print. This arrangement also enables the teacher to observe each individual's responses to the story. If there are multiple copies of a book, children can follow along, turning the page each time the teacher does.

Of course, children may want to sprawl on the floor and may even fidget—no matter how small the circle—but the objective is to convey pleasure in reading, not to teach children to sit perfectly still. The trade-off teachers must make to achieve an intimate arrangement will be repetition; for a class to accept the "small circle" reading situation, the children must be confident that everyone will get an opportunity at some point during the day (or maybe the next day) to hear the story. Aides or volunteers can take turns as story readers, as long as they understand the techniques for sharing literature with children and do not turn the time into a question-and-answer session. Children from higher grades make excellent storybook readers as well.

Storybook reading provides a bridge between oral language and book language and is a first stage in children's learning to read independently. It emphasizes two important concepts: that book language is similar but not identical to oral language, and that the individual words on the printed page each have a recognizable oral equivalent. Striving for a balance between instruction and informality is the key to reinforcing these concepts. Teachers may point out individual words, such as those emphasized by larger or different-colored print, or words like *Wow* or *Bang* or animal sounds that often receive special graphic emphasis. Teachers can use their voices to demonstrate individual words. For example, a description of a caterpillar "sliding—slowly—sneakily—silently—across a branch" should be read with particular, suggestive emphasis. Preparing for storybook reading allows teachers to develop and perfect these oral effects (see chapter 11 for more information). Books that teachers share with children should be readily available for quiet, independent browsing and for children's own initial attempts at reading. Having multiple copies of books encourages these behaviors, and inexpensive paperbacks make this possible. Paperbacks themselves can be cut apart, laminated, and rebound for longer use.

Shared-book experiences can also lead to more lively follow-up activities, such as acting out stories in dramatic play or with puppets or drawing or painting favorite characters or scenes. As they rework the ideas, children learn rudimentary comprehension strategies—that is, methods for extracting meaning from text. More structured, teacher-directed activities work well, too. Teachers might assign a few children roles for a dramatization or puppet show to be presented to the rest of the class. By planning and discussing, children are again strengthening their comprehension skills. They may even have to refer back to the story to clarify points of disagreement. Group art activities such as making murals, dioramas, or papier-maché can also be used as follow-up. Chapter 11 provides more information.

Storybook reading can also reinforce content area understanding. To illustrate, suppose the teacher has shared the book *Frog and Toad Are Friends,* by Arnold Lobel. A week after reading the book, the teacher introduces a science unit with tadpoles in a tank and notices several children conferring busily over one of the books placed in the science area. They walk toward her, holding the book in front of them, and announce that they can "read the book." The proof lies in their pointing carefully and correctly not to the pictures but to the labels for pictures of frogs and toads. Repetition of the Lobel book has paid off in interest in the science unit and the important realization that *f-r-o-g* and *t-o-a-d* are the same in two entirely separate contexts.

Big Books

Don Holdaway wrote (1979):

> Reading to a group of children in school has little instructional value simply because the print cannot be seen, shared, and discussed. A parent is able to display the skill in purposeful use and at the same time keep before the [child's] attention the fact that the process is print-stimulated. Teachers can do the same by using enlarged print for the experience of listening to stories and participating in all aspects of reading. (pp. 64–65)

Big books, with enlarged print and format, are available commercially; directions for teacher-made big books are outlined in Figure 8.1, which also shows the responses of two young learners to a big book developed by their student teacher.

Big books should be made only of favorite books, those with proven appeal. Predictable books or caption books are also good material for big books, as are books that invite "audience participation" so that children can easily "read" along with the teacher. Teachers may want to make original big books for their classes to introduce or reinforce units of study, commemo-

Big books are invaluable for shared book experiences. Here the teacher points to specific pieces of text, students respond to her questions, and she records information on a chart tablet to keep track of the students' discussion.

rate special events, or record ongoing class activities. Appendix A suggests many suitable predictable and caption books.

Informal instruction is easy and effective with big books. Running the hand under each word, pointing out space between words, emphasizing special words, and stopping at the ends of sentences are all easier with big book format. As teachers point out "words that begin the same," "long words," or "words like *slither* that sound funny," they are not interrupting the enjoyment of the story. The "lesson" reinforces children's enjoyment, strengthens their appreciation of the story, and increases their understanding of how books work. The interaction provides a scaffold that helps students become ready to participate in the more formal instruction discussed in the next chapter.

Big book versions of stories can be shared with groups for several days if children are enjoying them; they should also be left out on a chart stand or in a convenient place for children to review. Individuals or small groups "play school" with the big book or merely "read" to each other. The larger format of words in these familiar stories invites independent study and sharing and encourages the kind of familiarity from which children develop their first sight vocabularies. The large print of big books becomes like environmental print and strengthens emerging concepts about reading.

Materials:

Chart tablets or sheets of large, heavy paper
Magic markers with strong colors
Children's artwork
Rings or other devices to bind books together
Laminating equipment (optional)
Chart stand or easel

Procedures:

1. Decide on the contents of the big book; it may be an original book or duplication of a commercial book.

If using a commercial book:

2. At first, reproduce the pictures as closely as possible; using an over-head projection machine helps those whose art skills are weak.

3. Later, rough sketches or children's drawings can be used in place of duplications of original illustrations.

4. Duplicate the text in neat, clear handwriting; try to keep the same number of words per line of text that children will see in the book but definitely match text in original to pages in big book so that children can make a one-to-one correspondence between the original and the new book.

If using an original ideal:

5. Keep text and illustrations simple; make sure it will be relevant to the children.

6. Write text horizontally, usually across the bottom of the page.

7. As children become familiar with big books, use their drawings to illustrate.

8. Use pictures cut from magazines or other illustrations for books, especially if they are going to be laminated.

For either kind of big book:

9. If the book is in chart tablet form, display it on a chart stand or easel; punch holes in tops of pages of books made from large sheets of newsprint or tagboard, reinforce the holes, and use rings to hang them from chart tablets.

10. If books are smaller than chart tablet size and will be handled by children, laminate pages for durability; punch holes in pages, reinforce if neccesary and use rings, strings, or yarn to bind them together.

Displaying books:

1. Hang books on chart stands when presenting them to children; leave chart stands in clear sight so children can reenact the story.

2. Use an easel or chalk tray as support for books that cannot be hung; leave these readily available for individual and small group browsing and reenactment.

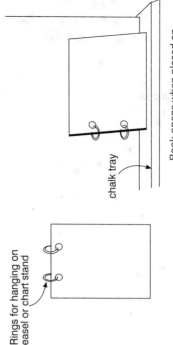

Rings for hanging on easel or chart stand

chalk tray

Book opens when placed on chalk tray of board

continued

Figure 8.1

Big book versions of familiar children's books or original big books written by teachers or teachers and children are easier to read than regular-size books. Children like to use big books to play school themselves. Big books should be made sturdy enough to withstand several years' use.

161

I think it is creative becusse
if your a teacher you can
read the little book and turn
the pages on the big book.
Be sides it fun, Little book is
are every comon. But big book
are easyer to read.

I think it's fun haveing
a big book and a litle book
becus you can rede awt
of the litle wune and
you can see the pichr
from the big oen and
I think ther friends are
nice.

Figure 8.1, *continued*

LANGUAGE EXPERIENCE APPROACH

Among the methods for encouraging emergent literacy, the **language experience approach** (LEA) ranks very high. The LEA (not to be confused with the general idea of children's *experiences with language*) can be defined as a method for encouraging reading growth that, in its early stages, uses materials developed by transcribing children's dictation. The process is simple: as children dictate, their teachers transcribe; then they guide learners in sharing or actually reading their stories. The LEA can be used with individuals or with small or large groups. This method accepts children's developmental levels and dominant language. It works because children like to see their words written down and are fascinated with the process of reading these words, and it builds upon children's experiences in and out of school and accommodates children's idiosyncratic language usage.

The most common use of the LEA is the chart story. Children and teachers share the act of composing and reading a story, often about a shared experience. Figure 8.2 presents possible activities and a series of charts that could be developed around a trip to the grocery store to get fruit for fruit salad; it sequences the activities to show how the LEA can be used in many sophisticated ways and summarizes guidelines for its use.

The language experience procedures can be the core of any preschool or kindergarten literacy program. (The next chapter extends the use of the LEA even further.) Classroom labels and charts developed with children's help are actually part of the foundation of language experience because they emphasize that just as one can say the name of a learning center or piece of furniture, one can also write the very same name. Commenting on children's work is another introductory use of language experience. As suggested in the essay in Table 8.1, children will frequently dictate a line or two about a painting or drawing or will welcome the teacher's labeling of objects in a picture. A day care director, writing in a log kept on one child's progress through a semester, reported transcribing the girl's story about Mickey Mouse: "She was thrilled—she giggled through my reading. When I copied her dramatic voice inflection, she hugged me. I certainly intend to do this again more often—talk about instilling a sense of positive self-concept!"

Guidelines for Preschool and Kindergarten LEA

Simple guidelines guarantee success with the LEA in preschools and kindergarten (see Table 8.2). Because children's sense of story is just emerging, their dictation may be confused, unsequenced, and redundant. Teachers can guide an LEA activity to reinforce concepts of time and sequence by prompting with questions such as, "Who can tell me what we did *first*. . . . What did we do *after* we saw the fire engine? . . . Tell me what

**Figure 8.2
An Illustration of the Language Experience Approach: Making Fruit Salad** Words and pictures can be combined for a rebus approach to a recipe that children can read easily. This recipe could be used in a cooking experience after a trip to a grocer to buy fruit. Children who are familiar with cooking procedures would feel confident as they read this recipe.

1. In preparation for a class walk to a neighborhood grocer, the teacher could elicit from the children safety rules that are recorded on a chart to be displayed in the classroom; these would be reviewed before the children leave on their trip. A map of the route could also be developed.
2. Because the purpose of the trip is to buy fruit for fruit salad, the teacher can work with the whole class or a small group to develop a shopping list for the trip; this is recorded on chart paper and copied.
3. The "committee" of students who will be responsible for making the fruit salad can develop a chart-sized recipe using words and pictures to guide their work.
4. After the trip and the cooking experience, children can dictate a story about what they have done.
5. Finally, children can dictate a thank-you letter to the clerks in the grocer if they were especially helpful.

Fruit Salad
You need:

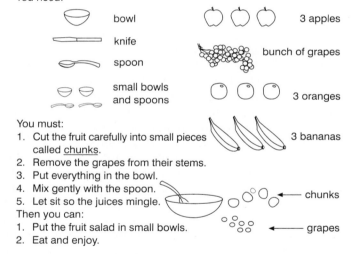

bowl		3 apples
knife		bunch of grapes
spoon		3 oranges
small bowls and spoons		

You must:
1. Cut the fruit carefully into small pieces called <u>chunks</u>.
2. Remove the grapes from their stems.
3. Put everything in the bowl.
4. Mix gently with the spoon.
5. Let sit so the juices mingle.

Then you can:
1. Put the fruit salad in small bowls.
2. Eat and enjoy.

3 bananas

chunks

grapes

we did *after* we left the store but *before* we got back to school. . . . *Before* we made the fruit salad, what did we do?" This behavior presents important models for children to use as they themselves begin to write.

Dynamic transcription of LEA stories, as described in Table 8.2, demonstrates many aspects of text production. The method becomes most effective when teachers use a "write aloud" process (Routman, 1991) and verbalize choices and the rationales for the choices as they actually transcribe an LEA story. A "write aloud" lets students see that writers plan, make choices about words and sentence structure, even move around and change words and ideas. Adding pictures to LEA stories lets children know that they, too, can use pictures to placehold words in their own writing.

Table 8.2
Guidelines for Using the Language Experience Approach

SMALL OR LARGE GROUP SESSION

Step 1

Teacher and students share an experience, such as the following:

- A trip
- A classroom visitor
- A classroom experience turned into a special event, such as observing a pet or cooking a treat

Step 2

Teacher and students discuss the event, with the teacher modeling or extracting from students key vocabulary and key concepts.

Step 3

Students dictate their ideas for the teacher to transcribe; teachers transcribe the stories on large chart tablets, using dark magic marker and clear, block printing; the teacher has two distinct styles of transcription to use:

- *Verbatim transcription*: the teacher writes down essentially everything the students say verbatim, stringing the statements together with children's names and verbs such as *said, remarked,* and so forth; the representation of children's ideas is accurate although uncreative. The disadvantage of this approach is that artificial-sounding, boring texts result; the method is traditional but *not highly recommended.*

- *Editorial transcription*: the teacher elicits comments, listens to students carefully, and combines comments to form more well-developed statements; some ideas may not be included in transcription immediately, but instead are woven into the story where they are appropriate; teachers focus the text production by stressing sequence ("Tell me what came **first**, **next**, **last**...."), quality of description or expression ("Who can tell me **another** way of saying that?"), or other rhetorical or mechanical feature; children's names are not used, but their ideas are clearly enough stated and acknowledged that they feel an appropriate sense of authorship. The advantages of this *highly recommended* strategy are that the teacher is modeling the composition process for the children and the resulting text is more interesting and conducive to teaching.

Step 4

Teacher and students read the resulting story.

With nonreaders: the teacher reads the text, pointing to each word and pausing to emphasize any words children might recognize or might find interesting to discuss; children are invited to read whatever they can, whether it is their names, phrases, or, as confidence increases, whole sentences.

With beginning readers: the teacher may read the whole story first, but the students are quickly invited to read as much of the text as they can.

---

continued

Table 8.2, *continued*

Step 5

Teacher uses the text for instruction, including work with word study, sentence construction, authoring, or reading subskills; strategies can include the following:

- Pointing out/asking students about the length, configuration, or composition of certain words, such as compound words
- Pointing out/asking students about punctuation or capitalization
- Eliciting words to replace words in the text, such as words that "describe better" than what was dictated
- Asking students to combine two short sentences and suggest appropriate rewording

This approach works especially well when teachers have used the Editorial Transcription model.

Step 6

The LEA chart story, on an easel or other stand, is left for students to reread, review, or illustrate.

VARIATIONS

Individual dictation: teachers may take dictation from individual children and record their work in small books or in notebooks; transcribing a caption for artwork falls into this category.

Sentence strips: transcriptions may be recorded on long strips of paper or on index cards; the strips are cut up into "word cards"; children use these word cards to create sentences on any flat surface or in pocket charts; children are encouraged to copy their sentences into a notebook.

Word bank: children request individual words from the teacher and keep then in a "bank" to study on their own, play with, swap among friends, and so forth; periodically the teacher and students review the words and discard ones that students cannot read; this approach complements the sentence strip strategy.

Daily calendar: each day, teachers take brief dictation about the day's happenings and record it on the classroom calendar (which may have to be specially made to allow enough space); this provides a model for children's own daily writing in journals.

Content area use: records are kept through LEA strategies of the work students do in content areas besides reading or language arts; observations of experiments, social studies observations, or even math activities are amenable to this approach.

The actual LEA chart story is less important in this dynamic process than the lessons children learn about text production. As they watch their teacher integrate oral statements into text, they also see their ideas woven into the total story. As the story itself unfolds, it doesn't matter who said what. Even children as young as three or four will benefit from this approach, for what they see confirms and expands their own ideas about writing.

Gradually, depending on the ages and abilities of the children in their classes, teachers can add more complex conventions to LEA transcriptions. "Writing aloud" again provides indirect instruction. For example, the differentiation between *big* and *huge* could be expanded to include choices such as *large, enormous, gigantic,* and *humongous.* Deliberate use of quotations in the transcription can introduce quotation marks to young writers. Asking children to "help" with a difficult word or suggesting that "we can look that word up in the dictionary" also demonstrates the dynamic aspect of text production. As children manipulate language in LEA sessions and observe their teachers fine-tuning their ideas for transcription, they confirm their hypotheses about writing and also learn new ideas. It is not uncommon for children to experiment with a convention modeled in an LEA story in their own writing.

WRITING IN PRESCHOOL AND KINDERGARTEN CLASSES

Language experience provides a bridge between reading and writing. As children dictate, they are actually producing texts, with their teachers doing the manual work. Children themselves often begin to commit "stories" to paper by drawing. When teachers offer to transcribe individuals' comments and stories on their drawings, they are helping learners do today what they will do alone tomorrow—that is, to move toward independent writing.

Drawing and Writing

Drawing is an important part of all preschool and kindergarten programs, one of children's primary modes of graphic communication. It is an essential element in helping children learn to write. Some of the advantages of drawing are as follows:

- Children use drawing to illustrate the "text worlds" they create in writing; drawing provides much of the context that they do not write in their stories.
- Drawing helps children think about what they want to write, serving as a prewriting warm-up; it helps them concentrate on what they are writing and on what they need to do to their stories.
- Drawing can provide an almost two-dimensional representation to parallel children's written efforts (e.g., a smiling face on a stick figure drawn by a beginning writer can represent several sentences that an older child might write out).
- Drawing can jog children's memories about content; they may draw a quick sketch as an organizer of a story they wish to write about; as they write, they refer back to the sketch to remember what they want to write.
- Drawing can help children organize their beginning stories; they may draw several pictures in sequence and use them as stimuli for writing labels or captions to flesh out their message.
- Drawing can motivate children to produce elaborate stories as they attempt to write, draw a little to help them think, and then write some more.

- Drawing that accompanies children's work can help young writers know what to say when they discuss their stories or seek transcription and elaboration from their teachers; discussions about the origin of the story/drawing itself and the decisions behind its production let teachers view children's emerging sense of how to orchestrate diverse aspects of text production.
- Drawing helps children stay on task as they write—some children may merely doodle little pictures to occupy their minds as they think about what they want to write or how mechanically to express their ideas in writing.

Dyson (1986, 1987, 1989) has extensively studied the relationship between children's writing and drawing. About one class, she wrote that "the children used drawing and its accompanying talk to serve an interactional as well as a representation function; children might, for example, engage in dramatic play with their friends during drawing. In addition, drawing and talk could also serve to evaluate the real world, as the children argued about the sensibleness of each other's drawings" (1989, p. 257). The following excerpt from a conversation reported by MacGillvray (1994) illustrates the powerful role that drawing can play in students' prewriting experiences. Two boys were asserting their sense of themselves as creators of meaning, negotiating a collaboration, and planning a shared story about a fantasy creature.

Arthur:	*Let me draw his mouth.*
Harold:	*No, I'm drawing his mouth.*
Arthur:	*I'll make him look cool, make him look this way. . . .*
Harold:	*You're making it look too angled.*
. . . .	
Arthur:	*Make him have an earring so he can take it off and throw them at somebody like pashooo (sound effect).*
. . . .	
Harold:	*No not on that one (ear) then it's a girl. Its [sic] supposed to be in the left ear. . . .*
Harold:	*This is my drawing, this is my drawing, not yours. . . . You're trying to make fun of me.*
Arthur:	*No, I'm noooooot (in a different voice, prolonged 'not').*
Harold:	*This drawing.*
Arthur:	*You want [the creature] to be like that?*
Harold:	*You draw him then. (p. 262)*

To encourage drawing, teachers should provide ample paper and a variety of writing and drawing tools. Many of the samples in this book were written with magic markers on the back of used computer paper. The markers themselves were motivating factors, and the computer paper was of high enough quality that it did not absorb ink and "bleed." The green bar lines of the computer paper showed faintly through to the wrong side, and some children used these as guides for letter formation. Teachers also need to provide time for drawing and to make it clear to students that their drawings are what Dyson calls "legitimate objects of their teacher's attention"—that is, valued parts of their literacy learning process.

Initially, teachers encourage youngsters to write by suggesting that children "write something" on their papers and by showing enthusiasm for all efforts. Dyson (1989) found that the majority (67 percent) of the written texts produced by kindergartners are "art notes," brief comments on their drawings. As children gain confidence, teachers might say, "Children in my class write a lot," to let children know that they are expected to write something on their drawings, to write little notes to each other, and to communicate with others through print. Spelling, handwriting, and other mechanics are of secondary concern. Teachers are merely encouraging children to *go public* with their literacy experiments.

After children have written something themselves, teachers can offer to transcribe the message and read the transcription back to the young artist-author. This must all be done without judgment about children's work. Teachers can, however, question and shape children's behavior. For example, children may begin to write *on* their drawings before they realize that they are supposed to write *about* them. If what children want transcribed seems to have no relationship to the drawing, teachers should question further by saying, "OK, but do you want me to write something *about* your picture? Tell me *about* what you have drawn." Gradually children figure out what is expected.

Keeping a Journal

All preschool and kindergarten students can keep journals in which they draw or write. A journal can be thought of as a collection of young learners' ideas, thoughts, and illustrations, an ongoing chronicle of their life in school and their emerging skills. Much of Dyson's (1989) research has been conducted in a classroom where the journals were simply "books with construction-paper covers; inside was alternating blank and lined paper. In [this] classroom, journal time was a regular activity. The children drew and wrote in their journals, as [the teacher] circulated. She talked to them about their story ideas and mechanics of production and . . . acted as scribe for the children's dictation. When individual children finished all the pages in their journals, she allowed time for them to share two or three entries with the class" (p. 16).

A journal provides students with a means of expressing their ideas in drawing or writing. Recording something in the journal—through teacher transcription or eventually in the child's own writing—establishes a habit that will eventually lead to frequent, fluent writing. Although children may not want to make journal entries daily, teachers should monitor their use and encourage reluctant writers to compose something at least several times a week. Additionally, journals also provide teachers with an excellent diagnostic tool for tracking children's progress throughout the year. Parents enjoy sharing the journals with their children and often gain real understanding from them about the developmental nature of literacy learning.

Writing to Communicate

Many children begin to write on their own by composing notes; they understand about mail, and they have seen adults writing letters. Children's notes are, of course, very personal, but they are still a primitive form of writing to inform, persuade, attempt to transact some business, or perform any of the other functions suggested early in chapter 7. A former student of mine reported an excellent example. She had been gently encouraging her kindergarten son to write on his drawings, but he maintained that he could not spell. When he could not find a tooth that had fallen out, he became very upset because he could not exchange it for money from the Tooth Fairy— that is, transact some important business. His mother wisely suggested that he could write the Tooth Fairy a note explaining his situation. That form of writing seemed acceptable to the child; he drew a picture of a tooth and wrote a note stating, "I SWOLD MI TT [I swallowed my tooth]." The Tooth Fairy made the appropriate exchange; business had been transacted.

The Social Nature of Writing

As children learn to write, they need to talk about what they are doing, thinking, and experiencing. Dyson (1989; also see Bibliography for other works by Dyson) has written about "friends learning to write" through their social interactions as much as through their independent efforts. She stated that although teachers may structure the environment for literacy events, the "children's own social concerns may come to infuse school literacy activities with social meaning" (p. 13). Even the youngest children she has studied commented on their own work, critiqued and sought help from each other, and competed in displays of knowledge. Dyson (1988, p. 58) called one kind of display among kindergartners a "spelling duel":

Regina:	*Do you know how to spell* sweet?
Maggie:	*I don't care if I don't.*
Regina:	*Just spell it.*
Maggie:	*OK. S-W-E-T.*

| *Regina:* | No, S-W-E-E-T. |
| *Maggie:* | Well, I was close but no cigar. |

Teachers can encourage children to talk about their writing by having them sit at tables or desks arranged in clusters or by establishing writing areas where children can sprawl on the floor. Asking students questions, commenting about their work, and engaging them in conversation provide oral scaffolds for students to use as they write independently.

And Since We're Thinking about Spelling . . .

For children who are just beginning to write, invented spelling is a powerful tool to encourage fluency. Being allowed to "spell it as best you can" frees children from the constraints of correctness and gives them room to experiment with many other aspects of print production. As they write more, participate in LEA sessions, and browse through and actually read more books, they realize that conventional spelling is driven by a definite set of rules. These same experiences, coupled with the kinds of instruction discussed in the next two chapters, help them move along the continuum from deviant to conventional spelling.

This movement is developmental, with some children making rapid progress toward spelling competency and others depending longer on the safety of invented spelling. Some, as Dyson found, even view spelling as a competitive activity in which accurate spelling of many words is a mark of excellence. It is, however, children's willingness to approximate spelling, rather than being hindered by fear of being wrong ("close but no cigar") that should be teachers' goal for young writers. Spelling can always be fixed later, but fear of writing because of fear of spelling incorrectly is far more difficult to eradicate.

What Can Teachers Expect?

The range of dictation and writing behaviors that teachers can expect in preschool and kindergarten classes is very broad. Factors such as children's interest in writing and drawing, their level of verbal skills, their dominant language, and their previous experiences with writing all contribute to their written output. Teachers are often disappointed that students do not write more, but they must remember that the development of all literacy skills takes time and does not happen overnight. Table 8.3 summarizes the sequence of writing development that spans the years in early childhood grades, along with teacher responses for each level. Some aspects of this sequence are discussed next, and others are elaborated upon in the next chapters.

Initially, children offer only brief labels or captions. Teachers can expand labels to captions verbally by restating and writing, "This is a _____." Children soon learn this longer statement and dictate captions themselves. Teach-

Table 8.3
Developmental Sequence of Writing

Child's Behavior	Teacher's Behavior in Response
1. Drawing and unrelated dictation	Transcription and discussion; asks *about* drawing
2. Drawing and related dictation	Transcription and discussion
3. Drawing and labels	Transcription; extends label to caption (see Figure 8.3).
4. Drawing and caption	Transcription and discussion; may question to stimulate thought; suggests topics such as "What You Like"
5. "I like…" stories (with or without drawing)	Transcription if asked; questions "Why?" for expansion (see Figure 8.4)
6. "I + [action verb]" stories (with or without drawing)	Transcription if asked; discussion (see Figure 8.5)
7. Use of multiple first-person subject (with or without drawing)	Transcription if asked; discussion (see Figure 8.6)
8. Use of third-person subject	Transcription if asked; discussion (see Figure 8.6)
9. Writing with no drawing	Request for clarification if needed (see Figure 8.6)
10. Exploration of ideas, format, narrative mode	Response as needed; suggestions for change, clarification (see Figures 8.6 and 8.7).
11. Editorial changes; revisions	Response as needed (See Figures 8.6 and 8.8).

ers should ask for additional information about children's pictures to model the process of "writing" longer and longer messages but must always be sensitive to children's levels of interest and motivation. Requesting too much information too quickly can take the pleasure away from beginning writers; dictated stories lengthen on their own as children gain understanding about producing texts. Figure 8.3 shows some beginning efforts.

Progression Beyond Labels and Captions

As children move beyond labels and captions, they begin to dictate and write sentences to accompany their artwork. Because children produce only single sentences at first, it might be easy to think of this stage as an exten-

Sample 1. Child wrote in deviant spelling and dictated label.

Rocket ship.

Sample 2. Child labeled parts of his picture: "VOLCANO FIRED" and "VOLCANIC ACTION."

Albert

FOKAO FASRE

dACSAENFOKA FOKAO

Sample 3. Child wrote her own labels on pictures of her friends. She also wrote "SCHOOL IS OVER. I LIKE SCHOOL."

Sckool isovrr I Loock Sckoo

Figure 8.3

The beginning of writing is labeling. Children may request that teachers label parts of their drawings or may use deviant spelling to label parts themselves. Gradually, labels expand to captions.

sion of caption writing, yet children are actually trying to share information or tell a story by using pictures as well as writing to create extended text. These sentences are the real beginnings of composition. Table 8.4, an excerpt from another teacher's essay, describes this process.

A common pattern after using labels and captions is the "I like . . . " story with its "I love . . . " variation. Suggested or spontaneous, these stories require few risks. The mere question "Why" is often enough to encourage expansion of the basic topic. "I like . . . " booklets can be used for more extensive writing.

Table 8.4
Beyond Labels and Captions

Many children bring beginning skills and an awareness about reading and writing to preschool. The extent of these skills is affected by factors the teachers often cannot control, but two factors a teacher can control are the quantity and quality of literary events offered in the classroom. Every time learners use language, they are learning language, learning through language, and learning more about language. My contention has been that children use literate language for learning, and they learn through literate language. Once a week we make a class book. The children are given a topic, draw something related to the topic, and bring their drawings to me to write what they tell me about the picture. Drawing is one way to provide a meaningful opportunity to use literate language and increases their understanding of the way oral and written language interrelate to represent meaning. The children in my classroom know their drawings represent ideas or things. For about the first three books the children orally "labeled" their drawings. At the beginning all I wrote were labels. Then I began restating the "labels" in complete sentences and writing them down that way. Soon, when the children described their drawings, they talked more in complete sentences.

The purpose of giving each drawing a caption has been twofold. First, we increase the child's vocabulary by taking his ideas and adding more words. Second, we show the child that writing is another form of symbolism for his ideas. Although drawing maintains a relationship of similarity to the object or occurrence it refers to, writing does not. Writing is a system with its own rules.

Gradually, the children began to "write" more freely, and it became obvious that all the children were drawing something related to the theme presented, sometimes even in the form of pictures rather than individual items to be labeled. It became safe to say that the descriptions of their drawings began to take on a "story-like" quality. Writing has varied: some added punctuation marks, others grouped letter-like symbols written together for words or phrases. None of the children said he didn't know how to write.

The children clearly began to feel comfortable with "writing." One important factor in the transition was the use of writing instruments. Crayons had always been used for drawing and writing. Now markers and pencils were placed at the tables for the children to use. They have been a major motivational factor.

Classbooks have opened up a whole new world of literature for the children. These books have become treasures that they want to share with others. Writing is indeed one area where I noted much progress....

H. Lopez. End-term report, ECED 3553. University of Texas at El Paso, 1986. Excerpted and used by permission.

The simplest version has the sentence starter "I like . . . " photocopied on individual pages. These become a variation of commercial caption books that can be shared among classmates or made into a big book. Alternatively, children can be given blank pages and the suggestion to write and draw about what they like and dislike. Figure 8.4 shows several examples of "I like . . . " stories.

A second pattern can be called "I + [action verb]" stories. These sentences are also safe and highly personal. The thought process to develop these stories probably goes like this: "What can I draw a picture of *myself doing?*" or "What have I *done recently* that I can draw?" or "What do I *want* that I can draw?" These stories begin with the first-person pronoun *I* and include action verbs such as *want, wish,* or *had a dream.* Children move easily between present and past tense and eventually begin to use the first-person plural (e.g., "My friend and I") as the subject. They vary other elements of the basic pattern to see what happens; they change the subject of their sentences; and they add extra sentences to expand their story and convey more information. Figure 8.5 shows this kind of writing.

Playing with Ideas and Conventions

The writing discussed so far has been in the first person because the writers have been concerned with topics close to themselves. Movement to the next developmental stage parallels the linguistic play of oral language growth, in that children begin to play with ideas, venture into fantasy, express outrageous wishes, write about supposedly taboo subjects, or attempt to shock, surprise, or even "gross out" their readers. Writing of this sort is riskier than verbal linguistic play because there is a written record of the child's thoughts. Stories may still be relatively short, but children are clearly making progress in text production. See Figure 8.6.

Children also manipulate words and sentence parts in an attempt to embed clauses into sentences, string more than one idea into compound sentences, or test ideas about grammatical rules or devices. Realizing that printed material contains punctuation, children may sprinkle periods, commas, exclamation points, and question marks throughout their stories. They may also attempt to vary sentence form by posing questions and answering them or writing in dialogue. (See Figure 8.6.)

Often these manipulations reflect what children have heard in storybook reading or have read themselves. Their writing begins to "talk like a book," indicating that children realize the differences between "book talk" and ordinary speech. Teachers cannot teach this difference directly, but well-prepared, enthusiastic oral reading of good children's literature provides the raw material from which children extract the concept themselves (see chapter 6). When children begin a story with "Once upon a time," teachers know that the important difference between talk and text has been recognized. (Figure 8.6 also shows examples of this kind of writing.)

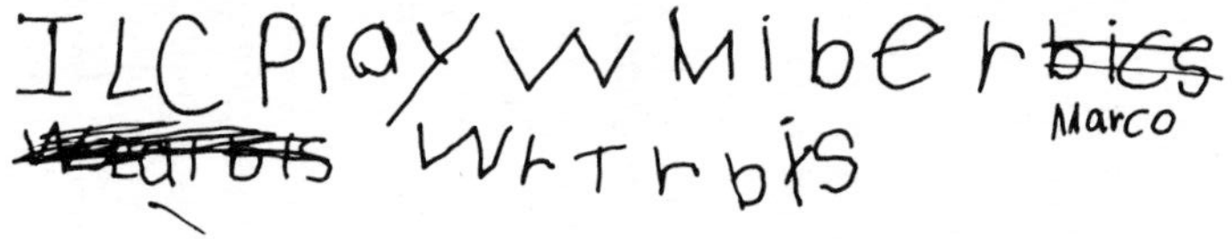

Sample 4. The child addresses her little red wagon and attempts to explain why she loves it; she changes number in the second part of her sentence but has clearly experimented with sentence construction; note two punctuation marks.

Sample 5. This child also states why she likes a toy, and she goes on to describe the kite and tell where she got it; notice how she corrects false starts. This is a later effort of the child who wrote Sample 4.

Sample 1. Child indicates what he likes to do; note correction of false start in spelling.

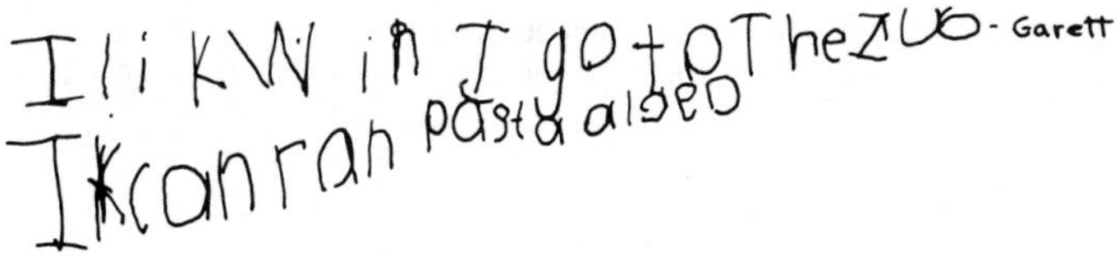

Sample 2. Child indicates what he likes to do and tells something about the activity; he is still uncertain about spacing between words.

Sample 3. Child thanks her kindergarten teacher for being so nice and tells her that she like(s) reading; this child leaves ample space between her words; notice the emerging spelling skills.

Figure 8.4

"I like . . ." stories allow children to write about things and events of special interest and significance. The basic phrase "I like . . ." may be expanded with reasons and description. At times, teachers may prompt this expansion by requesting more information. These samples were collected as part of the regular writing period in a kindergarten class; transcriptions were done by the teacher.

I W.ish I had a scatdord But I dont hav one
I wish I Rob on one
I wish I had a scate board, but I don't have one. I wish I rode on one.

Karla

Sample 1. Child indicates that he wishes he had a skate board; note use of negative construction and embedded clauses.

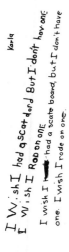

WinI KLIMDUP on mord
When I climed up a mountain, I fell down.

Sample 2. Child writes of climbing a mountain and falling down; note use of introductory clause; the simple line drawing contributes to the story because a mountain near the child's home has a cross and shrine on top; his drawing tells which mountain he climbed.

If I was a gasager on a shuti,
I wud flote afown in
The Sasshutl.

Sample 3. Child expresses wishful thinking: If I was a passenger on a shuttle, I would float down in the space shuttle.

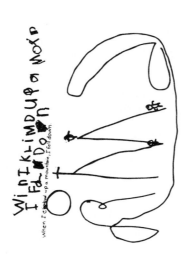

I Went to the Ice Cream Str
and My Sistr pickt Choclit
and I got Vanalaete,
and My mom Went
too.

Stephanie

Sample 4. The child gives lots of information about a family outing; her drawing gives additional information.

Figure 8.5

"I + [action verb]" stories tell about what children have done or want to do; they may also express wishes or ambitions. They are easy for children to think of and write because they are so personal.

Sample 1. The drawing conveys the action in this story; it is full of red and black and unhappy faces. The child's text (which he read tentatively to his teacher in case she might disapprove) was: A Dog was dumb enough to go in front of the racing track.

Sample 2. This child also tested his teacher's tolerance for gruesome subjects; his story, written without drawings, read: One day a boy was playing soccer with his friends and the boy was winning. All of a sudden, the boy fell. He fell again and again and again. He cracked his head open. He died. The end. The child might have been trying to imitate a sportscaster or merely shock his teacher. The writing (done without spaces between words) has a definite book-like tone that would not have been present if the child had been reporting on a real incident.

Figure 8.6

Young writers experiment with topics, story parts, and characterizations as they emerge into stages of confident writing. As this happens, they may not depend on drawing to help tell their stories. When confidence grows, they often attempt to shock, test, or even "gross out" their readers. Experiments with gruesome subjects or taboo words should be welcomed as signs of increasing skill and sense of authorship.

Sample 3. This is a much simpler story, written with less control of spelling; it reads: When Donald Duck did throw a tray on the people, the people screamed. What is unique about the story is the characterization of Donald Duck, unless the child was reporting on something he had seen on television.

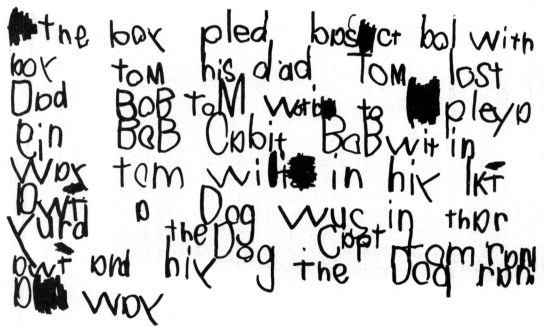

Sample 4. The left-hand side of this story lists a cast of characters. The story itself is not unique, except for the inclusion of one word. As the child read the story to his teacher, he paused and seemed to gauge whether to dictate what he had written; his teacher did not even flinch. The story reads: The boy played basketball with his dad. Tom lost. Tom wanted to play again. Bob couldn't. Bob went in. When Tom went he, he looked. A dog was in their yard. The dog crapped. Tom ran out and the dog ran away. Note the writer of this story was named neither Tom nor Bob.

continued

Sample 5. This child wrote about a dream: When I went to sleep I was dreaming about the dog in space. the dog was drawing himself flying after a cat in space. And the dog got scared and turned back and now the cat was after the dog and the cat scared the dog away. His dream includes made-up characters and considerable action. Notice the arrows to indicate which drawing is which character.

Sample 6. This child began on the back of his sheet of paper by writing a list of characters: Sheep, wolf, farmer (named Larry), Frank, and bob. His dictation read: There was a sheep. When he went to eat he would always find a wolf. The sheep ran away. And the wolf would get lost because the sheep was clever. Then he went back to eat, and another wolf found him again! Then the farmer came out and chased the wolf away. The list of characters gives information that is not included in the story, and the story itself may be a take-off on something the child has heard or read.

Figure 8.6, *concluded*

180

Children come to realize that books have authors, illustrators, divisions called chapters, and specific narrative sequences. They experiment with these concepts by calling themselves "authors" and "illustrators." To extend this experimentation, teachers can suggest that children divide large pieces of paper into several blocks or use separate pieces of paper to make a "chapter book." These separate blocks or pages help children to organize their thinking and to sequence stories. Knowing, for example, that there are four blocks to fill in with pictures and sentences tells children that they must think up four related parts for the story. If they draw and write in an inappropriate sequence, all they have to do is number the four component parts to show their order. The task, although difficult, has clear boundaries within which to function. It is risky but possible. Giving children this structured means of moving from single sentences to sequenced stories is a good example of Vygotsky's idea of helping a child solve linguistic problems today so that he can solve them alone tomorrow. Figure 8.7 illustrates children's attempts to manipulate space and ideas in early writing.

Even very young writers realize that what they write can be revised and edited. The "write aloud" process in LEA sessions and the use of magic markers rather than pencils foster this realization. The stories in Figure 8.8 show the ways kindergarten writers demonstrate their inclination to revise their work. The inclination to revise seems to differ from child to child, and many children will not purposefully revise their work until considerably later in their histories as writers.

SUMMARY

Even without a thorough understanding of letter–sound correspondences, young children can compose real stories and make sense from books. To accomplish these tasks they need appropriate adult support and appreciation of their developmental levels. Teachers in prekindergarten and kindergarten classes can provide this support by offering literacy-rich classrooms and activities that invite rather than push children into explorations of reading and writing. Through such experiences, children gain confidence in their abilities to communicate with print and reinforce the emerging sense of print production and use developed in their preschool years.

QUESTIONS AND TASKS FOR INDEPENDENT OR COLLABORATIVE WORK

1. Be sure that you can define each of these terms:

    • emergent literacy (update your definition based on this chapter)
    • shared literacy experience
    • language experience approach

Figure 8.7

Dividing paper into blocks allows children to begin to write sequenced stories. Each block presents an event or in some cases a "chapter" in a book. Paper may also be cut into small pieces and stapled together to form little writing booklets.

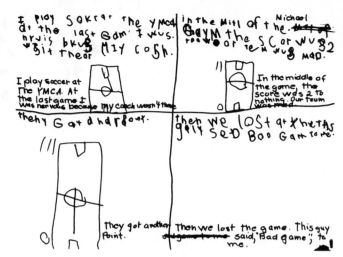

Sample 1. The child wrote and drew about a real event; having four spaces to fill rather than a whole sheet of paper made his task more manageable. Note that the drawing shows the layout of the soccer field rather than children playing the game.

Sample 2. This child drew individual "events" in his story in boxes like a comic strip; his writing was separated by dots rather than spaces: his story described the entire set of pictures: "A long time ago an old Model T just went putt, putt, putt along the road. All of a sudden a cat ran out in the road and splat the cat was gone." The child obviously enjoyed the gruesomeness of his story. Notice the HaHaHa in several blocks.

Sample 1. This child merely crosses out words she wants to change; the story reads: The elephant is going to the zoo. He is the man's helper.

Sample 2. This story has no drawing; the child had learned (through language experience) that he could add words by using arrows; his text reads: The man is cleaning the back yard and the man is playing soccer.

continued

Figure 8.8

Giving beginning writers magic markers instead of pencils is motivating and encourages them to cross out errors. Letting them know that this is an acceptable part of the writing process prepares them for the editing they will do later on longer pieces of writing. Crossing out and inserting words with arrows during LEA models this process for young children.

Sample 3. This child makes corrections by writing needed letters over the letters he has already written (as in FROG) or by crossing out.

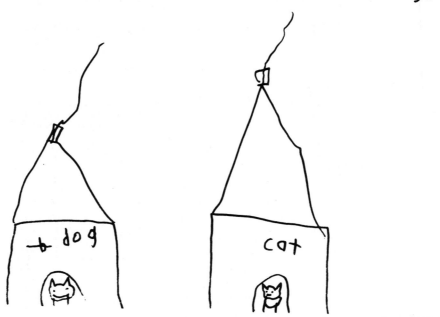

Sample 4. This story is interesting because the child corrected the text and his drawings so that they would go together; he began with The dog is in the box, changed the square box he had drawn to a house, and changed the word he used to describe the dog's vacation; then he changed the second part of the story as well.

Figure 8.8, *concluded*

2. In what ways can drawing be considered a "warm up" to writing for young authors? In what ways is the interaction of child drawing, child dictating, and teacher transcribing a true literacy event?

3. Visit several early childhood classes (including preschools) to assess the amount of writing going on. Is the amount adequate? What invitations does the teacher provide for the students through instruction and availability of materials? What opportunities have teachers missed for children's writing?

4. Pretend you are the teacher in either of the classes described in Tables 8.1 and 8.4. Parents do not understand what you are trying to do and maintain that their children are "too young" to write. Write a letter to the parents explaining what you want the children to do.

5. Find a children's story that would be appropriate for a big book. Make the big book and present it to a group of children. Record how they react. If possible, leave the book in their classroom and note whether they return to the book for storybook reenactments.

6. Find another book to present to young children. Read it to several children one at a time and invite each child to reenact the story. Observe their behavior as they "read the book" and tape record what they say. Notice how much prompting you have to do. Analyze the tape recording to determine what kind of storybook reenactment each child presented.

7. Visit several preschools and kindergartens and survey their libraries. Are there enough books to encourage browsing? Are the books appropriate for the children? How do the teachers feel about prereaders using books on their own?

8. In your visits, determine the extent to which language experience is used to develop prereading skills and concepts. What opportunities for LEA use are being missed? Ask the teachers how they feel about the LEA. Conduct several LEA sessions yourself to see how the children respond.

CHAPTER 9

Moving Toward Literacy

Themis chapter discusses how students grow as literacy users and how teachers can support this growth. Although the chapter concerns a transitional stage on the literacy continuum that often occurs during first grade, the principles, approaches, and techniques are developmental and hence applicable for children in earlier and later grades as well.

Children growing as literacy users are initiated into a learning community consisting of their teacher and peers. Comparing this with joining a special club, Frank Smith (1992) wrote: "Children must learn from people: from the teachers (formal and informal) who initiate them into the readers' club and from the authors whose writing they read. It is the *relationships* that exist within the classroom that matter . . . students' relationships with teachers and with each other and their relationships with what they are supposed to be learning—with reading and writing" (p. 440).

Although true, Smith's statement is deceptively simple. If students are to grow and mature as literacy users, their *instruction* must be grounded in theory about literacy growth and in knowledge of children's developmental needs (Durkin, 1990). Teachers most often provide focused instruction within classroom contexts—they ask the right questions, provide necessary information, model behaviors, and challenge learners just enough for them to move smoothly forward to more advanced levels of competency.

EXPANDING THE MODEL OF EMERGENT LITERACY INSTRUCTION

A primary assumption of this chapter is that, as much as possible, children spend part of every day in a literacy workshop setting. In that environment, focused use of the big books, storybooks, language experiences, writing, and drawing discussed in chapter 8 continues to foster students' literacy growth. The basic instructional "delivery systems" of the approach are teacher–student conferences, small groups of children working collaboratively or with the teacher, and brief, focused, whole class lessons. Other assumptions of this chapter are as follows:

1. Students learn to read and write from contact with more mature literacy users and other beginners like themselves; literacy learning is a social activity.
2. Students also learn from their own explorations of literacy and from formal and informal instruction.
3. As students read and write, they must draw extensively upon their background knowledge to help them construct meaning.
4. Learning to read and write does not involve learning a series of discrete, isolated skills; instead, skills should be combined into sets of strategies

from which students can select appropriate "tools" with which to accomplish their literacy tasks.

5. Students must learn to draw upon graphophonemic (letter–sound), semantic (word meaning), and syntactic (grammatical) cues as they read. As they write, they orchestrate these cues to express meaning.

6. As much as possible, students should be encouraged to develop strategies for independent work.

7. Reading and writing are related activities and should be practiced together. However, students do not have to be fully proficient as readers before they can write successfully.

8. Reading competency increases as students encounter a wide range of authentic reading materials. Writing improves as children progress from performing simple, personal writing tasks to engaging in more purposeful tasks geared to specific, more public, audiences.

Table 9.1 lists a range of activities appropriate for early primary-grade classrooms.

Effective Instruction

Effective literacy lessons are unified and coherent. Teachers must offer instruction that flows smoothly from classroom life and does not appear fragmented; students should see their work as meaningful and authentic so that they realize how their activities enhance their emerging abilities as literacy users. But reading and writing instruction should also be divided, however subtly, into three stages: prereading, reading, and postreading instruction and prewriting, independent writing, and postwriting instruction. For reading, each phase helps students learn how to tackle tasks by guiding them through specific pieces of text; they perform particular behaviors at each juncture of their reading and gain feedback on their success. The three-stage model of writing is known as the process approach and is discussed later in this chapter. Table 9.2 lists more information about the three stages of literacy instruction.

Assessing Children's Knowledge, Skills, and Strategies

Chapter 3 stressed that assessment is an integral part of good literacy instruction and should begin early in the school year, as soon as teachers feel they have adequate rapport with the children. Throughout the elementary grades, teachers should assess what children bring to the learning environment and what they are learning to understand as instruction progresses. In most cases, this form of assessment is low key and unobtrusive,

Table 9.1
Reading and Writing Activities for Early Classrooms

Logs and Journals

The major purposes of logs and journals are

- To give students frequent, if not daily, opportunities to produce writing that will not be graded; and

- To allow teachers to evaluate students' emerging understanding of the processes of writing and the content areas they are learning.

Possible uses include:

- Daily entries about topics children themselves select (see Table 9.4)

- Dialogue journals, which require daily responses from teachers

- Literature logs with entries about what children are reading

- Learning logs about content area work to record the stages of developing understanding (see Figure 9.4, sample 4)

Sustained Reading and Writing

During sustained silent reading and writing (SSR and SSW) activities, students and teacher read or write in silence. Children select the books they will read and write on topics of their own choice. Teachers must engage in silent reading and writing as well. The time periods for SSR and SSW are determined by children's age, skills, attention span, and motivation.

Used daily or as a routine practice several times a week, these activities have the following advantages:

- Students develop appropriate habits for focusing their reading and writing behaviors.

- Students see their teacher reading and writing.

- Students become more independent.

- Students realize that not all in-school reading has to consist of assigned work.

Reading and Writing as Part of Ongoing Content Area Work

Reading and writing activities in early childhood classes are often fragmented, so students do not see how literacy skills are tools to be used in all learning. By integrating reading and writing into all the content areas, teachers help students make the important realization that literacy extends beyond simple reading and writing work to encompass ways of

- Communicating with others, including experts of various sorts and the authors of books they read;

- Learning more about the world around them; and

- Enhancing their own learning in other areas.

Possible activities include:

- Reading as part of project work in content areas

- Writing, even dictation to teachers, as part of project work (see Figure 9.4, sample 2)

- Writing letters to authors of books that have been read or to solicit information related to other learning, so long as letters are directed toward real audiences and are actually sent

- Writing as demonstrations of comprehension in reading work

- Writing notes and process reports of independent work or small group work to keep track of what they are doing and learning; this would include individual log entries

Assigned Writing for Young Learners

Children in emergent literacy classes benefit from "free writing" and from more structured writing activities. Teachers must attend to developmental and motivational differences in assigning writing tasks and must be aware that some students may not readily draw upon background experiences as sources of topics and ideas for their work. Assigning specific writing activities encourages students to practice their skills but also establishes habits and discipline for ongoing development.

Possible activities include:

- Daily or regular writing in logs or journals
- Sustained silent writing
- Periodic assignments to write a story or a letter, so long as the assignments are clearly stated and within the grasp of the students (see Figure 9.4)
- Writing in preparation for peer or teacher conferences
- Writing with a friend

Assigned Reading for Young Learners

Children should read extensively in books of their own choice and books that the teacher selects. Instruction in supportive reading groups provides skills for independent reading and gives children confidence to read on their own. Appropriate tasks require reading in real texts—that is, in books or magazines, not in workbooks or on worksheets.

Possible activities include:

- Sustained silent reading
- Browsing through a big book
- Sharing a big book in small groups, often "playing school"
- Doing "research" for small group or class projects
- Reading in preparation for a conference with a teacher
- Reading with a friend either for recreation or to complete an assignment
- Reading with a student from a higher grade
- Reading in preparation for small group work with the teacher

with teachers making notes about their observations, fine-tuning instruction as needed, and providing intervention when children seem to need specific help (see "Help for Children When They Need It," later in the chapter).

Often children themselves provide excellent assessment data. They should be encouraged to talk about the processes they use as they read and write, to ask questions, and to voice confusion they experience. As they "think aloud" about their work, they may reveal misunderstandings or incorrect ideas that can be remedied before complex, deeply embedded problems arise.

Teachers should be alert for attitudinal signs: strong learners seem happy and relaxed, ready to meet the challenges of learning literacy with stamina and enthusiasm. Boredom, stress, and discomfort during literacy activities may signal difficulties. When a child seems uninterested in brows-

Table 9.2
Three Stages of Literacy Activities

Reading

Prereading Behaviors That Children Should Be Encouraged to Use

- Using clues from text (e.g., pictures, title) to determine what aspects of background knowledge to activate
- Using clues from text to make predictions about content and/or story line
- Using knowledge of the structure of stories or informational text to form a preliminary set of expectations about how material will be presented
- Setting a purpose for reading, either because of a child's own interests or in response to a question from the teacher

Reading Behaviors That Enhance Comprehension

- Confirming the accuracy of one's predictions
- Modifying predictions or making new ones
- Using context clues as much as possible to determine unfamiliar words
- Monitoring one's comprehension to make sure text is making sense

Postreading Behaviors That Further Understanding and Appreciation

- Confirming the accuracy of predictions
- Summarizing
- Assimilating new information into existing knowledge
- Rereading as needed to clarify comprehension
- Following up on reading by writing or talking about what has been read

ing through books or expressing him- or herself in writing, teachers should review the kind of instruction being offered, its pacing or content, or other factors outside of the classroom to direct the child's interest toward literacy.

CREATING GROUPS FOR INSTRUCTION

Because literacy learning is social, groups are essential, but they should be flexible, not static. The purpose of grouping students, besides the obvious goal of efficient delivery of instruction, is to tap the energy and intelligence of group members. Teachers must be willing to give some of the "control" of instructional groups to participants; and children must feel comfortable enough to discuss, share, and question what is presented and to take advantage of the highly social nature of literacy learning.

Teachers may work with either small or large groups or with individual children; groups of children may work independently. Some groups are

Writing

Prewriting Behaviors That Children Should Be Encouraged to Use

- Generating ideas
- Brainstorming with others
- Making notes or graphic organizers; drawing pictures
- Making preliminary rough drafts
- Setting a purpose for writing

Writing Behaviors That Enhance Comprehension

- Working independently
- Conferencing with others
- Working through initial ideas, adjusting and modifying as needed
- Organizing and reorganizing ideas
- Monitoring the development of the piece by reading and rereading
- Adding new ideas as needed to convey meaning

Postwriting Behaviors That Further Understanding and Appreciation

- Editing, revising, reading, and rereading
- Sharing works-in-progress and nearly finished pieces with others
- Making sense of peers' and teacher's critiques
- Adjusting piece to convey meaning more effectively
- Correcting grammatical and spelling errors
- "Going public" with finished pieces of writing

Though these behaviors may seem second nature to skilled literacy users, students need help developing proficiency at each stage of their reading and writing processes. The three-part model of literacy behavior should be reflected in instructional planning, and ample time should be allowed for students to engage meaningfully in each phase.

homogeneous, whereas others are heterogeneous, but in no case is group membership fixed. Children move in and out of groups as need and interest dictate. (Refer to Table 2.3 for suggestions of different grouping patterns.)

Supportive Reading Groups

In preschool and kindergarten, children participated in many shared book experiences in which they learned behaviors and concepts that allow them to move confidently into **supportive reading groups.** Such groups, consisting of five or so children, depend on the use of big books or other enlarged-print material. The point is to allow small groups of children to share reading. As one child wrote, "You can see the pichrs . . . big books are easyer to rede." The materials students encounter should be interesting, predictable, and accessible in terms of concepts and vocabulary. The time it takes to develop any background knowledge necessary for comprehension is well spent. When children gain confidence through supportive reading groups, they readily try out their strategies on unfamiliar texts as well.

Instruction in supportive reading groups is focused but always remains low key, with teachers constantly assessing children's emerging skills and making adjustments as needed. The objective is *to move from teacher-directed reading to students' independent reading* without sacrificing the support that teacher direction has fostered. In leading the session, the teacher runs a hand under the print and reads the big book text

(a) (b) (c) (d)

Sharon Suskin, a first-grade teacher in South Brunswick, New Jersey, is shown conducting a lively reading lesson with the whole class. She uses a pointer and slider to emphasize words that the students should study and presents large-format text on the chart tablet. Students sit on the floor around Ms. Suskin but are quick to jump up and assist at the chart stand and to answer her questions.

orally, while children track the print (follow along with their eyes). After the teacher has read a line, students *echo the teacher's oral reading.* In this way, the teacher is modeling fluent oral reading so that students hear and then practice appropriate intonation patterns. Students also hear how the teacher has "chunked" the language of the sentence into meaningful units rather than reading individual words. These chunks represent thought units that make up the sentence; they must be comprehended as units if the sentence itself is to be understood.

The best analogy for the process of teacher's modeling and students' echo reading is probably the use of training wheels on a bike. Training wheels let children feel safe and secure while they get the feel of pedaling, balancing, steering, and braking. By the time the wheels come off, children have gained the rudimentary skills to ride solo. They will still fall from time to time and probably should still ride on fairly level surfaces, but they are clearly on their way to being good bike riders. Table 9.3 outlines the procedures for structuring supportive reading groups.

Enlarged-print formats lend themselves to the use of sliders, or *masking devices* (see Figure 9.1). Systematically covering and uncovering words involves a *cloze* strategy, which is based on the idea that readers search for meaning in print and can fill in missing words if they are reading with comprehension. Guided by the clues inherent in the text, children figure out what comes next as the teacher slowly unmasks the words (this is discussed further in the section "Context Clues"). Teachers can also stop at appropriate places to elicit guesses about "what will happen next."

Masking can encourage attention to letter–sound correspondences. For example, as teachers approach a word starting with a blend, such as *small*, they stop the masking process and say, "Now, see if you can figure out this word. I'll give you a clue." Unmasking the *s* and then the *m* and hesitating while students blend the two letters into the *sm* sound encourages students to make guesses about the word. Children must use both their knowledge of letter–sound correspondences and the preceding words to ask themselves what word would fit and also begins with the indicated blend. Doing this successfully demonstrates the ability to use phonics and context clues, two approaches that are discussed later in the chapter.

Masking activities are open-ended. Slowly unmasking text and modeling a procedure for self-questioning and predicting the words that will make sense in text externalize for young learners the mental processes that more expert readers use as they attempt to figure out unfamiliar words. Teachers are in control of what children see, and they demonstrate the prediction strategies children should use in independent reading. Random wrong guesses from students suggest comprehension difficulties, whereas wrong guesses that are semantically or syntactically correct should be discussed with something like, "Yes, that word *would* fit here; but the word the author used is ___ ; they mean the same thing, don't they?"

Table 9.3
Structuring a Supportive Reading Group

Materials

Multiple copies of children's literature and enlarged-print version of what children will read

Procedures

Day 1

1. Teacher presents the enlarged-print version of the material and reads it in a normal, conversational voice, pointing to each word as he or she reads, emphasizing words like **POW!!!** with both voice and comments.

2. Children are invited to point out or guess at any words that they might know by sight.

3. Children look through regular-sized copies of the book for about five minutes; they should note and discuss the pictures and words they know. This gives them a chance to coordinate the teacher's oral reading and the regular text.

4. The teacher reads the text again as children follow along either on the enlarged print or in the regular books; children are encouraged to echo the teacher's reading as much as possible; the teacher should note who does not seem able to track the print in the text or the enlarged print and who can echo read most of the text.

5. Copies of the material are made available for browsing.

Day 2

1. Steps 1–4 from day 1 are repeated at a more rapid pace.

2. Echo reading behavior should increase during this session. Children should be called upon to read words, phrases, or whole sentences either from their books or from the enlarged-print version; approximations of the correct text are accepted.

3. The teacher provides appropriate low-key instruction by pointing out words that have a specific sound or represent a particular part of speech or grammatical principle.

4. The teacher observes the extent to which children participate and determines who needs advanced work and who needs continued close support.

5. Copies of the material are made available for browsing and rereading; peer reading and story reenactment are encouraged.

Day 3

1. A new book may be presented in the same fashion, or children may continue to work on the previous material.

2. From time to time, a familiar story is reviewed for fun and to reinforce past learning.

Alternative Procedures

1. A similar process can be used with dictated language experience stories; the teacher may or may not reproduce the LEA story for individual children, but the basic procedure of supportive reading is followed.

2. Again, with or without copies of the enlarged-print material, supportive reading strategies can be used to introduce poems; information on charts, posters, or bulletin boards; or song lyrics. Children follow along as the teacher reads; they read as much of the material as they can on their own.

3. Either alternative can be used with small groups or with the whole class; the echo reading process allows even weaker readers to participate.

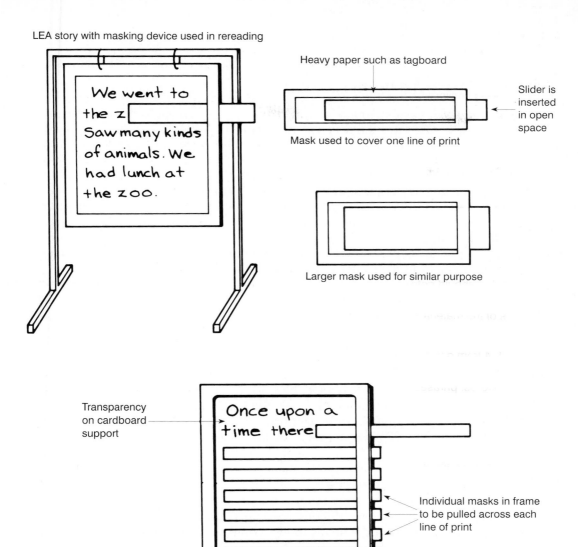

LEA story with masking device used in rereading

We went to the z▭ Saw many kinds of animals. We had lunch at the zoo.

Heavy paper such as tagboard

Slider is inserted in open space

Mask used to cover one line of print

Larger mask used for similar purpose

Transparency on cardboard support

Once upon a time there▭

Individual masks in frame to be pulled across each line of print

Masking used with overhead transparencies

Figure 9.1

Masking Devices   Masking devices can be used to cover individual words, single lines, or large pieces of text. They can be used with stories presented on chart stands or overhead transparencies. Teachers uncover text as children read orally or silently. The amount of text uncovered depends on the instructional objectives: to reinforce phonics skills, to demonstrate context clues, to encourage prediction of the story line, and so forth.

Various Types of Reading

Children in early primary grades ought to read extensively as part of daily routines. Many teachers set aside a specific time of day for independent reading that may or may not be part of the literacy workshop. During this time, *everyone* reads. The activity might be called sustained silent reading (SSR) or drop everything and read (DEAR). Ten to fifteen minutes of independent reading is enough to start; the length of time increases as students' competence grows. Routman (1991, pp. 44–51) suggests that sustained reading periods be extended to students' homes through the reading of Wonderfully Exciting Books (WEBs). She also stresses the importance of students' talking about their independent reading with their classmates. (Chapters 10 and 11 offer more information.)

In addition to periods when everyone reads independently, paired reading, or **buddy reading,** is an effective approach for young learners. During buddy reading time, two children read together, pooling their reading expertise, their background experiences, and their reactions to what they read. Sometimes the buddy may be an older student or even the teacher. Paired reading has many advantages, not the least of which is the shared enjoyment of children's literature. The approach is very powerful when a stronger reader is paired with a weaker reader. Because the two work together to construct meaning, it doesn't matter that one child may not know all the words. The stronger reader shares his or her strategies for identifying words and comprehending text, thereby serving as a reading model for the second child.

Transition to Silent Reading

Beginning readers have difficulty reading silently (just as beginning bike riders have difficulty on rough, pitted surfaces). Much of their initial work is

Sharon Suskin reads to her students each day. Here she is reading a book that supports the students' science investigations and answers their questions about the size of bullfrogs. Ms. Suskin had told the students that she would "look the information up," and the book provides the needed facts.

conducted out loud, and if the teacher suggests that they read silently, "to themselves," before they have learned how to do this, they might only stare at their pages. Just as finger pointing gives a visual assist, quiet vocalization seems necessary to help monitor and maintain comprehension.

Children will be receptive to suggestions that they whisper or mutter; gradually, their voices will taper off as silent reading begins. Teachers must be prepared for a low hum as children read independently and do other work. It is normal and usually indicates a productive class.

WHAT STUDENTS MUST LEARN TO DO

Students need to master techniques for analyzing words that they cannot recognize "at sight" or spell immediately, and they need to be able to use these strategies automatically.

Literacy Strategies

As children grow toward literacy competency, they acquire many skills. In this sense, *skills* are procedures learned for solving specific reading and writing puzzles. With time and practice, children's many skills merge into unified sets of strategies. The term *strategy* refers to thoughtful plans or operations that individuals can purposefully activate, adjust, or modify as needed to meet challenges presented by reading and writing tasks.

Inherent in this view is the idea that literacy users monitor their understanding. Faced with a challenge, they mentally "run through" a series of strategic behaviors to find the one(s) that will help them accomplish their tasks. If the selected behavior does not work, they know to search further until they have accessed the right behavior to meet their immediate needs. The next chapter elaborates on this topic. For now, here are some strategic reading behaviors that children engage in:

1. Previewing what they will read by looking at illustrations and other graphics and thinking about the title
2. Getting ready for reading by determining what they know about the topic or theme they will read about; often the title prompts this behavior, which activates relevant background knowledge and experiences
3. Drawing upon many cues to determine pronunciation and word meaning, rather than merely trying to "sound it out"
4. Developing useful strategies for helping comprehension, including slowing down their reading rate, running their finger under words as they read, subvocalizing (mumble reading), reading out loud, and talking about the material with another person

5. Reading to the end of a line when trying to determine unknown words; continuing to read to try to find meaning
6. Rereading text
7. Making predictions; confirming, rejecting, or revising predictions
8. Self-monitoring or asking themselves whether they understand what they are reading; asking whether text is making sense
9. Going to the teacher, peers, or other sources to check on information
10. Looking for connections and relationships among prior knowledge, real-life experiences, and other pieces they have read, had read to them, or seen on television and in movies
11. Recognizing that material may be too difficult for them to comprehend

Here are some strategic writing behaviors:

1. Planning what they will write about
2. Writing about topics and themes that are familiar
3. Sharing their writing with others at various stages to make sure they are communicating effectively
4. Spelling words as best they can and taking risks, knowing that work can be "fixed up" later
5. Learning to use external sources such as dictionaries to improve their work
6. Reading and rereading to make sure that their writing is making sense
7. Reading out loud to see whether their writing "sounds" right and whether they have left out any words or ideas
8. Paying attention to strategies or conventions for communicating meaning in stories that they read or hear and trying out those strategies or conventions to enrich their own writing

Teachers play a huge role in helping children become strategic literacy users by making sure that instruction and practice make sense. Teaching skills in isolation from real reading and writing and having students practice with worksheets and "skill and drill" activities that make no sense to them are not meaningful teaching methods. Routman (1991) wrote that teachers may think that a particular skill has been covered in their instruction, but "until the learner can discover how to utilize the skill in varied reading and writing contexts, skills teaching is largely a waste of time. *The learner must know how and when to apply the skill; that is what elevates the skill to the strategy level*" (p. 135). By asking questions such as "How did you know what the word was?" or "What part of the sentence helped you?" teachers make students conscious of the operations they are using. It is also important to give students "wait time" to figure out answers; this encourages them to make a selection from their store of strategies and figure out an answer independently.

To help students learn to be strategic, teachers can also engage in procedures called "think alouds," in which the teachers verbalize the strategies that are appropriate for figuring out aspects of text. This is similar to the "write aloud" process recommended as part of language experience sessions. Of course, texts appropriate for young learners will be relatively easy, so teachers must be careful to target the most perplexing, challenging parts. They may ponder aloud about how one might figure out a term or what a grammatical or literary construction might mean; in answering their own questions, teachers model strategies for their students. Questions should always invite students toward higher levels of thinking about text and about strategies for constructing meaning.

Alternately, teachers can invite students to use think alouds on their own to verbalize their thought processes. Students should be directed toward meaning-based strategies that will enhance their comprehension. When merely told to "sound out" unfamiliar words or when directed toward minor aspects of word analysis, students are discouraged from reading for meaning and understanding.

Cueing Systems

As children learn to be strategic, they learn to attend to three kinds of **cueing systems** to gain meaning from what they read:

1. *Semantic* cues, including word meanings and meanings conveyed by illustrations
2. *Syntactic* cues, including grammatical structure and other language patterns
3. *Graphophonemic* cues, or letter–sound correspondences

Children learn to use each kind of cue and to orchestrate the specific information each cueing system provides. They learn from many sources, including direct instruction. Exposure to many books and to good models of oral language helps children expand their vocabularies (semantic cues) and accustoms them to diverse language patterns (syntactic cues). Instruction in phonics and experiences with invented spelling make children more aware of the graphophonemic cues, and work with principles of structural analysis increases awareness of both semantics and syntax.

Eventually, readers attend to these cues automatically. They don't think much about them—that is, until they encounter an unfamiliar word. At that point, even the beginning strategic reader consciously draws upon his or her knowledge of the cues as a helpful way of figuring out the challenging word.

Word Analysis Strategies

While gaining immeasurably from their independent reading and writing, children also benefit from instruction in how to identify (decode) and spell unfamiliar words efficiently. Two categories of cues can help in decoding and in spelling: *graphophonemic* (sound–symbol) cues and *structural* cues. In decoding, readers are also helped by the context in which words appear in text.

As discussed in chapter 1, **phonics** has been a foundation of most reading instruction for many years; but traditional phonics instruction can leave many children wondering what "rules" of letter–sound correspondences actually have to do with real reading. They also fail to recognize that spelling and sounding out words are two aspects of the same behavior. Teaching phonics (i.e., "the sounds letters make") in isolation is a major contributor to students' lack of understanding the value of this cueing system. Words are composed of phonemes, or sounds represented by one or more letters. When the "sounds" of letters are pulled apart from real words for instruction, their inherent phonemic identity is distorted. Even when the letter sounds are orally blended together quickly, as in real speech, the result may not be recognizable as familiar words. Dialect and regional differences in speech can also confuse children even more (for example, consider the various ways "Park the car in Harvard Yard" can be verbalized).

Another drawback to traditional phonics instruction is that some children may come to depend on letter–sound analysis to the exclusion of other word identification strategies. Such children think that they must sound out every word, as though each word they encounter is new and unfamiliar; they do not learn to depend on context or the other cueing systems. The result is often laborious, plodding reading; students lose track of whatever meaning they have constructed from text. Other students may become very adept at rapid letter–sound analysis, but because they are focusing so intently on the letters in the words they see, they do not strive for meaning. Such students are often referred to as "word callers."

A more productive approach to teaching phonics is to emphasize to students that knowledge of letter–sound correspondences is a powerful strategy that can help them to become efficient at comprehending text and spelling words they wish to write. Children must understand that the goal for learning letter–sound correspondences is automatic word recognition and spelling so that they can use their literacy skills and strategies more efficiently. If children think that the goal is merely to match letters and sounds, they will not realize how helpful phonics knowledge can be.

For instruction to be really effective, teachers need to build on what children know about print production and about **phonemic awareness,** which is not the same as phonics. Whereas phonics refers to letter–sound correspondences in written language, phonemic awareness concerns knowledge about sounds in *spoken* words (Stahl, 1992). A child who cannot mentally manipulate sounds in words has little phonemic awareness. For example, the child who can string together words and nonsense words such as "ball, call, hall, spall, thall, wall . . . all" has a higher degree of phonemic awareness than the one who cannot do this relatively simple task.

To help children understand phonics in perspective as one of the many reading strategies they can use, teachers can provide both direct and indirect instruction. Direct instruction should be clear, with simple and intelligible explanations for what principles that are taught. Stahl (1992) suggested that instruction can become ambiguous when teachers try to pronounce single phonemes, such as the sound made by the letter *b* that ends up sounding like *buh*. To alleviate confusion, teachers should provide instruction primarily with written words rather than isolated words and help students to see how the letters in words function together to create the words we recognize in visual and auditory forms. Stahl also states that less than 25 percent of any reading lessons should be devoted to phonics instruction and practice, with the majority of time spent reading and discussing extended text.

Indirect instruction and practice can be accomplished in many ways. Teachers can easily engage children in phonics games or compile lists of words that demonstrate certain sounds. As mentioned previously, masking is also an important instructional strategy for phonics. Teachers can even pull words from text for specific study—for example, by pointing out a number of words that demonstrate a specific letter–sound pattern that has been previously taught. The words might be recorded on a "word chart" that illustrates the specific sound–symbol relationship. The important point in this kind of activity is that students recognize that applying knowledge of the specific phonetic pattern helps them decode individual words, comprehend them when encountered in text, and spell them in their own writing. In this way, phonics instruction is purposefully embedded in the everyday literacy instruction in the classroom. The ultimate goal that should guide teachers and students is automatic word recognition so that young learners can concentrate on reading comprehension and spelling of words they wish to write. (Appendix D can serve as a reference for teaching phonics.)

Structural and Morphemic Analysis

Structural and morphemic analysis is the study of small parts of words, such as "root words," prefixes, and suffixes. Through observation and instruction, children come to recognize that little word parts have consistent meanings that will help them figure out unfamiliar words. For example, *un-*, *dis-*, *non-*, and *anti-* all mean approximately the same thing. Learning word parts as "mini sight words" is useful for word construction in spelling and word identification in reading. (Again, refer to Appendix D.)

Determining What to Teach in Phonics and Structural Analysis. When teachers do not have to rely fully on commercial materials to teach phonics and structural analysis, they face the question of how to offer the best possible instruction. The answer to the question goes back to the role of teachers as observers of children and decision makers within their own classrooms.

Instruction should balance what students know, what they need to know, and what they are ready to understand. For example, a teacher might decide to offer direct instruction of homophones during a mini lesson. The decision to do so might stem from either of two sources: informal assessment that students are misspelling such words in their writing and need to have some clarification about the words, or the teacher's perception that the students are *ready* to make sense of this instruction. In either case, presenting the new information should provide students with the necessary tools for both reading and writing. Homophones could also be taught during a small group lesson to students who are ready to learn about them or to an individual child who consistently confuses the words *their, they're,* and *there.*

Instructional sessions on principles of phonics and structural analysis should always be kept relatively short. Many examples should be provided, and students should engage in interactive practice with real (not nonsense) words presented in sentences, paragraphs, poems, jingles, and other kinds of text. Some teachers use lyrics to popular or folk songs, presenting them first in chart form or on transparencies. Children study the familiar text carefully and use their awareness of its rhythm to help them read with fluency. Teachers then point out specific words to illustrate aspects of phonics or structural analysis.

Teachers might use think alouds to demonstrate how specific strategies can be applied. Doing so demystifies the procedures students need to master and helps students create strategies for monitoring their own progress. Not only do they see that talking one's way through reading and writing is appropriate behavior but they learn to determine when this self-talk can be most valuable.

Context Clues

Children need to learn to look at the entire context of what they are reading to find aids for identifying unfamiliar words and constructing meaning from text. **Context clues** involve using the words around an unfamiliar word to come up with a "ballpark" meaning that is good enough to allow reading to continue. If the meaning students derive does not make sense, they know they need to go back to the word and try again. Children use knowledge of all cueing systems to figure out the word. Masking provides ongoing demonstrations of how context clues work.

Children's first context clues are probably book illustrations. Teachers can lead children's discussions of the pictures and how they relate to the text. Children know intuitively how this works because they have used drawings to convey meaning in their own early writing. "Look at the picture" is often a good clue to give when a child encounters an unfamiliar word. If the picture stimulates a different but appropriate word, teachers acknowledge the attempt with "Yes, but, what *other word* would work? Look at the first letter of the word you don't know." Prompts such as this help children realize that they must be flexible in their selection of strategies to help them read.

Although learning to use context clues is important, there are certain limitations to their use. If the target word is relatively technical or specialized, the context in which it appears may not help readers determine a meaning simply because the meaning of the word is the focal point of the sentence in which it appears. The same drawback often occurs when the target word is a low-frequency word or the particular definition required in the sentence is infrequently used. (Appendix D summarizes the kinds of clues children can often find in text and the questions readers should ask themselves as they attempt to use context to determine the meaning of unfamiliar words.)

Vocabulary Growth

A child's vocabulary can be thought of as the storehouse of words that he or she can use correctly in speaking and writing and can recognize in print and speech. This includes both the *denotative* meanings commonly found in the dictionary and the *connotative* meanings—those specialized, technical, or personal meanings that words often come to have. Being able to recognize and produce words' graphic representation is crucial for literacy; but it is more important to understand that words convey their meaning through context. "Learning a word means learning the meaning *potential* for that word—the possible meanings connected with various social settings. . . . Knowing the word 'table' means knowing its meaning in context: for example, 'table the discussion,' 'check the water table,' 'table and chairs. . . . 'There are no context-free, static meanings of words when language is actually *used*" (Edelsky, Altwerger, & Flores, 1991, pp. 32, 33).

One of the best ways to help young students gain large, useful vocabularies is for teachers to read to them frequently, point out interesting words, and help them develop meanings from the context in which the words appear. Instruction and discussion about vocabulary are interwoven in the reading itself, where definitions and word identification skills can be seen as most meaningful.

Teachers can also encourage students to read broadly themselves (Nagy, 1988). Children can often figure out unfamiliar words independently if motivated to do so. They should also be encouraged to keep track of words whose meanings they want to check. By figuring things out on their own, students truly make new words a part of their reading, writing, and often speaking vocabularies. Additionally, they gain confidence in their strategies for finding meaning on their own. Students may want to make personal dictionaries of words they learn and would like to use in their own writing.

Actual word study can increase the depth and breadth of students' vocabularies. To be most productive, word study activities should integrate "new" words with other knowledge that students already possess, thereby emphasizing the meaning of words at the conceptual level. Instruction should also give students many opportunities to encounter new words through meaningful, authentic use so that they can really see the utility of expanding their vocabularies (Nagy, 1988). Activities such as semantic mapping can be very effective (these methods are explained in appendix D).

Whatever approaches teachers take, vocabularies should always be taught in context and as naturally and unobtrusively as possible. Drill activities simply do not produce lasting, meaningful vocabulary growth.

LANGUAGE EXPERIENCE IN EARLY PRIMARY GRADES

The value of language experience for both reading and writing growth extends throughout the early primary grades. The approach can be especially beneficial for students who seem to be developing reading and writing competence more slowly than their peers. Even more than supportive reading groups, language experience dictation and transcription make reading and writing processes very concrete. Children can see their words being translated into text that they and others can read; they experience themselves as part of this process of constructing meaning with and from abstract symbols and feel more confident to write on their own.

Language experience also has particular worth for second-language learners and for those who speak a nonstandard dialect. Because the language experience approach allows children to use their own regional or code-switching dialects, reading materials are personalized. They do not present the cultural, semantic, or syntactic conflicts that texts written in standard English might pose. Teachers in bilingual classrooms can take dictation in children's dominant language and help them produce appropriate, relevant beginning reading material that fully reflects their own language community. Teachers shape dictation toward standard usage and provide a bridge between "home" and "school" language.

Teachers can also introduce *word banks* or "key" vocabulary activities as part of language experience. Each day, children request one word or more, which are written on cards to be stored on key rings (hence the term *key* vocabulary) or in word banks made from coffee cans, shoe boxes, or any other sturdy container. Word banks become children's personal dictionaries as they add words they need for composition. Having this resource gives young writers independence and also personalizes their spelling program. The merit of word banks for children learning English as a second language is motivational as well as educational.

When teachers sense that students need extra support, they often take dictation individually and enlist the students in creating a personal library of very special books. Students are encouraged to build a personal vocabulary in their word bank while still being included in supportive reading groups. Additionally, teachers make sure that students take part in class story reading (especially of big books), write in their journals daily, browse through books in class, and take books home—to ensure that students have gained something from these valuable literacy experiences.

Of course, language experience is also beneficial for students whose literacy development is progressing smoothly. Teachers can model various ways of expressing ideas—such as using quotations, combination sentences, embedded clauses, or other elements to vary word choice or sentence and paragraph patterns. (Language experience as a vehicle for teaching revision strategies is discussed later in the chapter.)

WRITING IN EARLY PRIMARY CLASSES

Writing is an important part of the literacy workshop approach because it so fully complements beginning reading work. Students have a second path by which to absorb different concepts and subject matter, test their understanding, and reinforce their learning. Additionally, teachers have an additional "window" into what students know and can do.

Teachers encourage writing by providing ample writing supplies, word lists and other such stimuli, bulletin board space for displaying students' writing, reference materials—and time. There must be at least one secluded, quiet place for private work. All students should keep a writing folder for their work. Work kept in this way may become raw material for later work; it also may find its way into assessment portfolios as documentation of the real progress learners have made.

The Writing Process

Teachers want students to realize that the act of writing is a process and that *doing* writing is more important than the final product. The **process approach to writing,** like reading, consists of three stages: prewriting, independent writing, and postwriting (review Table 9.2).

Prewriting periods are times for discussing, generating and organizing ideas, and often instructing. The prewriting stage helps students understand the decisions they must make, the options they have, and the expectations placed upon them (such as who their audience will be or for what purpose they are writing). Mapping procedures can be very beneficial during prewriting. A map is a graphic organizer that provides a rough outline or skeleton of what will be written, often composed of only key words and ideas that students have brainstormed. A similar device, called a story map, can be used to guide story writing. (Appendix D gives examples of the many different kinds of graphic organizers that can be used in writing.)

The first part of the *independent writing* stage involves getting ideas down as quickly as possible, in *draft* form. When teachers ask children to draft or "write it the best way you can," they ask them to subordinate aspects of "correctness" to the expression of ideas. They are also promising that beginning efforts will not be graded; instead, teachers will offer help in making the writing stronger. Drafting allows children to take risks and to be playful with words because they know there is a safety net of peer and teacher feedback to help them refine their work. Some teachers even provide a stamp saying "DRAFT" to designate papers that are still in progress.

Accepting the idea of multiple drafts means accepting the chores of *revising*. Revising involves more than copying over for neatness—it involves making changes at many levels of text production. Teachers must realize that many efforts by young writers are single expressions of feeling that can stand on their own, untouched by revision. Sometimes, too, a piece of writing represents a false start, a dull topic, or an experiment gone awry with a technique the writer cannot yet control. These papers should often be filed in an inactive work folder to be looked at again, perhaps, in the future. Other work is prime for revision.

Not all children learn to revise readily, and children seem more inclined to revise work that concerns personal experiences or topics they have selected themselves. Having a peer audience or a teacher–student writing conference contributes to children's revision—when children must share their stories, they tend to revise more intensely. To become comfortable with revising, children must realize that when a piece of writing needs revision, it is the *writing*, not the writer, that is being questioned. They also need to realize the fluid nature of writing—that there are many ways to express ideas and that some are clearer and more appropriate than others. Additionally, young writers must develop a repertoire of strategies for "tinkering with" their writing to make it better: means for inserting words, taking words out, rewording, and reorganizing by crossing out, drawing arrows, and using other simple editorial devices (see Figure 9.2, which shows a student's revision marks on a typed second draft of a story and the third, final version).

Teachers can model revising strategies during language experience sessions. They can also make chart-size or individual copies of stories dictated in LEA sessions or taken from other sources (anything other than class members' own work). Using think-aloud procedures to test ideas, students revise the piece collaboratively. The story that emerges will be different from the original, and students will have shared their insights about the role and function of revising. (Chapter 10 discusses revision in greater detail.)

The *postwriting* stage is a time of sharing and receiving feedback, although additional focused instruction may also be provided. As will be

THE TIME I WENT TO PLUTO

IT ALL STARTED ONE DAY WHEN I SAW A HOLE. SO I WENT IN TO SEE

WHAT WAS IN IT / I SAW A SPACE SHIP SO I GOT IN IT AND THEN IT

SHOT UP LIKE A ROCKET. I HAD TO SIT ON A THING I DIDN'T KNOW

WHAT IT WAS. ALL OF A SUDDEN IT STOPPED SO I GOT OUT OF IT.

I SAW A LOT OF DOGS ONE OF THEM CAME UP TO ME AND SAID <u>WHO</u> ARE

YOU? I SAID "ROBERT." BY THAT TIME THE SPACESHIP HAD GONE BACK.

I WISHED THAT JASON WAS HERE ALL OF A SUDDEN THE SPACESHIP WAS

BACK AND MY BROTHER AND TOMMY WER HERE. I SAID HI TO THEM AND

THEY SAID HOW DID YOU GET HERE. THE SAME WAY YOU DID. "OH WHO

ARE THEY, THEY" SAID AND I SAID, I DON'T KNOW. LETS FIND OUT AND

SO WE ASKED ONE OF THEM. HE, SAID "THE PLUTONS.' SO I ASKED IF

WE COULD GO BACK TO EARTH" HE SAID "YES". BUT HOW I ASKED THE

LEADER OF <u>US</u> WHERE IS HE OVER THERE HE'S NAME IS PLUTO OK AND SO.

WE DID AND HE SAID ONLY ON ONE CONDITION OK WHAT. THAT YOU WILL TELL

EARTH TO KEEP ON PLAYING DISNEY OK. THE END

in the junk yard. ✓

It was big as a elefant and as soft as a fetery

w What did the abs

Sample 1. The student had written his first draft in pencil; it was then typed, double spaced, so that he would have ample room for revision.

The Time I Met Plutons

I all started one adventurer Saturday when I saw a dark gloomy hole. I looked inside it. I saw a read with purple rocket ship. I got in and saw computers all over the place. The made me sit on the lumpiest bed I've ever seen. And then it took off. Afer a few minuts it stoped. I escaped and jumped many mean PIT BULLS. One said, "Who are you kid!" I said David. I saw more gods. I wished my freind John was here. All of a sudden I was home. John was there. John said, "Who are they?" I said, "who are you?" One said, "Pluton?!" I said, "can we go back to earth?" He said yes. But how? I asked the leader. He said one one condition. "What's that" I asked. "That you tell earth to keep on playing at Western Playland."

Sample 2. Completed revision (third draft).

Figure 9.2

This student undertook the process of drafting and revising his work; he used revision marks to guide his efforts and drew pictures to help him remember his ideas. Note that having a clean, typed version helped him gain some "neutrality" as he worked to make his story better.

discussed in the next chapter, children may present their stories orally to their classmates, "publish" them on bulletin boards, and bind them into books. Figure 9.3 offers procedures for making simple bound books.

Helping Children Achieve During this Stage

Chapter 8 suggested a series of stages through which beginners' writing progresses and gave examples of what teachers might expect in preschool and kindergarten classes. Writing samples presented in Table 9.4 and Figure 9.4 illustrate the kinds of writing that are common in early primary-grade classrooms when writing has become a routine part of students' work in all content areas.

Classrooms should feature a well-stocked writing center, mailboxes for student communication, and bulletin boards for displaying writing. Time should be built into each week for students to experience all the stages of

Simple Books

Materials: Paper, stapler, construction paper for cover (if desired)

Procedure: Staple several sheets of paper together between a plain cover; a long-arm stapler works well to make books that open flat.

OR: Punch holes in paper and use brads or yarn to hold the book together.

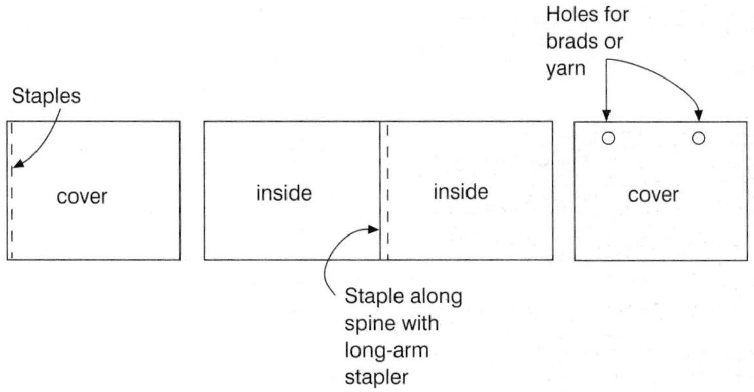

Staples

cover

inside   inside

Staple along spine with long-arm stapler

Holes for brads or yarn

cover

More elaborate books

Materials: Paper for pages of book and cover; stapler or sewing equipment; contact paper or laminating machine

Procedure: Cut paper to desired size.

Stack several sheets together and fold in half; staple along spine or sew; use heavy thread or sew on machine with #18 needle.

Cut two pieces of cardboard or other heavy paper for cover (see diagram).

Cover the cardboard with contact paper or laminate.

Place stapled or stitched pages in the center so that the folded spine is between the two covers.

Use rubber cement or glue to attach the end pages to the cover.

Tape end pages for decoration and sturdiness.

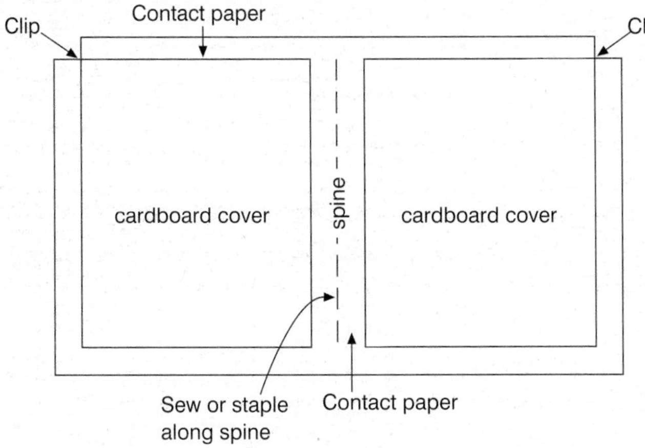

Clip

cardboard cover

Contact paper

spine

cardboard cover

Clip

Contact paper

Sew or staple along spine

Figure 9.3
Making Books for Young Writers   Teacher-made books may be either simple or elaborate. Teachers should present very simple, stapled books first so that children feel they can practice their skills. More elaborate books can be used to "publish" work that has been carefully written and revised. Publishing software or simple word processing programs allow teachers to make uniform pages easily.

the writing process, including the publication of their best works. These and many other activities emphasize that writing is a regular part of classroom life (more specific details are provided in chapter 10).

First graders who have had many writing experiences should be well on their way to becoming enthusiastic, competent writers. However, it is unfortunate that not all children have the advantage of preschool and kindergarten teachers who believe in young learners' abilities as writers.[1] Teachers do not need to lower their expectations for what children can accomplish as writers during first grade so long as they structure the literacy workshop

Sample 1.   The child was so enthusiastic about having a journal that he proclaimed the fact for all to see; most of his classmates decorated their journal covers with pictures.

Figure 9.4
Writing by First-Grade Authors

---

[1] The writing samples in this book represent the work of many students from early childhood classes around the country. Most, but not all, of the children were enthusiastic writers; few of the children would have been categorized as "gifted." What these writers have in common is that they all attended classes in which writing was expected from all students on a daily or near daily basis. Their teachers understood the writing process and welcomed invented spelling and all the other placeholders children use in expressing their ideas.

Mon. Oct. 6, 1986

today one of
my seeds is
starting to get
green.

Oct. 9, 1986

Today two of
my seeds you
can see the
lea f.

Oct. 10, 1986

today one of
my seeds is
a plant.

Oct. 14, 1986

today three of
my seeds are
groing to plants.

Oct. 15, 1986

Today one
of my plants
is 18 :centim
eters.

Oct. 24, 1986

today my
plant is
bigger than
the rooler.

Oct. 29, 1986

today I
have new
leaves com-
ing out.

Sample 2. One use of journals is to give children practice observing what goes on in their world. First graders kept a "plant journal" as part of their science work and wrote observations at regular intervals.

Figure 9.4, *continued*

Figure 9.4, *continued*

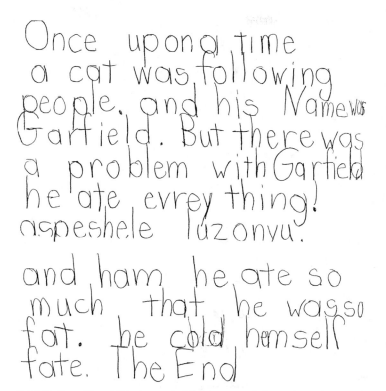

Once upon a time a cat was following people, and his Name was Garfield. But there was a problem with Garfield he ate evrey thing! aspeshele luzonyu.

and ham he ate so much that he was so fat. he cold hemself fate. The End

Sample 3. The child who wrote this piece wanted to write on her own, but her teacher had over emphasized the importance of neat handwriting and correct spelling. As I observed in the class when the teacher was not present, this writer and others asked me to spell many of the words they wanted to use. As an experiment (and to demonstrate a point to the teacher), I left after about ten minutes, bidding the class to continue without my help for a moment or two. The point at which I left is very obvious in this story, for the writer began to use her invented spelling strategies to continue her story.

Figure 9.4, *continued*

Sample 4. The class had been given the story starter "A flower was growing." This writer understood this easy task but was clearly more interested in drawing. This sample illustrates that inauthentic tasks will not motivate students to good, productive writing.

EL   paso

The mowntens
sit up hiy. we eat
a lots of piy. The
grows green we
play rite betwen.
The End.

Sample 5.   This child has written a brief description about the city
where he lives and has elected to do so as a poem. When
the child read the poem to the teacher, he noticed that he
had omitted the word <u>grass</u>, and he inserted it with a green
squiggly shape on the fourth line.

Jan. 21, 1984

Dear: president

I will like you to help the poor
And to put the prices down.
And the persons that don't have
work to give them work. That's
what I think you should do.
And to be nise to others.

I will like you to do
all this things. Because
you will make my
family happy.

Sample 6.   Even young children can express their ideas about important issues.

215

Figure 9.4, *continued*

The Magic Broom
One day a cat found
a broom. From a witch.
The witch went and
got the broom. She saw
the cat. Then she turned
the cat into a frog. The
frog bouced away. Into an
opened window. He went
into the pond. Then the
witch went with the
broom. She met a man.
The man got a bucket
of water. He poured it on
the witch. Then the
witch melted
                    They End

Sample 7.   Here is a simple, straightforward story showing that the child had a good command of basic mechanics and spelling. The child might have meant the cat to "steal" a broom from the witch, which would have made it more exciting; there is some action but no character development to involve the reader in the story.

Micky the nice Pirate

Along time ago there was a pirate he was not a mean pirate he wa a nice pirate. he and his croow were sailing the Atlantic Oceon. It was cold and win windy and waves would come in. One day anathor ship was shooting at them. Then mickys croow started. And mickys croow won the battel. They found a place to live and staed.

Sample 8.   This child has written an action story but has not used enough description to help the reader really "see" the pirate and his "croow." She has, however, given Micky some personal attributes and concluded her story with a specific "happy ending." The work is a revision, based on comments from the teacher.

Figure 9.4, *continued*

period to provide instruction and support as young learners try out their writing skills. Students should write in a log or journal every day. Entries are never graded; they may be personal, fanciful, or informative; and they should be written in children's most "comfortable" language. Writing should be a standard follow-up activity to reading, and other content areas should be presented in ways that invite authentic writing activities.

Once upon a time my dad bought a robot. Dad bought it at robot publicing store. I was jeles (jealous) cause he treated me like a ghost! He always said "Bring me a glass of water and a steak" but he told it to the robot. Once some visitors came. I said "Go bring 19 glasses of orange juice and 19 steaks." He went in the kitchen he jumped and I disconected a little bit of things and after he got the plates he threw them the meat was raw. My dad said "STOP thet crazy robot!" So I stopped it. It said "Crazyyyyy, crazyyyyy I am a crazy robot." So we kicked it out.

Sample 9. This child enjoyed writing the story to such an extent that he lost control of his skills in the middle and used a long run-on sentence; the story has emotions (jealousy), a problem to solve, and a logical solution, right down to kicking the robot out; details, such as the raw meat, strengthen the story.

The Imaginary Land

I was in a little girlscout troup, and I was just tagging along not paying any attention and all of a sudden my troup turned, and sense [since] I was not paying any atention I didn't notice and kep on going the wrong way. Then I noticed that nobody was in front of me. I looked all around me but I couldn't not see anything or anyone. I decided to sit down and think. Then I decided to go left. I finally saw something. I walked up to it, it was some kind of round red thing just handing there. Then a dust devel [dust devil, swirling dust cloud] came and swooped me in the red thing. Before I could catch my bruth I saw myself falling threw the air, then thump! I landed on a strange planet, and boy I was pretty thirsty so I went to look for some water, I saw a lake, and I saw the prettyest thing I ever saw. It was a unicorn with wings. I went over to it and asked her what her (inserted with an arrow) name was. Unis she said so I told her my name to. We became very good freinds and she told me how to get back home and when we got to the place, I asked her if she would come whith me and she said yes, so we went home and lived happily ever after. THE END.

Sample 10. This story progresses logically but lacks details and emotions to let the reader "see" the action; "land" implied in the title stays "imaginary" and does not materialize; the writer could benefit from "showing writing" activities and needs to read her work out loud to get a better sense of the flow of language and its relation to punctuation.

Figure 9.4, *concluded*

As they write, first graders often explore their own "self," express emotions and concerns, and come to better recognize who they are as individuals. Equally, students may create "text worlds" in stories that combine elements of their own experiences; recollections of what they have read, heard, and viewed; and fragments of their own imagination. Because of these many reasons for writing, children should have opportunities to write narrative and expository prose, letters to real audiences and for many purposes,

Table 9.4

The Ongoing Story of Bun-Bun   These stories were completed in a composition book as part of the writing work done in a first-grade classroom. Children wrote at least once every week about the characters the class had created together—Bun-Bun, a rabbit, and Leafer, a leaf. Other characters were created and introduced as needed. The samples were collected from September through November and are arranged chronologically. Note that this young author lives in New York. Her invented spelling reflects her speech patterns and differs slightly from that of the Texas children presented elsewhere in this chapter.

Entry 1
On day Bun Bun and Leafr war tacei [taking] a wak. Bun Bun Saw Brd Bode and crase carit [Bird Buddy and Crazy Carrot].

Entry 2
On day Bun Bun had a BaeBey. She neamd hem Baebey Boney. Bun Bun got efeawon [formula], Bae Bey Bone was qut [cute].

Entry 3
My Cagashen [Composition] buuk

Own day when Bun Bun and Lefar was takkn a wak BunBun git qat in a trap. Lefr sed I ul help. Lefr git Bard bade and crase carts. finle tha cam weth Help. Thn tha ol wen too Bun Bun hows. thn the had denr. then tha ol went hom. To go to slep. crease carets cad [could] not saep. he gost help from Bun Bun to hem to qaunt [count] sheep.

Entry 4
One day Bun Bun was plannting a garden ahd she asked Leafer to help. Tha planted carets and string beans and lettuse. And tha saw it gro.

Entry 5
One day wen Bun Bun and Leaker wos takn a wake. Tha kam to a plas war that havr never Ben befr. Bun Bun sed hew wl we get hom?

Entry 6
On day Bun Bun and Liefr and Bird Buddy and Crzy carrots wor tacing a walk and tha got lost. But Bun Bun sed I no the wea to liefor haws. so tha ol went to lefrs haws and tha ol went home.

the ind

Entry 7
It was thacsgeving and Bun Bun had bord Bodee and Krasee Karit and Liefr ofr for dinnr. tha had torkee and kramberee soes and pomken pei.

Entry 8
It was thacsgiving in yellow land and Torce gobol and sara sweet potatou and Bun Bun and Leefr ol had denor togegthr. But Sara sweet ptat and toke gobol got aiten up.

the ind

---

poems, plays, and other kinds of texts. These exercises in exploring different writing modes help them recognize the important role writing should
play in their lives.

The idea of collaborative writing was introduced in the last chapter; it
remains a powerful way to encourage students toward fluency. Collaboration may take the form of parallel writing activities with two or more friends
writing independently but commenting on each other's emerging efforts.
Collaboration may also produce one mutual effort, pieces written by two or
more authors who have pooled ideas, and writing strategies, just as
"buddy" readers share their understanding. Through collaboration, students exchange concepts and understanding about the purposes of and procedures for creating written works. Sharing understanding in this way provides powerful learning experiences. In their own language and in their own
ways, student collaborators review what teachers have taught, try out procedures for themselves, and support each other's explorations of what it
means to be a writer. Consider, for example, this report of two first graders
who were sitting opposite each other as each wrote a nursery rhyme:

> Darlene, looking back to her own paper, says softly, "Little Miss /mm uuff/." She
> continues to draw out the sound of the word she is writing. Ann stops writing and
> returns to the top of the page, pointing to a single letter and a cluster of letters as
> she reads aloud the nursery rhyme she has written. Darlene leans across the table
> and points to Ann's b, "Hey, that's not Diddle, need a 'D'" for diddle /d/." Ann
> ignores her. Darlene points to a part of the picture and asks, "What's that?" Ann
> explains, "That's the sport man, 'to see such a sport.'" Darlene says, "If you need to
> spell something with m's or s's you can copy [mine]." (MacGillivray, 1994, p. 254)

Responding to Students' Writing

Teachers' responses to students' writing should encourage, not stifle,
growth. Drawing a "happy face" or writing "Good Job" on a piece of writing
insults young writers' efforts; and evaluations that "bleed" all over beginning
writing ultimately convince children that their teachers are more concerned
with how correctly and how neatly they express their ideas than with the
ideas themselves. Still, teachers need to help students realize the interconnectedness of content and form. Comments addressing *what* children are
writing and *how* they are expressing themselves convey this connection and
let children know that good writing can take many shapes.

Conferences between teachers and students provide an excellent way
for teachers to respond to writing. Students bring one piece or more of writing to the conference, and teachers question students about their work,
offer immediately useful instruction, and perhaps gain diagnostic information that can help them fine-tune instruction for each individual. Confer-

ences do not have to be long (maybe five minutes per student); they can be scheduled during workshop time, with teachers trying to meet with each child once a week. Notes taken by the teacher during the conference become part of the assessment documentation for each student, and teachers and students may set specific goals toward which students will strive.

Peer response is a valuable tool for motivating writing, so long as children know how to respond constructively to their classmates' work. Teachers model the appropriate ways to talk about writing through their conferences with students and set the tone and suggest the language that will provide the most beneficial peer responses. Talking about a group-constructed language experience story provides another model. At a beginning level, teachers can lead small peer response groups at which children talk about works in progress. These, however, must be kept very informal and nonthreatening, so that students learn procedures for making kind, equitable, honest comments that focus on the appropriate aspects of their peers' work. After a child has read his or her story to the group, the teacher guides group members to formulate questions and comments about the piece. Their purpose is to help the author revise the piece to communicate more effectively.

Another means for sharing student writing is to save a few minutes at the end of literacy workshop sessions for students to share their writing with others. During this brief circle time, willing students may read what they have written and listen as their classmates comment. As in small groups, teachers can model how to respond to the writing. In general, responses should be directed at three points:

1. What did listeners really like about the story that is presented and what parts did they think were well written?
2. What parts did listeners not understand?
3. What can the writer do to make the story better?

As students generate these kinds of comments, they learn to think seriously about each others' writing and to talk about writing in thoughtful, constructive ways. Learning how to give peers appropriate feedback prepares students for the more formal peer response groups that are discussed in chapter 10.

PROCEDURES TO ENCOURAGE CHILDREN'S INDEPENDENCE

Helping children move toward independent reading and writing is an important task for early childhood teachers. It is the essence of Vygotsky's concept of teaching. As a starting point, children need to be reassured that they will encounter many words they do not recognize or cannot readily spell. They also need strategies to use in such situations.

In reading, teachers should encourage them "to read to the end of the sentence" to see if they can identify the word. This simple behavior is often enough; even beginners can often pull together information from the cueing systems and from the context to be able to decode the puzzling word. If that fails, children should have alternative strategies to draw upon. A teacher in South Brunswick, New Jersey, posts a chart similar to the one in Figure 9.5 to remind students of the strategies they can use on their own.

There are parallel behaviors for writing. From the very start, students are empowered to "spell it as best you can and fix it up later—you are the boss of your own spelling" (MacGillivray, 1994, p. 254). As they become more competent, they learn to use their emerging knowledge of letter–sound relationships in more precise ways. They ask themselves questions about the consonant and vowel sounds they hear in words they are trying to spell and about words that "sound like" their target word. They realize that tinkering with the structure of a familiar word is often a successful way to spell a new word: substituting a letter or adding a different affix can pro-

1. Think about the story.

2. Look at the pictures.

3. Reread the sentence and get your mouth ready to say the first sound in the word and keep on reading.

4. Take a guess.

5. Look at the vowel sound in the word and take another guess.

6. Get your finger ready under the word and CRASH THROUGH THE WORD by concentrating on making sense of what you are reading.

7. Skip the word, keep on reading, and take another guess in a few minutes.

Posting directions such as these, adapted from those of a first grade teacher in South Brunswick, New Jersey, help children become independent readers. They reassure the beginning readers that it is acceptable NOT to know all the words and give them ways to try to figure out words they do not know immediately.

Figure 9.5
Helpful Chart for Young Readers   Directions such as these, developed by a first-grade teacher in South Brunswick, New Jersey, help children become independent readers. They reassure the beginning readers that it is acceptable not to know all the words, and they give them ways to try to figure out words they do not know immediately.

duce the desired word. They also begin to look at their spelling analytically to see whether it looks "right" or "funny"; then they decide either to leave it alone and continue writing or to keep trying to fix it up. Using the dictionary is a valuable ability that should be taught as students move toward independent writing.

Teachers also use *prompts,* helpful comments or questions that give students the information they need at the time they need it to continue with a task. Examples of using prompts include supplying a word that has baffled a student, suggesting that students look for context clues, and reminding a young writer of steps for figuring out how words are spelled. Prompts help shape students' self-regulatory and monitoring processes because they convey that it is really all right not to know a word immediately and to have to reread or edit one's writing. Prompts reassure learners that there are many ways to solve puzzling aspects of reading and writing.

Even when children read material at the appropriate level and apply numerous strategies to maintain momentum, their oral reading often contains many omissions, insertions of words or word parts, or substitutions of new words. At times, readers will catch themselves and self-correct; at other times, they will continue reading. These deviations from text can be thought of as **miscues** rather than errors. Accepting that students' oral reading does not have to be a word-for-word replication of text liberates teachers to help students focus on making meaning, the real goal of reading. The idea that reading should result in a coherent, meaningful message is one of the "big ideas" of literacy acquisition, an essential understanding that children must fully grasp if they are to achieve independence (see Table 5.2 for other "big ideas").

Analysis of children's miscues gives teachers insight about whether children are progressing in a normal, developmental fashion or need more focused instruction. This is the principle underlying the use of running records as diagnostic tool (see chapter 3). Analysis also provides information about how children orchestrate the cues they derive from print. For example, if a child seems consistently to miscue by saying words that mean the same thing as the target word but that have little or no graphophonemic resemblance, it is clear that the child is attending to semantics to the exclusion of letter–sound correspondences. This child is constructing meaning from text successfully but needs to broaden his or her range of strategies to include more attention to other cues. In a case like this, the teacher must help the child see the utility of other strategies without sacrificing the strong use of semantics. Too heavy-handed instruction on phonics would tell the child that her reading strategies were "wrong"; prompts, offered as gentle "nudging" toward a wider repertoire of strategies, would be appropriate.

Teachers must understand that children who speak nonstandard dialects or who are reading in their second language will frequently "translate" standard text into their own dialect or use code-switching in their oral reading. So long as children's comprehension seems adequate, acceptance of nonstandard oral reading is absolutely necessary if children are to progress with reading. The key is comprehension, no matter what the oral, surface utterances might be.

Students' invented spelling may also provide insight into how they are processing letter–sound correspondences. By looking for patterns of misspellings—equivalent to written miscues—teachers can fine-tune instruction to help students become more independent spellers and hence more confident writers.

Help for Children When They Need It

Sooner or later, every teacher encounters students who are not achieving to their maximum capacity. Some will be difficult to identify at first; others may be more obvious, such as the six-year-old child quoted by Lyons, Pinnell, and DeFord (1993), who said, "It's too late. Everyone is reading in my class but me. I tried to learn the letters and sound but could never remember anything" (p. 1). Teachers want to help children who are experiencing frustration and difficulty, and individualized approaches like language experience can indeed be successful. But with large classes and many subjects to teach, instructors often cannot take enough time to work intensively with each needy child.

For many children, "pull out" programs that provide intensive, individualized assistance on a regular basis for a few months or longer can be highly beneficial. Many pull-out programs are modeled on the Reading Recovery program developed originally in New Zealand (Clay, 1979, 1993; Lyons, Pinnell, & DeFord, 1993). In Reading Recovery and similar programs, children work one on one with a highly trained teacher in carefully planned lessons that focus on *reading for meaning* and *communicating meaningfully in writing.* Children read simple but motivating books that present clear, interesting language patterns; teachers and students discuss the books to enhance understanding. Teachers model reading strategies and talk about what they, as literacy experts, do in various literacy situations. Children write extensively. Skills instruction is offered but within the context of real reading and writing and with the goal of enhancing strategic behaviors. Students are not bored; they work hard at what they do and are helped to see the purpose of each new aspect of literacy they are learning.

The advantages of programs such as Reading Recovery are their immediacy (they serve students as soon as difficulties are detected) and their emphasis on reading and writing for meaning. They do not require students to engage in repetitive drills of isolated skills but instead involve them in pleasurable and meaningful tasks from which strategies can be readily generalized. When students seem to be ready to progress on their own, they are discharged from these focused programs, often after only a few months (Clay, 1993; Lyons, Pinnell, & DeFord, 1993).

Still, such programs are expensive. Teachers must be highly trained in diagnostic and instructional strategies; Reading Recovery training takes a full year of study. After training, teachers can work with only a few children a day because the work must be individualized. Many books and other materials are necessary for the program to function smoothly. Yet, this kind of intervention—offered early and intensely—seems to work for many children. If later difficulties can be thwarted, then the expense is most definitely worthwhile.

In students' own classrooms, approaches like one-on-one language experience, buddy reading (when one buddy is a stronger reader), and collaborative writing projects can provide support to young learners who may need a little extra time, some extra help, and a few more models to put all the pieces in the literacy puzzle together.

SUMMARY

Being part of children's beginning mastery of reading and writing is exciting. When teachers give support to beginning readers, young learners will take the risks needed to bridge the gap between "play" and "real" reading. They discover books in new, stimulating ways and expand their sense of themselves and their world. As they explore what books offer them, they practice their emerging skills in purposeful, self-motivating ways.

Writing should be part of every early childhood class. Students' work gives children opportunities to express themselves and allows teachers to gain insight into what and how children are learning. Students will progress at different rates, but when they are expected to write often, they will gain confidence in their abilities and their skills will grow. From this early confidence will emerge their own sense of themselves as competent communicators in this important mode of expression.

QUESTIONS AND TASKS FOR INDEPENDENT AND COLLABORATIVE WORK

1. Be sure that you can define each of the following terms:
    *   supportive reading groups
    *   buddy reading
    *   cueing systems
    *   phonics
    *   phonemic awareness
    *   structural and morphemic analysis
    *   context clues
    *   process approach to writing
    *   miscues

2.   To what extent do you think language experience could be the total reading program in an early primary class? What advantages and disadvantages would you anticipate from its use as a total reading program?

3.   Discuss the difference between a miscue and an error when children deviate from text in their oral reading.

4.   Interview several early primary teachers to find their criteria for grouping children. Observe their reading groups. How do the children respond? What are the rest of the children doing while the teacher works with one group? What suggestions for improvement could you make?

5.   Why is supportive reading important? How can supportive reading strategies help children make a natural transition from prereading to competency? In what ways should an early primary writing program also be supportive?

6.   Understanding the concept of miscues is essential for supporting children's emerging reading skills. What behaviors in young children's writing are similar to reading miscues? What does teacher acceptance of these aspects of beginning literacy demonstrate to young learners?

7.   Visit early primary classrooms where students write a lot. Observe how teachers evaluate students' work and provide feedback. In what ways do teacher behaviors encourage or inhibit writing growth?

CHAPTER 10

Independence and Collaboration in the Literacy Workshop

This chapter is about children who are gaining competence and confidence as literacy users. Margaret Meek (1982), a British educator and authority on children's literature, wrote:

> The first years of school pass in a flash. As soon as they find their place in the classroom and the playground, children become working members of a real community, for school is the society of children. . . . [T]he general assumption is that reading and writing will be firmly grounded by the time children have passed their seventh birthday, and most parents expect them to be able to read on their own shortly after that. (p. 109)

Of course, as Meek knows, not all seven-year-old children are reading and writing well; but in many classrooms, even if students are not all achieving at the same level, they all are making real progress toward literacy. The level of these classrooms may be second or third grade, a combination of these grades, or even earlier grades. As was the case in the last chapter, much of what is discussed next is applicable across several grades because of the developmental nature of literacy learning.

FOSTERING INDEPENDENCE

The ultimate goal for all students' literacy development is **automaticity**, the point at which individuals can perform complex tasks without paying too much attention to the component parts of the activity. Think back to the bicycle-riding analogy in the last chapter. When children achieve automaticity in bike riding, they can orchestrate the various aspects of keeping a bike moving forward safely, virtually without thinking about what they are doing.

Automaticity in literacy means that readers and writers readily call up the appropriate strategies to perform literacy tasks. They can, for example, recognize words in a text without stopping to figure out individual sounds. Of course, because the texts that young learners encounter are increasingly more challenging throughout the early childhood years, children do not achieve full automaticity at this point. But the momentum they have acquired in reaching for this goal must be maintained.

Classroom Environments

As always, the classroom must be a literate environment. Students are busy, active learners, often self-selecting the material they read and many of the topics about which they write; they spend increasing amounts of each literacy workshop time working independently. Time with teachers may be spent in guided reading groups or in individual reading or writing conferences, both of which are discussed later in the chapter. At other times, students may be reading or writing alone or working with classmates. When they work with others, they often engage in specific activities designed to enhance their reading and writing abilities and their capability for thinking about literacy.

During workshops, students engage in both required activities and what Routman (1991) has called "invitations." Students know that they must complete the required activities and that the invitations represent tasks from which they may select. Activities presented in Table 9.1—writing in logs, working independently or collaboratively, preparing for a conference with the teacher, and so forth—continue to be appropriate for young learners. (Chapter 11 presents even more reading and writing activities to consider for workshop time.)

As children become more sophisticated literacy users, teachers decide which of many challenging activities should be required, how often during each week certain activities must be completed, and which activities may remain optional invitations that students are encouraged to undertake after they have finished other tasks. Thus, first graders might have had to write in their journal only twice a week, but second graders are *required* to write on a daily basis. First graders might be asked to draw about a story they read independently, but second graders are *required* to make an entry in a literature log expressing their reactions to what they read; further, second or third graders might be asked to read a minimum number of books each week. Determining the balance of invitations and required activities is an important decision that teachers make and refine throughout the year. Criteria teachers use in making these decisions include students' motivation, self-direction, level of independence, and acquired skills and strategies; the number of students in the class; the size of the room; the availability of resources; the amount of time that can be dedicated to workshop activities; and many other context-specific variables that contribute to the classroom atmosphere.

Content area activities such as science or social studies projects provide students with challenging opportunities to refine their reading and writing abilities. The teacher may pose a question to be investigated, or students themselves may suggest challenging research opportunities. In pursuing answers to these questions, students use reading, writing, and collaboration skills in purposeful ways. Much of students' time may also be spent working on activities related to a particular thematic unit (see chapter 2 to review this approach).

The Role of the Teacher

Teachers play many roles as students become more independent literacy users. They are still the supportive "expert" and model for young learners, but, increasingly, they are discussion leaders, resource people, and coaches who encourage students toward independence. Additionally, teachers give students insight into the intricacies of learning to read and write. They continue to use direct instruction and think alouds to explain complex literacy strategies in ways that learners will find comprehensible, relevant, and accessible. Statements about reasoning and other cognitive processes are always offered in clear, understandable language, with many examples of how the processes can be useful. Students are encouraged to verbalize their own strategies and to ask questions about how to construct meaning. Through this process, they expand their sense of how to make use of the many cues found in text.

Explicit explanations are effective in writing instruction as well. For both reading and writing, students need to continue to have many opportunities to engage in purposeful tasks. What they do must make sense to them and be readily seen as valuable. Workbooks and skills sheets continue to have no place in this kind of classroom.

The Nature of Instruction

As should be clear, many different kinds of groups meet during the literacy workshop time. Much of students' work is collaborative, as students share

Sometimes children need help learning to schedule their time during reading and writing workshops. The teacher is helping these students sign up for work in the classroom writing center.

ideas and construct common understanding of reading and writing. Equally, they share understanding of other content areas, of the interrelatedness of what they study, and of the role of reading and writing as tools to foster learning.

Teachers offer instruction in focused lessons and in planned and impromptu conferences that provide on-the-spot instruction as needed. Although teachers carefully plan both required work and "invitations," they remain responsive to students' needs, their interests, and the many "teachable moments" that occur when interested young learners explore books and ideas independently and with their peers.

GUIDED READING SESSIONS

The supportive reading groups that children have already experienced have prepared them for the more focused work in **guided reading groups** (Routman, 1989, 1991). Students do more silent reading in guided reading groups, but they still read orally to firm up their emerging strategies. They engage in discussions about their reading, and they participate in interesting and challenging extension activities. In guided reading groups, an increasingly important goal is for students to learn to think critically and creatively about their reading and writing.

Conducting Guided Reading Sessions

As discussed previously, instruction should consist of three stages: prereading, directed reading, and postreading (see Table 9.2).

The *prereading* phase of guided reading sessions is the time to assess background knowledge, develop needed concepts, and generally prepare for reading. Questioning is essential at this point to prompt certain kinds of thinking and direct students' attention to specific textual challenges. The prereading phase may begin with a set of generic questions that can be asked about almost any piece of text:

1. What do students expect from the piece of text?
2. How might the new text be similar to or different from other things they have read?
3. What do they know about the kind of text they will read (e.g., narrative or informational)?
4. What do they already know about the topic or theme?
5. What do they think will happen (for narratives) or what do they think they will learn (for informational texts)?

Teachers help students develop more focused questions by using the illustrations and title of the material to be read. Especially with informational texts, students also learn to pose questions (often factual) for which they want answers; these will guide their progress through the text. As they become more sophisticated, readers may jot down answers to such questions, or they might use a Know–Want to Know–Learned chart to help them as they read (see appendix D).

During the second phase, *directed reading*, students' silent reading is interlaced with discussion and more teacher questioning. Questions focus primarily on complex, interesting, or puzzling aspects of text; their purpose is to emphasize the variables students should consider in monitoring their own reading. Questions should teach, not test. They may ask readers to refocus at the word, phrase, sentence, or paragraph level; activate prior knowledge or relevant experiences; or integrate information across text. Students should draw on evidence both from the text and from their experiences as they answer questions, and they should be encouraged to raise their own questions as well.

It is also important to remember that as students move from supportive to guided reading groups, the teacher must repeatedly and thoroughly model self-questioning strategies to help students understand how and why such strategies are helpful. The think-aloud procedure can again be invaluable.

During the *postreading* phase, teachers check on comprehension and offer provocative questions to spur discussion. In discussing *what* they have read, children also share *how* they have accomplished their reading, thus cutting through the "language of instruction" to present workable explanations of individual reading strategies. By collaborating, they expand their strategies for reevaluating and analyzing text. For example, students may share personal experiences similar to events in the story and tell how they used their own experiences to help them understand the characters or plot. Other students may relate how they interpreted specific words—such as descriptors of characters' personalities—and how these specific words were keys to understanding a story.

Part of the flexibility of guided reading sessions is that the postreading phase allows for review and expansion. Children review their initial predictions to see which were right, discuss differences they found, and offer their own questions about the text. One way to stimulate student questioning is to suggest that they raise questions they would ask the author if he or she were present. This idea does not seem strange to students who have been writing extensively themselves. To quote a second-grade author/reader's realization: "Before I ever wrote a book I used to think there was a big machine, and they typed the title and then the machine went until the book was done. Now I look at a book and know that a guy wrote it. And it's been his project for a long time" (Newkirk, 1982, p. 457).

Realizing that there has been a real person behind a written piece seems to give students permission to identify flaws, gaps, inconsistencies, and inadequacies in what they read. They may suggest that an author assumed that his or her reader would know some piece of detail and minimized it in the story; because information is missing, comprehension is difficult. For example, students who have never experienced snow will have difficulty understanding the joy expressed in Ezra Jack Keat's *The Snowy Day*.

Questioning is only one form of postreading activity. Some texts lend themselves to critical thought through dramatization, puppets, art, pantomime, or choral or dramatic reading—what Jim Trelease (1985) refers to as the "third dimension" of students' reading. Here are some ideas for extension activities; many are designed to be completed independently or in small groups during workshop time:

- Letters to authors
- Posters about books/stories that students have enjoyed
- Letters or notes to classmates about books/stories; these may include either positive or negative comments
- Independent reading of additional works by a favorite author
- Independent reading of additional work on a favorite topic
- Buddy reading for pleasure
- Working on a project related to what students have read
- Drawing/painting related to students' reading
- Creating puppets based on what has been read
- Writing in literature logs
- Writing new endings to books/stories
- Rewriting stories/books to add characters, change settings, and so forth
- Rewriting stories/books to change format (e.g., story to poem or play)
- Preparing for Readers' Theater (see chapter 11)
- Preparing for dramatization of story

Students should also be encouraged to respond to text at an affective level. As Rosenblatt suggested, "Frank expressions of boredom or even vigorous rejection is a more valid starting point for learning than are docile attempts to tell what the teacher wants" (1985, p. 70). Young readers need to realize that negative responses to a book they read are valid reactions that do not mean they do not like reading itself.

Negotiations in Guided Reading Groups

The processes suggested for guided reading groups make as concrete as possible the mental processes that skilled readers use in trying to make sense from text. Children are helped to think about what they do when they read, to monitor their understanding, and to employ a wide range of literacy strategies. As teachers learn to use guided reading groups, they realize that in many ways the approach involves complex negotiations among students, teachers, and the instructional situation itself. Teachers want their instruction to make sense to their students, and the students themselves are trying to fit new information into existing models of how reading and writing "work" and to make sense of what they are reading.

Negotiations work like this: Teachers may sense that students are not understanding instruction or are having trouble comprehending a text. The wisest move in such situations is usually for teachers to back off, assess what is going on, and quickly determine the most appropriate next steps. Sometimes, the best approach is to stop instruction entirely; at other times, teachers may fill in missing background knowledge, teach or reteach a needed skill or fact, or listen carefully while students try to think aloud and talk their way out of their confusion. It is unfortunate that teachers sometimes make three errors at this juncture:

- Explaining too much and losing children's attention,
- Not saying enough to make strategies or content clear, or
- Not listening to what students are trying to say about their confusion.

Teachers need to bring all their kidwatching skills to the fore during situations like this to determine when children actually "get it." Children can then move on with their real task: actually reading and thinking about the text before them. This process of renegotiating instruction shows responsiveness to students' needs as learners and is evidence of the teacher's role as kidwatcher and decision maker.

FOSTERING THOUGHTFUL WRITING

Children learn to write by writing, but they also need help in shaping their work toward increasingly sophisticated forms. Help comes from teachers' use of direct and indirect instruction and from external models such as language experience work and children's literature. Without help to refine their skills, children's writing may grow in length but still be little more than expansions of the "I like . . . " and "I + [action verb]" inventories mentioned in chapter 8. Such stories are loosely connected strings of sentences tied together without a logical flow to show what the writer thinks, knows, or has experienced.

Teachers who recognize that reading and writing are intricately related processes can most effectively help young learners improve their literacy skills. As mentioned in previous chapters, classrooms that motivate writing offer quiet places to work and confer, ample supplies of writing equipment, reference materials, display space for students' work, and the expectation that all students will write every day. Students continue to keep logs or

As children's skills and strategies improve, they often work independently. Note the troll on the child's pencil—probably a symbol that she feels good about herself as a learner.

journals, write about their reading, and write many different kinds of pieces as assigned work, invitations, and free-time activities.

Writing in Different "Voices" and for Different Purposes

For children to move beyond the beginning phases of writing, they must start to understand the different categories or voices of writing and understand the characteristics of each type. Reading instruction that makes students aware of text structure contributes to this understanding, but children need opportunities to try out these different forms themselves. The content of young writers' work comes from many sources, including stories they have heard or read, television and movies, and their own imagination, experiences, wishes, and fantasies. Letters, articles in newspapers and magazines, and other real-life texts provide additional models for beginning writers. Children also need to learn to write for audiences other than their

Table 10.1
Audiences, Purposes, and Formats for Young Writers

Audiences for Young Writers

- Oneself: journals, logs, notes prior to writing, personal notes
- One's teacher: journals and logs, other assignments
- One's peers: writing to be shared in workshops and conferences, personal notes, collaborative projects, writing published on bulletin boards
- One's parents: personal notes, assigned work
- Other members of the school community: writing to other students, teachers, and administrators
- School newspapers, newsletters, and magazines
- Magazines that publish student writing

Purposes for Writing

- To entertain oneself or others, usually in story format
- To state one's view or perspective
- To persuade
- To ask for information or permission
- To provide information, as in reporting on science observations
- To reinforce learning, as in making notes and keeping a log
- To reconsider material, as in reports

Formats for Writing by Young Writers
Narratives or stories, consisting of the following:

- Theme or what the story is about
- Characters
- Statement of setting, including time action takes place
- Statement of problem to be investigated and solved
- Major events that advance the story and constitute the plot
- Minor events
- Resolution, stating how the problem is solved
- Conclusion, stating how the story ends

Expository formats, providing information, seeking to serve a particular purpose such as to persuade, or discussing ideas. In general, such writing consists of the following:

- Introductory paragraph, setting forth the basic information or purpose
- Explanatory paragraphs, providing information, description, explanation, definition, procedures, or support; these may be full of description, details, or facts
- Transitional paragraphs, changing ideas or focus (as needed)
- Concluding paragraph, tying ideas together and often summarizing

---

teachers and peers and to recognize the different constraints imposed by distinct audiences.

Table 10.1 is an overview of the range of appropriate writing for students at this level. See Figure 10.1 for analyses of many writing samples.

Writing Across the Curriculum

One important way to encourage students to write for many different purposes and audiences is to integrate writing into all content areas. The term **writing across the curriculum** is often used for the approach to planning that exploits every opportunity to encourage students to write. They can write factual reports; letters; diaries; learning logs; science reports; math problems; annotations for graphs, charts, or artwork; and imaginative, fanciful pieces. Through these activities, students learn to view writing as a means of communicating many different kinds of information and to recognize it as a tool to organize and test their thinking. (Figure 10.1 includes several examples of this kind of writing.)

In many ways, writing across the curriculum is a state of mind that teachers adopt when they are committed to having their students engage in wide and purposeful writing. It places writing at the very center of the curriculum, and it answers teachers' frequent questions about when they will find time to allow their children to write. They find time as part of instruction, as a follow-up to instruction, and as a means of evaluating learning.

One common writing across the curriculum activity is *report writing.* Some reports result from students' observing and recording various phenomena; others are written as an extension to content area learning and demonstrate the value of linking reading and writing. Teachers may assign a simple topic for young learners' reports, but it is also beneficial to allow them to select their own questions or issues to investigate. Teachers need to ensure that topics are not so broad as to be staggering and that appropriate resources and references are readily available. A Know–Want to Know–Learned graphic organizer is often a good starting point for young researchers (see appendix D). As will be discussed in chapter 11, report writing can be a fine introduction to the library and its diverse resources, introducing children to literary genres they have not previously encountered.

To be successful, this kind of writing must always be authentic; that is, it must come from the processing of facts that make sense to student readers and writers. Too often, teachers ask children to "write" as a follow-up to content area work but have not provided enough information to produce a valid writing experience. If information is merely spoon fed to children and their follow-up writing assignments simply ask them to feed the information back to their teachers, the writing experience is invalid. The samples presented in Figure 10.2 (see pages 246–247), all produced by second graders,

Samples 1 and 2. These are samples of two children's journal entries. They were both in bilingual classes and had only recently begun to write in English. Notice the use of drawing as a supplement to their writing.

Figure 10.1
Writing Samples from Second and Third Graders

The Mean Salerie

Once there live a mean old calerie. He didn't like people to buy him. Then a little man past buy. He said to his hive "I am goin to buy salerie for the pic nic. Buying the salerie bit the man. The man said to the casher that there are bugs in the salerie. No there not bugs in the salerie said the cashe. They called the ditectives they said this salizie has eyes, mou and a nose. They took him to inapect him. They put him in a table a nose came out of a hole and ate the salerie.

Sample 3 (Second Grade). There is some confusion between English and Spanish syntax; verbs shift between present and past tense; punctuation is weak. The child knew about quotations but did not use them consistently. The story is very creative and develops a "psychology" for the celery; ideas and actions progress logically to a good solution to the problem.

The Football game

Once apone a time there was a football game in the super bowl! 7 o Q.B. his name was Goergie V and a cheer lenter her name was Olga F. and a tackler his name was Hector Z. and a rusher his name was Gabe B. and the teams name was Dallas cow boys and seahawks and the scor was. 3839

Sample 4 (Second Grade). Even though the student was going to offer straightforward reporting of a Super Bowl game, he began his "story" with "Once a pone a time." This is essentially an inventory, although the writer offered details from a real event. The illustration provides the only action and detail. The writer could benefit from instruction on descriptive words, as well as on the use of uppercase letters to start sentences. He could also benefit from instruction on different modes of writing.

Figure 10.1, *continued*

A happy ending

One day Jenny Vicki
and ~~Jeanette~~ were
waking on the play
groud and we were eating
lunch then Mickell
came aloge then
he shtated chasing
us then he cot
Jenny and kissed
her then Jenny
ran an hit him
then he said
I am sorry

Sample 5 (Second Grade). This, too, is an inventory of events, a straightforward chronology leading to an apology at the end. The writer could benefit from instruction on descriptive words, maintenance of first or third person, and other means as on express action, as well as on conventions of writing. Note that similar to sample 8 in Figure 9.4 (Micky the nice pirate), this story has a happy ending; Dyson and others have found this a common convention in writing by girls in early childhood classes.

illustrate the difference between authentic and inauthentic report writing. Note especially the report that begins with its writer's honest statement of ignorance "abwt germany."

OPPORTUNITIES TO SHARE WRITING

It is essential that young writers share their work with others. Sharing provides real audiences, whether peers or the teacher. Knowing they will have real

Figure 10.1, *continued*

My Life As A Foot is not very sweet smelling. Every day my oner puts on his socks and that is how it all starts. Wean he gets home from school I don't smell very good. and at night I relly don't smell very good! Oh! I don't smell very good right know my oner just came home from a soccer game. Oh! that is one thing that is wrog about being Mr. Smelling Foot. I aways get kicked.

The End

Sample 6 (Second Grade). This student felt very comfortable with himself as a writer. He selected his fanciful topic and wrote with real enthusiasm.

audiences for their work motivates young writers to stretch toward increasingly sophisticated strategies for expressing their ideas. Students are inclined to make revisions when they realize that real audiences will be trying to make sense of what they have written. Further, members of an audience ask questions that can help the writer shape his or her work toward greater clarity.

Sharing with Peers

As students get ready to share work with their peers, they evaluate their writing from the perspective of their intended readers to determine whether the work is in fact communicating meaning as intended. Perhaps they have left out some information, not offered enough description, or not sequenced ideas logically. Reading in this way is a sophisticated task, for it requires that students distance

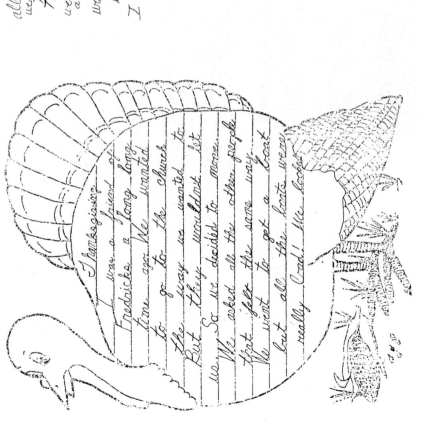

all over get a good boat. The olny place
we could get the guen was from
The guen kit. So we went to the guen
we lied to the guen We sailed because
a long way the name of boat boat
was longthe May Flower. We sailed, but
long way. Every body was happy. but
I ww not. It was cold! We had no
home we had no food no
along people would
say that They were right
would diy They were right in the
my brother died of no food
cold and died We were all sad
and no home We were all sad
It was summer and we made
friends with the Indians
The Indians told us
how to plant corn the
right way We got to
like the Indians.

After a long we
started to see

more and more of
each other

Thanksgiving
was a friend of
Fredricks a long long
time ago. We wanted
to go to the church
the way we wanted to
But they wouldn't let
us. So we decidid to move.
We asked all the other people
that felt the same way.
We went to get a boat
but all the boats were
really bad. We looked

242

Sample 7 (Third Grade). The writer of this story refused to be confined by the turkey shape; he considered himself a writer and had a story to tell. The story presents many elements of the traditional Thanksgiving story. This piece was written by the same child who wrote sample 6.

Figure 10.1, continued

Long ago live a handsom
boy from Mexico. He looks
for dragon One day as I
was going home I saw a
dragon I did what I can
do but I lost her he
died I will look for it
today so he with to the
woods and he saw three
baby of the mother I took
on home but I did not
know what to with it
I took it to the moo-
I took he I will get
two more he died and the
mother to oft died the moo
keep I will take good
of them I will come
right now but comfort I
will he got the tri baby
and took them to the
moo.

**Sample 8
(Third Grade).**

The writer of this story also spent grades one and two in a bilingual classroom. His sample in English shows that he was comfortable writing and had a lot of imagination. He switched from first to third person in his attempt to balance first-person narrative and his imaginary story. He left out some words and would benefit from reading his story aloud. He used quotations to advance his story and could benefit from the suggestion to put each person's statement on a separate line. Note the confusion between cursive "I" and "b" in line 7.

Figure 10.1. *continued*

Figure 10.1, *continued*

Mold

One day I brought a
bread to show my class. The
bread head spots on it. Then
one week passed and the bread
had more spots of mold. At
last the bread got all full
of mold.

Sample 9

Mold   Spois   Food

At   first   Mrs. Proven
brought   a   tortillas. Then It
had   a   little   bit   of
mold.   At   last   it   has
a   lot   of   mold.

Sample 10

Mold.
First angelica brought a bread and it was not to much green but now is very green.

Sample 11

El Moho y el Hongo
Primero Mis.Provensc
trajo una tortillas.
Y luego tenía un
Poque De moho.

Despues el moho
tenía más. Al último
las tortillas se mcieron
moho

Sample 12

Figure 10.1, *concluded*

Samples 9, 10, 11, and 12 (Third Grade).

The writers of these pieces were in a transitional year from instruction in Spanish to instruction in English. Their teacher wanted to use writing across the curriculum to enhance their literacy skills and their content knowledge. She encouraged them to write in the language in which they felt most confident and provided them with many stimulating experiences about which to write. Note that the writer of sample 9 brought a piece of bread to the class to replicate the lesson her teacher had provided and that the writer of sample 11 wrote a commentary on his classmate's demonstration. Samples 9, 10, and 11 show evidence of the children's first language but also show confidence and enthusiasm for writing.

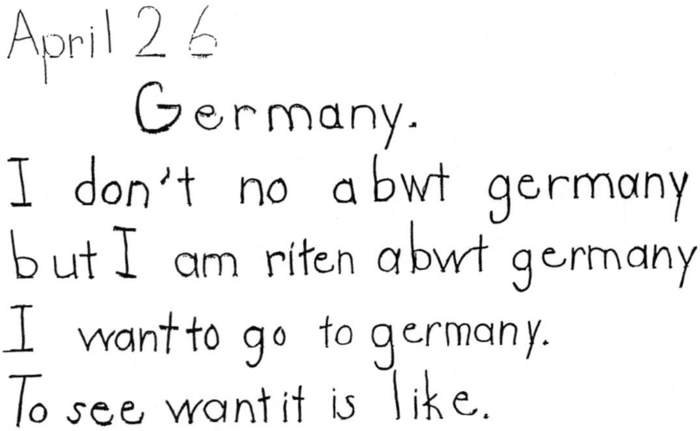

April 2 6

Germany.
I don't no abwt germany
but I am riten abwt germany
I want to go to germany.
To see want it is like.

Sample 1

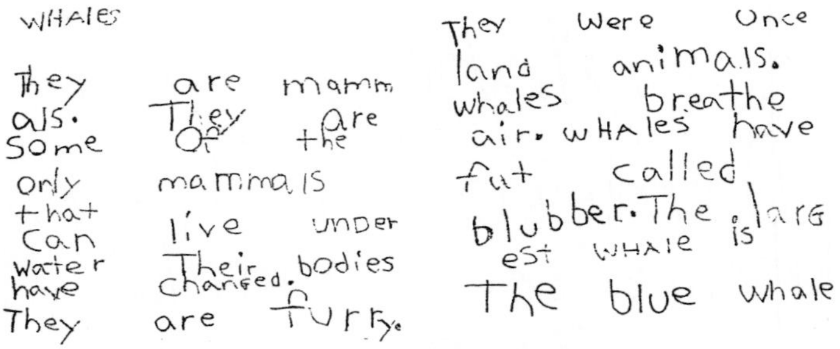

WHALES

They are mamm
als. They Are
Some Of the
Only mamma, IS
that
Can live under
Water Their bodies
have Changed.
They are furry.

They were once
land animals.
whales breathe
air. wHALes have
fut called
blubber. The larg
est WHALE is
The blue whale

Sample 2

Figure 10.2

Examples of Authentic and Inauthentic Report Writing   When children do
not do real research in preparation for writing reports, the resulting writing
can be sterile and dull. The students have not learned useful skills and have
not had the satisfaction of finding information and restating it in their own
words. The report on whales was written near the beginning of second grade
by the child whose work is shown in samples 6 and 7 in Figure 10.1. The
report on trout reflected the writer's strong interest in tropical and other fish.

TROUT

Trout eggs are vary tiny. 14 to 16 trout eggs can be as big as I penny. When they are I or 2 weeks old they're called eyed eggs because you can see the fish's eyes. A look up close shows the whole embryo. They will hatch in about two months.

When trout are young thay have up and doun lines called parr marks. The parr marks camouflage the fish in tall grasses. When the trout gets older insted of the parr marks it has spots. The spots help the fish blend in with the pebbles at the bottom of the stream. The trout has 8 fins. It is red, yellow, blue and sometimes green. It eats minnows, insects, wrms, tadpoles and even frogs. The trouts teath are tiny and sharp. They are used to keep prey inside the trout's mouth. The trout has good senses to catch its food. It has good eyesight and color vision. The trout uses its nostrils to smell its pray.

It has ears inside its head. It can still hear very well. The trout could even hear a worm wiggling at the bottom of a stream. Moste fish have a sense that humans don't have. It is called the lateral line. It helps the fish know when something is near by. One other way the trout catches its food is that it is a fast swimmer.

Sample 3

Figure 10.2, *concluded*

themselves from what they are doing enough to evaluate their efforts. "Going public" by sharing motivates writers to think long and hard about what they have written and to reach for increasingly higher levels of clarity in their writing.

Several forms of peer interaction about writing can be very beneficial, even to beginning writers. In these interactions, students think together about their writing as it emerges from its initial draft form, in almost final form, and as a completed piece. Each level serves a specific purpose, requires distinct preparation, and focuses students' thinking on different aspects of the writing process. Steps for several forms of interaction are listed and discussed in Table 10.2.

Table 10.2
Types of Peer Interaction

Authors' Circle

Participants: Several children

Teacher's role: Initially, models interaction and sets tone; maintains tone and moderates as students become more adept

Writing: In draft form

Questions: Is the writing conveying meaning? How can it be made clearer?

Purpose: To encourage students to talk about their writing and realize the importance of an audience

Editorial Conferences

Participants: Designated "assistant" and classmates

Teacher's role: Helps designated "assistant" to understand role and responsibilities for helping others; selects students who will serve the role each day

Writing: In first-draft or somewhat polished form

Questions: How can the writing be made clearer and more polished? What aspects of the writing should be changed to increase readers' understanding?

Purpose: To encourage students to talk about their writing processes while focusing on their own and others' writing; to encourage collaboration

Peer Conferences

Participants: Author of piece to be discussed and other students

Teacher's role: Initially, models interaction and appropriate tone for discussion; focuses students' attention on aspects of the writing; asks relevant questions; provides support for writer by recasting questions and responses as needed; continues to set tone

Writing: Nearly finished

Questions: How successfully has the piece conveyed meaning? What might be confusing to the audience? How can confusing parts be fixed? What should the author attend to? What has the author done well?

Purpose: To develop students' awareness of the many ways meaning can be effectively conveyed; to help students read their own and each other's writing more critically and deeply; to establish a spirit of collaboration about writing by building trust among students

Teacher–Student Conference

Participants: Teacher and one student

Teacher's role: Asks questions about writing; to listen to what student is trying to do; to offer instruction as needed

Writing: Any phase

Questions: What are you working on? What are you having trouble with? What are you trying to say? How can I help you?

Purpose: To give teacher a close look at students' processes and to offer immediate instructional help

Publication of Student Work

Participants: Any students who are willing to let their work "go public"

Teacher's role: Provides suggestions for ways to publish work; sometimes to type work into cleaner format; to establish a climate in which students feel comfortable putting their work out for public display

Writing: Finished form, highly polished, often illustrated, sometimes typed

Modes of publication: Bulletin boards in classrooms, halls, or other public places in school; in teacher- or student-made books, for inclusion in classroom library; in school newsletters or schoolwide books produced for special occasions; in magazines that publish student work, such as *Stone Soup, the Magazine by Children* (see Stoll, 1994)

Teachers have many responsibilities as they introduce these peer interactions to young learners. They must establish a tone of respect and helpfulness by creating an open exchange of ideas and modeling the kinds of questions students should ask. Students should think of themselves as a community of learners sharing the common goal of literacy competence. In some sessions, students may present work in early drafts; in others, the work may be more polished. Students need to be sensitive to the different levels of completion of the work they are sharing and discussing and make comments accordingly. An important element for students to understand is that the work—not the authors—is what's being discussed during these interactions.

As students work through the process of bringing a piece of writing from draft to publication form, they should be encouraged to turn to their peers for editorial assistance. Emphasis is on improving work in draft form. The seemingly impromptu nature of *editorial conferences* belies their value in encouraging critical thinking about writing. Because student writers turn to their peers to solve writing puzzles as they occur, the experience of thinking together about a piece of writing is authentic and purposeful. If students have learned the essential protocol for thinking about writing, the immediacy of the editorial conference challenges them to use their skills and strategies on their own, without teacher instruction or intervention. When students serve as editors for each other's work, they "develop an appreciation of audience and the communicative commitment [writers] make to their readers" (Harste, Short, & Burke, 1988, p. 257). How well students can apply what they have learned about thinking about writing will be reflected in the extent to which the piece of writing succeeds in communicating to others.

When students complete a piece of writing, they may want to present the work to a group of peers to see how they—a real audience—actually respond. Initially in *authors' circle* sessions, only one student brings a piece to the circle, where he or she shares the piece and engages in discussion with other classmates. Children are interacting as authors and audience, offering and receiving critiques about what is clear and unclear in the writing. At first, teachers guide the sessions carefully to provide models of how to talk about the writing in helpful ways. Gradually, students can meet independently, and two or more pieces of work can be presented during one session.

Publication of students' completed writing provides excellent motivation and affirmation for young writers. In addition to publication on bulletin boards and teacher-made books (see Figure 9.3), teachers may compile stories into books to be distributed to parents. Many magazines for young children also welcome submissions from beginning writers. Typing students' work for publication is a productive activity for parent volunteers.

Sharing with the Teacher

Student–teacher writing conferences are tremendously valuable and do not necessarily take a lot of time. If students understand that they are expected to come to the conference prepared to discuss a piece of work in progress and if a schedule for conferences is posted and adhered to, individual conferences need not take more than five to ten minutes each.

During conferences, teachers and students work together, with teachers providing impromptu instruction on needed aspects of writing. Yet, in many ways, control of the conference situation is given to the students themselves, whose responsibility it is to prepare for the session and to lead the discussion as much as possible. Silent "wait time" helps children to remember their writing behaviors and organize what they will say. As they read a piece to the teacher, they may discover and change awkward or incorrect expressions, faulty word choice, or even spelling errors previously undetected. Teachers' gentle questioning prompts students to recognize that they need to analyze and evaluate their work. Teachers note strengths and weaknesses, offer reteaching on the spot, or plan for later instruction.

TEACHING THE CONVENTIONS OF WRITING

Chapters 5 and 6 emphasized the importance of students' home language and dialect, both as a mark of who they are and as a powerful bridge to literacy learning. Valuing the linguistic diversity that is evident in many early childhood classes, however, does not preclude teachers from offering instruction on grammar, the mechanics of writing, and standard spelling.

Grammar and Other Mechanical Aspects of Writing

Lucy McCormick Calkins (1981) wrote:

> When children write, they reach for the skills they need. When children ask the questions and raise the dilemmas, [mechanical] skills are learned in context—young writers need time to run into their own problems, to ask their own questions. Only then can skills be learned in context—for the context is not the subject matter, but the child's questions, the child's need. (pp. 89–90)

The balance between direct instruction, indirect instruction, and children's own needs results in understanding and mastery.

Instruction in grammatical and mechanical conventions of language can be offered during mini lessons, small group sessions, language experience dictation, or individual conferences on an as-needed basis. Instruction should help students understand that mastery of the conventions of writing provides them with invaluable tools for communicating their ideas more clearly and precisely.

Oral language is the most powerful means of teaching children correct grammar and the mechanical aspects of writing. Grammatical and mechanical errors often make writing that sounds "wrong" or "funny" or that does not "make sense." Also, because major marks of punctuation (commas, periods, question marks, exclamation points, semicolons, colons, quotation marks) indicate pauses that have direct parallels in oral language, oral reading may reveal errors that might go unnoticed in writing that is read silently. This is a strong rationale for encouraging students to read their work aloud to peers or to themselves so they can detect places that need to be revised.

The language experience approach is also helpful because it provides concrete examples of how and where certain conventions should be used. For example, LEA can be useful to formalize understanding of punctuation, paragraph structure, and conventions such as indenting. Transcription demonstrates punctuation use, and spirited rereading of LEA stories reinforces its importance. Teachers can start by emphasizing full stops—periods, question marks, and exclamation points. Next, they should stress internal punctuation—commas, dashes, apostrophes, and quotation marks. Names and uses should be presented, but teachers must remember that using the marks correctly is more important than remembering what they are called. The first grader who called exclamation points "out loud marks" and used them correctly was well on her way to mastering punctuation.

Spelling and Handwriting

Appropriate spelling work in early childhood classes offers a balance of formal and informal instruction and student discovery of spelling principles. It is fortunate that there are several very practical guidelines for helping children move toward spelling competency. The first should sound familiar by now: *Children learn to spell most efficiently when surrounded by print in a literate classroom environment.*

The second suggestion is to encourage *active involvement in language* through word play and noncompetitive spelling games. Children should be encouraged to continue to form hypotheses about spelling, just as they did in the early stages of invented spelling. Classroom charts and lists of words tailored to thematic units, holidays, or students' interests and personal word banks also involve children in thinking about words.

Frequent writing is the most productive way to involve students with language. As they write, students often develop a "spelling consciousness" (Gentry, 1981, p. 380) that enables them to evaluate their work, recognize nonconventional spelling, and have numerous strategies available for changing an incorrect word. Spelling consciousness also assures them that writing a word incorrectly is not a big deal (remember the kindergarten child in chapter 8 whose attitude was that words could be "close but no cigar").

The third suggestion is to *deemphasize standard spelling.* This is easy advice for kindergarten or first-grade teachers to follow, but second- or third-grade teachers may shudder at the thought. Deemphasizing standard spelling encourages children to write. The instruction to "spell it the best you can, we can always correct the spelling later" gives children the freedom to experiment in writing, take risks, use their imaginations, and refine their skills. Through writing, they refine (and speed up) their ability to break words into component sounds and to match those sounds with letters. They learn to look at their spelling and match it visually with their memory of how the word "should look." They develop a spelling consciousness.

Additionally, nonconventional spelling gives teachers a reflection of children's knowledge about letter–sound correspondence and irregularities in the spelling system. Spelling "errors" of this sort can be thought of as written parallels of miscues in oral reading. Viewing nonconventional spelling diagnostically, teachers attempt to find an underlying system or pattern rather than count the total number of misspellings. For example, children may hear phonemes incorrectly because of speech problems, hearing loss, or temporary hearing difficulty (colds, allergies, etc.), or they may be matching phonemes and letters according to their own pronunciation, which is influenced by regional dialects, second-language learning, or speech difficulties. Additionally, children have not learned certain concepts, such as silent letters (lam*b*, *w*rench), consonant digraphs (*ph*one), double consonants (swi*mm*ing), and changes to the terminal *y* (pennies, ponies);

they may need review and reteaching. Finding an underlying error pattern allows teachers to focus instruction.

The idea of looking at spelling diagnostically implies that each child may need an individual prescription to remedy his or her spelling difficulties. In all probability, this will not be the case, for patterns of errors will clump together to allow for whole class, small group, and individual instruction.

Having a *well-planned, logical instructional program,* with adjustments made for individual help, is the final suggestion for helping children learn to spell. Bissex (1980) made an important point about teaching spelling: "[Instruction] may be useful or crucial at only some stages. . . . [Y]oungsters have a sense of how they learn and [should] be allowed and encouraged to take more control of their own learning. The teacher's function would then include more helping children listen to themselves and less the entire burden of diagnosing the needs of every student" (p. 114). Children will differ, she stated, and teachers should be sensitive to whether students are experimenting or seeking focused help and direction. She added, "Development of spelling ability may not rest on any particular sequence [of instruction] but on an ever-changing concept of spelling that increasingly approaches the actual nature of [the conventional spelling system]."

Such a program limits daily study time but encourages ample practice, through writing. That some words are more difficult to spell than others is acknowledged, as are differences in students' abilities to spell easily. A program goal is to strengthen children's vocabularies and store of sight words that they can spell independently. When writing and reading are integrated for instruction and practice, children spend considerable time each day practicing their spelling skills and strategies in purposeful ways. Lists of words tailored to children's interests or needs can be useful; such lists are used as part of the "environmental print" in the classroom.

Learning to use the dictionary is also important, and the excuse that "I don't know how to spell it, so how can I look it up?" should never be accepted. Children who have been forming hypotheses by "spelling it as it sounds" can easily apply the same process to dictionary sleuthing by thinking of the many possible ways a word might be spelled. Group modeling is a good way of teaching children to do this. The teacher selects a difficult or irregular word and together the group generates and discusses possible spellings. The correct spelling can then be found in the dictionary. Demonstrating the process shows children what they should do individually and helps them realize what they know about spelling.

Subvocalizing as an aid to spelling is modeled, along the lines of a whispered "spelling think aloud" that children must learn to use. Children who view spelling as memorization may be especially reluctant to subvocalize, as are children who have not realized the connection between sounding words out in reading and in spelling. Teachers must acknowledge that subvocalizing is part of the spelling process for many words and that it is not, as one child told me, "cheating—you know, you are supposed to be able to spell the word from your memory." Some children will need scrap paper so that they can write down the results of their subvocalizing to compare the various possible spellings for unfamiliar words.

Many early childhood teachers are confused about handwriting instruction. They wonder whether it is necessary, whether it helps, whether it merely makes children want to stop writing. And when specific handwriting programs are mandated, do they have value? The most important point that teachers can emphasize to students who are just becoming literate is that good handwriting is worth achieving for one simple reason: *When one's handwriting is legible, one is better able to communicate ideas in writing.* Remember the little vignette cited in the last chapter in which a child tells her classmate, "If you need to spell something with m's or s's you can copy [mine]" (MacGillivray, 1994, p. 254).

Handwriting is merely a tool for composing—the process of being an author. When children see its value (and see the benefits of being an author), they will strive to achieve readable handwriting. Their handwriting may not be perfectly neat and well formed, but it will show attempts to communicate. When children understand handwriting as a tool, teachers can remind them individually about spacing, letter formation, staying on the lines, maintaining margins, and so forth. They can offer direct instruction as needed during mini lessons or small group work to ensure that students learn good habits. As they remind and offer instruction, teachers need to remember that neat handwriting is an important but still relatively small aspect of students' emerging ability as writers.

SUMMARY

Helping students become proficient literacy users involves balancing support and challenge. As it has from the time children enter school, teacher support enables students to take the risks needed to grow, and the challenge of interesting reading and writing tasks motivates them forward. The most productive climate for growth is one in which students encounter authentic materials and real tasks to perform. They read real books and write for real purposes and real audiences.

In addition to practice in authentic, self-selected, and motivating tasks, students also grow from teacher instruction. Teachers assume a diagnostic stance toward their students, a refinement of their kidwatching skills that enables them to tailor instructional sessions to students' immediate academic needs. By giving students help when they need it, teachers enable young learners to maintain the momentum their early experiences with literacy have fostered.

QUESTIONS AND TASKS FOR INDEPENDENT AND COLLABORATIVE WORK

1. Be sure that you can define each of the following words:

    - automaticity
    - guided reading group
    - writing across the curriculum

2. This chapter discusses "negotiations" in instruction and the need for "balance" between support and challenge. What do these terms mean to you as you think about the style of interaction with students that you want to attain as you become a professional?

3. Find a piece of children's literature that you think would be appropriate for use in a guided reading lesson. Plan how you would use it instructionally but then present it informally to one or more students. Do you think your instructional plan would have been appropriate for the literature you selected? How might you now change your plan?

4. Think of as many "authentic" writing experiences as you can for students in early childhood classes. In what ways are they authentic, as opposed to contrived or teacher driven? What skills will students gain from them? Discuss your list with others in your class.

CHAPTER 11

Children's Literature

More and more early childhood teachers are choosing literature as the core of their literacy program, and administrators at local and state levels are supporting this choice (Alexander, 1987). Reasons for the increased use of literature are many and varied. Although researchers and teachers recognize that instruction in strategies for figuring out unfamiliar words and achieving comprehension is necessary for young learners, they also understand that children need opportunities to experience real, authentic, challenging examples of age-appropriate literature. These experiences with real literature provide opportunities for personal reflection and response and for the construction of meaning with small groups of peers. Reflection, response, and collaboration are powerful means for even the youngest learners to figure out the intricacies of literate behaviors. They provide meaningful opportunities for students to read (and write) purposefully.

These instructional experiences also demonstrate to young learners that they must question the texts they read, bring their own knowledge to bear in constructing meaning, and essentially read and probe beyond the words printed on the pages before them. Literature exposes young listeners and readers to new ideas and provides vicarious experiences with unfamiliar places, events, and times. Children compare their own experiences with those of the characters they meet to gain insight into emotions, motivation, and behaviors. Literature can be the bridge from one content area to another—for example, when students become interested in art from looking at illustrations in picture books or want to learn more about specific individuals because they have discovered biographical literature. Nonfiction—informational literature—can expand students' knowledge base, increase their understanding of diverse areas, introduce them to new topics and ideas, and generally enhance their learning in content area subjects. As they read, children may find ideas that they want to challenge, information with which they disagree, and styles of presentation that they simply do not like. These findings motivate young learners to become stronger, analytic thinkers and more willing to take on intellectual challenges than students who are fed an early diet of carefully sequenced, vocabulary- and concept-controlled reading material.

Literature also familiarizes children with "book language," which is structured differently from speech and which must be understood to gain comprehension from free-choice and content area reading. And, of course, literature is a tremendous source of personal pleasure for children and adults. For many reasons, then, authentic literature, encountered in a classroom where the teacher monitors student progress and provides developmentally appropriate instruction, helps create strong readers and writers.

This chapter discusses children's literature from several perspectives.[1] First, it presents a brief, practical overview of children's literature (references for more elaborate compendia about children's literature are provided

---

[1] The term *tradebooks* is often used interchangeably with *children's literature*. This term refers generically to books other than textbooks.

in appendix A). The chapter concludes with specific suggestions for using literature to enhance reading and writing growth in a literacy workshop.

AN OVERVIEW OF CHILDREN'S LITERATURE

Helping all learners develop an appreciation of literature is an important goal of the literacy curriculum, and the place to start is to help learners understand what literature is. People who read widely realize that "literature" as a concept is very broad but also has distinct parameters. Certain *common attributes or patterns* are found from the very beginnings of recorded literature: heroes with magical powers, wise women, the apparent fool who triumphs in the end, love as a more powerful force than evil. Transmitted from culture to culture over time, these attributes and patterns are easily recognized in their various guises in contemporary and traditional literature.

Also, authors use specific *conventions* for manipulating attributes to achieve a certain effect or purpose; these contribute to literary unity as well as diversity. Examples include clues in a mystery; a larger-than-life main character accomplishing superhuman feats in a tall tale; a somber, dank, dreary locale in a horror story; and charts, graphs, and figures in certain kinds of nonfiction. Finally, there are broad categories of literature referred to as *genres*.

Specific patterns and attributes are found in nonfiction as well. Books that tell how to do something use a different organizational pattern than joke books or biographies; renderings of historical events follow still other patterns. Young children need exposure to nonfiction as well as to stories, although some informational books for children are written in a distinctly narrative style (Rosenblatt, 1991).

Young children gain a sense of the basic patterns and conventions of narrative and expository text from being read to, from oral storytelling, and even from television. Understanding these aspects of literature, at even the lowest level, gives listeners and readers tangible means by which to increase their appreciation and comprehension. Intuitively, children anticipate a particular kind of structure in what they hear and read, much like benchmarks that guide understanding. Thus, reading widely can be considered the best method to strengthen reading skills—the more students read, the more they appreciate the common elements of all literature and the more they perceive themselves as capable of in-depth comprehension.

FINDING AND EVALUATING LITERATURE FOR CHILDREN

Several criteria for evaluating children's literature cut across all age levels and genres; other criteria pertain to specific kinds of books and stories, purposes for use, and children's developmental levels. Guidelines for selecting children's literature are presented in Table 11.1.

Table 11.1

General Criteria for Evaluating Children's Literature

General Questions to Ask About All Literature

- Is the work developmentally and conceptually appropriate for its intended purpose and audience? Are concepts, vocabulary, or language patterns too difficult? Does the work assume more background knowledge than the students probably possess?

- Is the book sturdy and attractive? Will it withstand handling by many students? Can you laminate the cover or in other ways make it sturdier?

- Does the work compare favorably with others about the same topic or of the same sort? How has the work been reviewed—by professional reviewers, by other teachers, by students?

- Are all characters and situations presented fairly and without stereotyping?

- Is the work accurate, current, objective, honest, nonsexist, and nonracist? Is it well written? Is the point of view appropriate for the purpose of the book?

- Will this work appeal to children or does it seem to have been directed primarily toward an adult audience?

More Specific Questions

Illustrations

- Are the pictures in the book necessary to tell the story or teach the concept or skill emphasized in the book?

- Do they contribute to the book's effectiveness?

- Are they aesthetically pleasing, uncluttered, clearly defined? If pictures are murky or faded, is there a definite point to this style?

- Are illustrations and graphics used in nonfiction books appropriate to contribute to children's knowledge?

- Will children be able to identify the pictures and use them as necessary to aid comprehension?

Information about children's literature is available from many sources. Journals such as *Language Arts, The Horn Book,* and *The New Advocate* offer reviews of current books, as does the *New York Times Book Review,* which is available in bookstores and libraries. The International Reading Association (IRA) and the Children's Book Council provide yearly summaries of recent books, and several excellent bibliographies are readily available (see appendix A). The IRA summaries cite books that have been rated superior by teachers and children.

Picture Books

The first books that most children encounter, including squeezable bath and toy books, are usually **picture books**. Picture books may be of many sorts:

Narratives (Fiction)

- Is the story worth telling? Is it developmentally appropriate for the age for which it is intended?
- Is there a recognizable theme?
- Does the work have a clearly developed plot? Is it original, rather than trite or predictable?
- Are characters, setting, and plot introduced and developed appropriately?
- Is there a recognizable conclusion that resolves the story?
- Is the story realistic in terms of all story elements, including dialogue?
- If the story is fanciful, do story elements work?
- Does the story sound right when read aloud?
- Will children be able to relate to the story or, if its purpose is different, will it introduce children to new experiences and enlarge their vision?

Nonfiction

- Will informational books lead to greater understanding? Can they be used in content area instruction? Are facts, procedures, and other elements accurate? Is content up to date? Are there any significant omissions? Is the author qualified to write about the topic?
- In **history** and **historical fiction**, are dates, places, events, and so forth correct?
- In **concept or alphabet books**, is the format of the individual pages appropriate to assist students in learning? Are illustrations clear, identifiable, and attractive? Are objects to be counted clearly defined?
- In nonfiction **activity books**, are activities safe, easy to understand, and meaningful?
- Are **joke** and **humorous books** tasteful?

Style and Other Elements

- Is the style appropriate for the nature of the book (picture or chapter book), the subject of the book, and the age of the students for whom it is intended? Is the language realistic and rich? Will students understand it?
- Is the format (e.g., narrative or expository) appropriate for the topic and purpose of the book? Does the format invite reader involvement?

number books, alphabet books, concept development books, wordless books, and simple story or informational books. Mother Goose and other nursery rhyme books introduce children to traditional literature. Picture books can teach values, behavior, concepts, and skills; they stimulate language development, expand vocabularies, foster intellectual growth, strengthen observational skills, and increase children's perception of art and beauty.

In picture books, illustrations complement and enhance the short text and carry much of the message, instruction, or story line. Text is more prominent in *picture storybooks*, in which the story itself cannot be garnered through the pictures alone. Picture storybooks are excellent for beginning readers, and several publishers produce series of "easy readers" for this audience.

Children can enjoy picture books alone, with peers, or with adults. As adults share picture books with nonreaders, they foster understanding that is a prerequisite to literacy. Children just starting to read gain models of reading strategies when adults read to them, along with the enjoyment of sharing literacy with others. Many picture books have been made into big book format for use in beginning reading work; because many picture books are available in inexpensive paperback versions, it is easy to have multiple copies for the class.

Picture books can also be used as an integral part of instruction. Alphabet, concept, and counting books, for example, reinforce instruction; and other books can expand students' background experience and knowledge base. A teacher might present a different book on a particular concept each day as part of language arts work; counting books and books on shapes and size differences belong in math work. Contrasting books on the same concept can be interesting and fun. For example, alphabet work with *On Market Street* (Lobel, 1981), with its highly detailed, intricate illustrations, might be followed by William Wegman's (1994) *ABCs*. This book features photographs of the author's Weimaraners rearranged to represent the letter forms and scenes—such as "Fay is *U*nder [the cushion]"—to illustrate words beginning with the letters. The contrast in styles provoke considerable inspection and conversation, but they also invite deliberation about the reasons why authors and illustrators make certain choices in creating their books.

Picture books can be the starting point for many discussions. There's a Nightmare in My Closet (Meyer, 1968), Do You Want to Be My Friend? (Carle, 1971), and The Rainbow Fish (Pfister, 1992) all encourage children to talk about their personal feelings. Books like The Runaway Bunny (Brown, 1942/1972), Time for Bed (Fox, 1992), and Where the Wild Things Are (Sendak, 1963) focus specifically on relationships with one's mother, while Grandfather's Journey (Say, 1993) deals with grandparents from a different culture. Children can also be encouraged toward more "literary" discussions as they experience and talk about picture books by the same author or on the same theme. Series such as Hoban's Frances, Lobel's Frog and Toad books, Keat's Peter books, and Wiseman's Morris the Moose books introduce characters with strong, identifiable traits and recognizable problems to solve. Through reading and discussion, children learn to like specific characters, make judgments about them, and evaluate how authors craft their stories.

Many nonfiction picture and picture storybooks are available, and they need to be part of young children's libraries as well. They help young learners expand their sense of literature in general and of the purpose of books for school learning and enjoyment as well. (These are discussed later in the chapter.)

Traditional Literature

Mother Goose and other nursery rhymes, folktales, fairy tales, tall tales, myths, and legends introduce children to **traditional literature.** The many forms of such literature have been handed down from generation to generation—in oral, written, and visual form. Common themes and recurring structural patterns appear in all traditional literature, with specific manifestations depending on the cultural and social groups in which the story originally developed.

Traditional literature should be a fundamental part of students' literary experiences, as stimuli for storytelling, dramatics, art, and writing and as part of the study of different cultures. Once they have understood the basic elements to be manipulated, students can dictate, write, or enact their own versions of traditional tales. Tall tales are especially good for this purpose. Spontaneous or planned dramatic activities based on traditional literature invite students to become swashbucklers, wise and beautiful princesses, gods and goddesses, evil witches, demons, and dragons. Art activities, pantomime, and dance also accompany traditional literature quite naturally.

Over the years, traditional stories have been translated into many different forms. Numerous versions of traditional tales exist, for example, about runaway food (e.g., "The Gingerbread Boy"), wise and strong animals (e.g., "The Three Billy Goats Gruff"), and the consequences of greed or stupidity (e.g., "The Fisherman's Wife"). Recently, contemporary versions of several traditional tales have been produced. Examples include William Wegman's versions of *Cinderella* (1993) and *Little Red Riding Hood* (1994), which, like his *ABCs,* are illustrated with pictures of his Weimaraners. Young readers and listeners appreciate the humor of the books and the twist on familiar stories. In many ways, "translations" such as Wegman's are more accessible to young learners because of their conversational and informal style. For example, children can readily savor text such as, "Then the Fairy Godmother pointed the magic wand at Cinderella and with a simple 'ta-da' turned Cinderella's frock into the most beautiful gown in the world, complete with matching corsage and tiara"; and they will be reassured to know that Cinderella's famous shoes were "not the kind of glass slippers that could break or cut you" (unpaged). Children could compare Wegman's story with *Princess Furball* (Huck, 1990), another Cinderella retelling. They also appreciate *The True Story of the Three Little Pigs* (Scieszka, 1989), the traditional tale told from the perspective of the big bad wolf. There is even *The New Adventures of Mother Goose: Gentle Rhymes for Happy Times* (Lansky, 1993), a supposedly "scrubbed, tidy, and polite version of the rhymes that were raucous and rude for centuries" (Lipson, 1994, p. 27). Not only do books like these amuse children, they also demonstrate that writing is not sacred—that writers can change, modify, and personalize stories, often to suit their own whims.

The variations of traditional stories and themes that appear in numerous cultures offer teachers excellent ways to use literature as part of a culturally sensitive curriculum. For example, *Mufaro's Beautiful Daughter* (Steptoe, 1987) presents a Zimbabwean version of the Cinderella tale. By sharing different versions of the same story with students, teachers demonstrate common themes and issues across cultures and the ways national and ethnic characteristics shape literature.

Fiction

Two basic kinds of **fiction** are available for young listeners and readers: realistic and fantastic. Together, they offer students important opportunities to explore their emerging selves, experience adventures vicariously, and expand their views and knowledge of the world.

Characters in **realistic fiction** act like real people; animals act like animals; the environment is real; and plots revolve around everyday occurrences and common problems, conflicts, and tensions. The antagonists in these books may be the main characters themselves, siblings or parents, other children or adults, or nature. Even if readers have not had similar experiences, they do not have to suspend disbelief to read with comprehension. Indeed, actively constructing meaning from examples of this genre can help children learn to understand life situations and empathize more fully with others; students can also vicariously experience escapades and pleasures and escape into mysteries and adventures. Novels about sports, family chronicles, and animals suit other interests and needs. **Historical fiction,** such as that written by Jean Fritz, introduces students to different periods by chronicling real adventures.

Fantastic fiction, on the other hand, requires readers to suspend disbelief. If the main characters are real people and are introduced within a normal, everyday context, readers quickly find themselves transported into extraordinary, imaginary adventures, confronting extraordinary difficulties and solving superhuman problems. Some main characters are off-size people, personified toys, or supernatural beings. Other forms of fantasy include talking animals that get in and out of very human predicaments; Winnie the Pooh, Peter Rabbit, and Paddington Bear are favorite animal characters for young children. Books like *The Cricket in Times Square* (Selden, 1960), *Stuart Little, Charlotte's Web,* and *The Trumpet of the Swan* (White, 1945, 1952, 1970) appeal to young children as "read alouds" and are easy enough for many young readers to comprehend independently. Because the animal characters possess human characteristics, encounter human difficulties, or launch upon human adventures, children can readily accept their behaviors, responses, and reactions.

Books in this category are often referred to as *chapter books* because, unlike picture storybooks, they contain distinct chapters. Some chapter books are excellent for teachers' daily reading because they contain complex, engaging plots and intriguing characters. Shorter chapter books are often children's first "difficult" books. Moving from picture books to multi-chapter books is often considered a real rite of passage for young readers. (Table 11.1 suggests evaluation criteria for children's fiction.)

Nonfiction

Many children enjoy **nonfiction** books, whether they are how-to or informational books, joke and humorous books, books about specific content areas, biographies, or other samples of this genre. These books serve many purposes: they increase children's knowledge about the world, satisfying their curiosity, stretching their imagination through vicarious experiences, and providing insight into the lives of people about whom they read. Children gain confidence in their abilities as they replicate experiments and observations presented in science books, make things described in how-to books, and strive to emulate the people whose biographies they read. Many children who do not enjoy fiction become readers when they encounter nonfiction books. For that reason alone, every classroom library should have a balanced selection of nonfiction books. (Table 11.1 lists criteria for evaluating nonfiction books.)

The range of nonfiction books for children is truly amazing. For example, DeGroff (1990) cites informational books with titles as provocative as *Sam Goes Trucking* (Horenstein, 1989), *Horses in the Circus Ring* (Saville, 1989), *The Skeleton Inside You* (Balestrino, 1989), and *How to be an Ocean Scientist in Your Own Home* (Simon, 1988). Authors such as Aliki have tackled a full range of topics in clearly illustrated, well-researched, easy to understand books. From her works, students can learn about dinosaurs, corn as a crop common to many cultures, medieval life, mummies, the five senses, and many other topics. One topic that may be of particular interest to beginning readers and writers is the process of making books. Aliki's *How a Book Is Made* (1986) provides correct terminology and fascinating, factual information about the production of books by publishing companies. Students can easily contrast that with information in *Making Books: A Step-by-Step Guide to Your Own Publishing* (Chapman & Robson, 1991), which also gives young learners advice on making their own books.

Books within a distinct content area, such as books in the Crowell "Let's Read and Find Out Science Series" and science books in Harper and Row's "I can read" series of picture storybooks show learners that factual information can be obtained from books. Sage (1993) reviewed many picture books that dealt with social studies topics; their value rests in the diversity of books that students can read on a single event or theme and the quality graphics that enrich text and expand students' repertoires of ways to obtain information. Included in the bibliography presented by Sage are books about the Americas, Europe, Asia, and Africa; folktales; biographies; and books about topics such as foster parents, immigration, the Vietnam War, and the eruption of Vesuvius. Many of the recommended books give young learners a sense of place (e.g., Cairo, a small steel town, the African rain forest, an Inuit village in northern Canada). The common social studies theme of changes can be reinforced with books about the cycle of time played out in various urban and rural venues. Such books also help students understand the differences between narrative and expository text structure.

Books to Expand Students' Sensitivity and Knowledge

As suggested in chapter 5, many books can support a culturally sensitive or culturally responsive curriculum. Appropriate books broaden students' sensitivity to others, their viewpoints and perceptions, and their knowledge about individuals and groups that differ from their immediate surroundings. These books may deliberately strive to instill positive values in their readers or dispel stereotypes. Or they may simply present stories or information about different ethnic groups; show girls and boys in varied, often nontraditional roles; portray the aged positively; or dispel false information about people with disabilities. Through such books, young children learn about models and information that will help them recognize both the connectedness and the differences between all people.

Multicultural/Multiethnic Literature.   Literature that meets two important criteria can help students appreciate the multicultural aspects of their society. First, books should present characters from many different cultures and races accurately, realistically, and respectfully. Characters of all ages should be depicted engaging in many different kinds of activities. Teachers may want to start with books about the cultural heritage of the students in their class; during the course of the school year, books and stories about many other different groups should be presented and discussed.

Second, literature should provide accurate, current, factual information about different cultures and people of color. Information should concern all aspects of customs, beliefs, and life-styles, from historical and contemporary perspectives. Teachers need to scrutinize books about different cultural and ethnic groups very carefully to be sure that they do not perpetuate stereotypes. Some stories overemphasize the efforts of immigrants and people of color to assimilate themselves into mainstream American life, often at the cost of the characters' ethnic and racial heritage. This perspective tends to minimize the distinctiveness of unique groups of people and thereby inappropriately validate a "melting pot" view of culture. Additionally, some books dwell entirely on the past, overlooking the way different groups of people actively engage in contemporary life.

Nonsexist Literature.   Children's literature can help young learners develop a positive, nonsexist attitude toward people around them. To accomplish this goal, literature must show a balance of male and female characters in both text and illustrations; this balance must be achieved in both fiction and nonfiction books. Until quite recently, male characters (boys and men) have predominated in children's literature, with girls and women relegated to minor roles. To help children develop nonsexist attitudes, females must be depicted in major roles in children's books—for instance, as main characters of stories and as subjects of biographies.

Good children's literature must also help to break the mold of standard gender-related stereotypes. Girls and boys, as well as women and men, should be presented in the full range of human diversity that exists in the population at large. Girls should be tough and do interesting, exciting things; they should climb trees, solve problems and mysteries, excel at mathematics and athletics, become scientists and doctors. Boys should be nurturing, sensitive, and kind; they should be teachers, librarians, and caregivers to young children. By establishing in literature that females and males demonstrate many different behavioral styles, aspire to many professions, and accomplish wide-ranging feats, teachers help students reach beyond stereotypical expectations for who they can be and what they can achieve.

Defeating Other Stereotypes and Biases.   Children's literature is also important in portraying older people in positive ways. The relationships between young children and grandparents and in general across generations within a family should be presented as warm, nurturing, supportive, and respectful. Older people should be shown as capable, vigorous, energetic individuals who contribute actively to their families.

Literature should also depict children and adults with disabling conditions in positive ways. They should be shown setting and accomplishing goals and living their lives in the least restrictive environments possible. Finally, books such as *Heather Has Two Mommies* (Newman, 1991) help students recognize that there are many different life-styles, many different definitions of "family," and many different ways of experiencing close family ties.

DEVELOPING A LITERATURE-BASED LITERACY PROGRAM

Developing and maintaining a literature-based instructional program is no small task. Teachers must accumulate materials representative of different literary genres; having approximately one hundred books is a good start for a literature program, with a goal of four hundred or so by year's end (Routman, 1989; Veatch, 1968). Many schools offer teachers "start-up" funds to build classroom libraries, and teachers can take advantage of book club offerings, library sales, garage sales, and flea markets. Teachers might consider having subscriptions to one or more magazines and should encourage students to bring in magazines they get at home (Stoll, 1994).

Keeping track of materials in the permanent class library and materials borrowed from other sources is essential. Books and materials might be categorized according to genre or topic—but not according to difficulty. Even young students quickly recognize that some books are harder than others and they select accordingly. Books should be stamped with the class name or number, and if they will go home with children, sign out cards and card pockets should be affixed to the book. Teachers may also want to keep a record of comments about books in the library by jotting down brief notations and cross-references on each book; such notes enable teachers to make recommendations to students as needed, plan effective thematic units, and add to the library collection books that are similar to those that have proven successful.

One excellent way to organize books and keep track of what students read is with the use of *text sets* (Harste, Short, & Burke, 1988). A text set includes two or more books related in some way. For example, the two books mentioned earlier about making books could be the start of a text set;

A well-stocked classroom library is essential for young learners.

this set might also include books about making paper and several magazines like *Stone Soup* that publish student writing and artwork. Table 11.2 suggests some of the dimensions around which text sets can be created. Text sets are an excellent addition to thematic units, especially when students can read independently. Not all books in sets must be read by every child, but if students read several books in common, they can discuss similarities and differences, preferences, and what each has learned from individual reading.

Students should also be encouraged to keep track of what they read and how they respond to each selection. A literature log makes this easy. Students should share their opinions about what they read by having brief discussions before guided silent reading sessions or by making weekly or monthly entries on a bulletin board. A class roster kept in a file box keeps a year-long record and helps teachers evaluate and expand their library. Individuals or small groups can compile "reviews" for inclusion in this roster or for publication in student newspapers or other publications.

Literature in the Literacy Workshop

A thoroughly planned and carefully organized workshop, as discussed in chapter 2, is the best environment for a literature-based program. Many of the activities appropriate for a literature-based literacy workshop have already been discussed and listed in previous chapters. Depending on their developmental level and the structure of the class itself, students will spend time pursuing several different activities: reading independently, often through focused literature study activities; writing independently about what they have read; and discussing literature with the teacher and classmates. In many instances, students themselves select what they will read and determine what aspect of their reading they will discuss in writing. In other cases, students read designated material to prepare for reading with the teacher or peers or to complete language arts or content area assignments.

Teachers also introduce thematic units consisting of several books about a common topic or theme. Thematic units allow students to study topics in depth. Usually there are more books suggested for a thematic unit than for a text set, although the idea of grouping books for focused study is similar. A designated topic might be literary, such as a unit on folktales; or it might be tied closely to work in science or social studies and give students experience with informational books.

In selecting books to include in thematic units, teachers need to think about breadth of choice—that is, having many different books central to the theme so that students have real choices. They also need to think about depth of coverage so that students gain real understanding, not superficial tidbits of information. Think back to the student reports cited in the last chapter; some reports reflected superficial treatment of three countries, whereas the others showed the results of students' reading deeply about a topic of interest. If

Table 11.2
Text Sets

Text sets are composed of books that vary along these dimensions:

- Presentation of the same story, differing in the form of the retelling, the cultural perspective presented, the author or illustrator, and so forth
- Story structures or basic organizational patterns
- Thematic similarities, such as books about families, friendships, being afraid, starting school, and so forth
- Text types, such as folktales, tall tales, how-to books, and science experiment books
- The same topic, regardless of genre
- The same illustrator or author
- The same character in many different stories or adventures

Possibilities include text sets of the following:

- *Amelia Bedelia*, *Nate the Great*, *Frog and Toad*, *Frances* books to be compared and contrasted; books by the same author, such as Maurice Sendak, Arnold and Anita Lobel, Daniel Pinkwater, and many others
- Books that teach concepts such as the alphabet, colors, and numbers in many different ways
- Books about issues, themes, content area topics, and so forth, especially to supplement content area study by increasing independent reading
- Books to increase students' awareness about issues such as health, civic responsibility, cultural diversity, and so forth

A Boston/Revolutionary War text set might include the following:

- *And then what happened, Paul Revere?* (Fritz)
- *Sam the Minuteman* (Benchley)
- Other easy-to-read books about the period
- *The Midnight Ride of Paul Revere* (Longfellow) (to be read by teacher and illustrated by class)
- *Johnnie Tremain* (Forbes) (to be read aloud by teacher)
- Several nonfiction books about the period
- Maps about colonial America

---

there are many books from which to select, students refine the focus of their selection process as they gain understanding about what the theme involves. They take on manageable "chunks" of study at each phase of the unit.

Activities for Focused Literature Study

A major goal for literacy workshops is to have children engage in *focused literature study.* This type of study actually begins early, within the bedtime storybook learning cycle, when a child spontaneously expresses a reaction to the story or the reader poses a thought-provoking question to the young listener. The child realizes that it is appropriate to respond to literature in some overt and thoughtful way. When children enter school, focused literature study helps them learn to analyze; judge; synthesize; evaluate, form, and express opinions; and compare works across genres, themes, and topics. Teachers know that students' responses to the literature are central to their growth and that responses will vary in form—a question or comment, sharing or retelling, an original composition, a drawing, a dramatization, or any other art form. Literature study is based on the principle that there may be no correct answers to questions posed and no single right way to respond to a text. "Meaning does not reside ready-made in the text or in the reader; it happens during the transaction between reader and text" (Rosenblatt, 1989, p. 157). By using literature study activities in a class, teachers encourage this transaction.

Teachers play an important role in helping students learn how to discuss and write about literature. Having brief *book talks,* presented by the teacher during mini lessons or to small groups, is one way of doing this. Teachers essentially talk about a book, telling a little about the plot or the contents of nonfiction, perhaps a little about the author or illustrator, and any other information that would motivate students to want to spend time with a particular book. It is also important for teachers to mention their

Children benefit from many experiences with literature, including listening to a tape as they follow along in a book. These children are listening to a book about Clifford, the big red dog; listening to the story might make them want to find other books in the series.

affective response to books they discuss by telling how much and why they liked what they read. Providing reasons to substantiate their statements lets students know that they, too, should reach for substantive comments to make about their reading. Teachers' book talks thus become a model for students' conversations about books. Specific activities can be introduced as scaffolds for young learners to supplement the models that teachers provide for discussing and writing about literature. A guide for literature discussions is presented in Table 11.3.

Having discussions about books is important for beginning readers because they provide a relatively safe environment to share the processes of making sense intellectually and emotionally about what one reads. As students tell what they think and how they have gone about comprehending what they have read, they strengthen their understanding about literacy. Students who seem reluctant to share ideas might read parts of their literature log as a starting point for shared questions and comments. Even if students' initial participation seems superficial and inauthentic, the processes of reading deeply, thinking about text, and expressing ideas will eventually develop.

Activities such as *Readers' Theater* also encourage students to think critically about what they read (see Table 11.4). The approach involves oral interpretation of pieces of literature or scripts, and even very young readers can participate. Only a few simple props—such as chairs, a hat, a flower, and so forth—are needed. Children use facial and body gestures to accompany their interpretation of what they read. To be successful participants in Readers' Theater, students must comprehend what they will present from two perspectives: that of their "part" and that of the story as a whole. Additionally, Readers' Theater enlivens—gives voice to—literature. The auditory component of preparing and listening to the presentation deepens students' sense of the literary "register," which may be vastly different from their own vernacular language. Increasing their sense of the cadence and pattern of "book language" can help students monitor their silent reading more effectively.

Dramatic or *choral reading* will foster meaningful interactions with literature for students who are not quite ready to undertake a Readers' Theater project. Simple parts can be assigned to weaker readers so that they, too, can participate. Stories that lend themselves to choral reading foster fluency—students hear the cadence of language and can follow along as they tract text visually. Teachers might also plan to read a story to the class but assign parts to specific students, who then read their sections dramatically at designated parts of the story.

Using the arts as follow-up activities can be very beneficial. Consider, for example, a situation in which some of the class members have read a book while others have listened to it. Students can still work together to create a mural, a piece of music, a dance, a pantomime, or other movement activity to recreate the story. Additionally, students can analyze and discuss

Table 11.3
Literature Discussion Groups

Participants:
- Teacher and students
- Students without teacher

Materials:
Multiple copies of high-quality literature that can withstand intensive discussion

Context:
Literature-based classroom that uses a workshop approach to instruction; several groups of students may be preparing for discussion at one time; in early childhood classes, teachers may read some or all of the story to the students and make a tape of the story available in a listening area.

Duration:
One day for a picture book; several days to a week for longer works or if works are being compared

Instructional Goal for Students:
To prepare for and participate in focused literature study during group discussion sessions

Instructional Goal for Teacher:
To increase students' ability to read deeply and with comprehension; to express their ideas fully and support them with reference to what they have read and to their personal experiences; and to engage purposefully in focused literature study

Procedures:

1. Teacher gives a short "book talk" about several books to stimulate students' interest; students sign up for the book they wish to read.

2. Students prepare for their discussion group by reading independently during workshop time or at home.

3. Students reading "chapter books" may meet daily or every few days to discuss several chapters; alternately, students must complete the entire work before the discussion period.

4. When first using the approach, the teacher asks open-ended questions such as "What is this book about?" and serves as moderator and model for discussion; as students become accustomed to the process, the teacher can play a less dominant role; the teacher may want to offer opinions rather than ask questions and should encourage students to question each other and voice what they have found satisfying and/or confusing about what they have read.

   Throughout the discussion, students offer their ideas, possibly referring to their literature logs and contrasting the meaning each participant has derived from reading.

5. At the end of each session, the teacher helps students summarize what has been discussed and set goals for the next discussion; these goals include what aspects of the book students want to discuss and may provoke students to reread parts already discussed; students may want to write in their literature logs and bring their notes to the next discussion.

6. At the end of the discussion period, students may be asked to prepare notations about the book to be kept in the class book roster or posted on the bulletin board.

continued

Table 11.3, *continued*

Alternate Approach:

If there are text sets available, students may prepare for discussion by reading one or more books in the set. Although not all books in each set must be read, at least two students should read each book that will be discussed. Then, during discussion, teacher and students compare and contrast books according to content, style, format, and other variables.

To use this approach for reading instructional groups, make these changes:

Participants:
The teacher and several students who are reading at about the same level

Materials:
Books that the students have prepared the night before

Context, Duration, and Goal:
Same as above

Procedures:

1. Students take a few minutes to review their reading before the session begins.
2. Teacher leads a discussion of the reading; the discussion seeks to establish common background knowledge, affirm purpose for reading, and check comprehension.
3. Students take turns reading whole pages of text; teacher asks high-level questions.
4. Teacher may use an overhead projector and masking strategies to engage students in a more focused interaction with difficult parts of the text.
5. Students may again take turns reading whole pages of text or the group may read orally together to "get the sounds" of the text.
6. Teacher provides focused instruction on strategies students need, with specific references to aspects of text where they would be useful.
7. Students are given a written cloze to complete independently or in pairs; the exercise consists of several paragraphs in which the teacher has blanked out all but the beginning letters of particular words that illustrate graphophonemic, syntactic, or semantic principles that need practice. Any reasonable response is accepted for completing the cloze.
8. The session ends with additional group reading for pleasure.

---

the artistic elements of children's literature. They might, for example, contrast illustrations by Chris Van Allsburg and Maurice Sendak and develop language for discussing these (and other) examples of dense, intricate art. Monson (1982) cautioned, "It is not important or encouraged that we teach children to analyze *each* piece of art, music, literature or drama closely. But it is important that we recognize some of the *commonalties among art forms and give children guidance in appreciating them*" (p. 256; emphasis added). Table 11.5 suggests activities that allow students to respond to literature through drama, the arts, writing, and other content areas.

Many follow-up activities reflect higher levels of appreciative comprehension than a child's merely saying, "Yes, I liked that book." They represent real involvement in thinking about a book and about the craft that went into constructing it.

CHILDREN'S LITERATURE AND WRITING

Enjoying, discussing, and studying literature can help children become better writers. More than a decade ago, Donald Graves (1983) wrote, "All children need literature. Children who are authors need it even more" (p. 67). Through experiences with literature, students become familiar with the

Table 11.4
Readers' Theater

Participants:
Students in a literature-based classroom

Materials:
- Multiple copies of literature or scripts
- Simple props to enhance presentation

Context:
Early childhood classroom, with strong literature focus

Duration:
A week or so for preparing the script and practicing prior to performance

Students' Goal:
To offer an interpretation of a piece of literature in a pleasurable fashion

Teacher's Goal:
To foster interpretive comprehension

Procedures:
1. Select material to present as Readers' Theater.
   - The piece should have an interesting, ideally suspenseful story line, rich language, considerable dialogue, and strong characters; folktales, especially humorous ones, are good sources.
   - Prepare the script by removing any extraneous parts from the material, shortening long speeches, and eliminating unnecessary descriptions or transitional material; the part of a narrator can be written in to provide transitions and maintain flow.
2. Prepare multiple copies of the script; participants should have the entire script, but their own parts should be highlighted for easy reading.
3. Gather minimal props, such as hats, shawls, jackets, chairs, a lamp, and so forth, if they will enhance the presentation; decide upon background music if any will be used.
4. Have students practice their parts and help them adjust pitch, intonation, volume, and so forth for a smooth delivery.
5. Present the Readers' Theater to other class members and to other audiences.

Table 11.5
Interdisciplinary Responses to Literature

Drama Activities
- Making puppets for favorite characters and presenting their story as a puppet play
- Using puppets to act out events from stories
- Writing scripts to dramatize stories
- Performing improvisational dramatics based on stories
- Performing Readers' Theater
- Developing storyboards for dramatizing stories

Art Activities
- Drawing or painting representations of what has been read
- Creating murals about individual stories or about several pieces of literature
- Designing cartoon representations of what has been read, either fiction or nonfiction
- Making dioramas
- Designing illustrations for books that have few, if any, pictures or designing new illustrations for picture books
- Creating shortened versions of stories in the form of picture books
- Drawing what characters look like based on descriptive evidence presented in stories

Writing Activities
- Developing alternate endings for stories, including adding new characters
- Adding or taking out characters and rewriting stories
- Writing letters to authors or illustrators (send in care of their publishers)
- Writing letters to characters in books
- Writing letters, diaries, and so on from the perspective of characters in fiction or nonfiction books
- Turning narratives into scripts; writing scripts about nonfiction books, especially history books
- Writing newspaper accounts of real events

Other Content Areas
- Developing long-term research projects
- Finding other books, newspaper accounts, and nonprint sources to supplement what has been read
- Finding primary sources about what has been read

skills and devices of writing and discover themes and topics to write about. Two forms of writing evolve directly from literature study: writing *about the literature* and writing *based on the literature*. Additionally, literature has many less direct influences on young writers' choice of words, sentence structure, and literary devices; children learn to write with flair and confidence, with accuracy and precision.

Writing about literature is not the same as writing dull, inauthentic book reports; it involves responding to a whole book or to favorite characters or events. If teachers allow drawing as well as writing, even beginners can respond in this way. Children who keep journals on a regular basis should be asked to make entries about their reading and may even keep a *literature log;* these are records of their thinking about their reading and their questions and observations during reading. Literature logs are never graded; they may be shared with peers during book discussions and used in writing about what has been read. When literature logs are first introduced, children might draw and write only the title; but eventually they write questions about what they read, reactions to ideas and characters, and indications of difficulties they have had. Literature logs provide a written trail of students' processes of constructing meaning from text. They also help teachers understand what students are learning about reading and can be part of the classroom-based assessment process. By combining the raw evidence in students' logs, knowledge of the students, and familiarity with the books being read, teachers can draw preliminary conclusions about students' reading skills, strategies, and preferences.

Students may also write *literary letters* to be sent to the teacher and peers. These focus on what students have read and on their responses. Because these are more public than literature logs, they must be more carefully crafted. Students may also write letters to authors and actually send them through book publishers. Figure 11.2 shows a series of such letters that I have treasured over the years.

Literature can also be a springboard for writing. It provides beginners with direct models, which students may initially just shorten and copy. Yet, copies gradually become "liftings" as children personalize another author's ideas or adopt phrases, choice words, or imagery. In time, children edit or revise stories; change plots, settings, or characters; or use only the basic framework and title. This writing is not as derivative as it may at first seem. Far from being a passive activity, such writing involves analysis and reconstruction of the text itself and of the author's craft, the illustrations, the ideas presented, and the format for presenting those ideas. Sometimes, as shown in sample 3 in Figure 11.1, young writers use characters they have encountered on television as well as in books; their writing can often take on unexpected twists.

Children can adopt characters from books in series like Hoban's *Frances* or Lobel's *Frog and Toad* and write new adventures. Sample 4 in Figure 11.1 shows a story written in response to *Alexander and the Terrible, Horrible, No Good, Very Bad Day.* Most children are fascinated by the "terrible day" theme, but they differ widely in the extent to which they experiment with it in their own writing. Some generate relatively bland stories with perfectly possible, not really "terrible" events. Others are more creative in their terribleness. Still others, like the child whose writing is shown, reverse the theme entirely. Literature like the Alexander story lets children

Figure 11.1
Influence of Literature on
Children's Writing

He
Ham
HAS
A
C ¢ t

Sample 1.   A kindergarten writer combined elements of Dr. Seuss books to create a story of his very own.

Max was wearing a wild coat.
And mother sent max to bed without any supper.
And maxs bedroom grew until it was a jungle.

Sample 2.   A reluctant first-grade writer drew upon his knowledge of *Where the Wild Things Are* as an aid in creating this short story.

continued

My Wondeful, Most, Good Super Day

You know want happen to day When
I woke up I woke up bightander lyy
befor my. Mommy and Daddy soerly
it was 5:00 o dock I got dresst
and ate my brefeest and when.
I was thow with at my mommy
woke up and my daddy woke up too.
Then at school and I had super
work. I now want a My Wondeful
Most Good super day. and at
lunch a good thing happen I had
a good dsert.

The Plan

Once upon a time
ther were a bun/ named
Big Burd and a grouch
named o scur the grouch.
One morning they
went in a plan and
the plan crashed
Big Burd died ocur died
even the pilot died loo
The because one other
plane came.

Sample 3. This writer borrowed characters from Sesame Street books and television shows but put them in a totally unique situation on a plane. She had carefully planned her story using a story map and seemed to take great delight in doing away with characters whom she claimed she had never liked. Her story map indicated that the plane crash occurred because "annoter plane went in front," but this reason was not transferred fully to the story itself.

Sample 4. A second grader enjoyed listening to and reading *Alexander and the Terrible, Horrible, No Good, Very Bad Day* and then wrote her own version of the story.

Figure 11.1, *concluded*

279

Figure 11.2
Letters Written by First
Graders to E. B. White

to mr. E. B. White,
I want to tell you How
much I enjoyed reading
Stuart Little, Charlottes web
and trumpet of the swan
thank you for writing These
FabbaLas Books!!

June 3, 1976

Dear, Mr. E.B. White,
I liked your books, The
Trumpet of the Swan,
Stuart Little, and Charlotte's
Web. I like Stuart Little
the best. If you wrote any
more I diden't read them
yet.

Sincerely. Jessika

realize that stories do not have to be about "nice" things only, helps them externalize feelings, legitimizes discussing them, and affirms that these themes can be written about. With models of ideas, models of writing style, and permission to "lift" from favorite literature, children are caught less frequently with "nothing to write about."

If a classroom library has ample supplies of nonfiction books, periodicals, and other print reference materials, students will come to view literature as a source of information about which to write. They will learn to go to the classroom library to find ideas for stories, information about topics they want to consider in writing, and data to support the points they want to make.

Children also need to be surrounded by the *sounds of literature*. There are many excellent recordings of children's literature, some of the authors themselves reading their work. Multimedia presentations can also make literature real and exciting to children. This kind of treatment of children's literature should not be merely a replacement for teachers' oral reading, Readers' Theater, and other interactions with real books; however, carefully selected and judiciously used, audiotapes and videotapes can be excellent tools for involving children in literature.

The Library

A classroom library is essential for a strong early literacy program, but teachers would do well to extend students' experiences beyond their own school room. A school library is a good place to accustom children to the card catalog, shelves of books, and personal criteria for selecting books to borrow. School librarians are usually very helpful and welcoming.

If there is a public library located within walking distance of the school, teachers might take students on a field trip to get library cards, listen to a story, and begin a lifelong habit of library use. As a beginning teacher in Brooklyn, New York, I took my first and second graders to the big, main library every three weeks. And it was indeed big! Many of the children had never been inside such a huge building. At first dwarfed by the marble main entry, the students quickly became comfortable in the smaller-scale children's room. Over time, they learned to use the card catalog independently and to turn respectfully to the librarian as a resource person. They felt at home, and they felt competent as they applied their alphabet skills to the card catalog, found familiar books on the shelves, asked for help finding books on interesting topics, and learned to make choices based on their emerging preferences for different kinds of books.

SUMMARY

Early childhood classrooms need to be filled with books so that young learners can practice their beginning skills and strategies with the real stuff—books, ideas, stories, science experiments, social studies facts, and so forth among the wide range of topics and themes found in children's literature. Children's reading in real books gives them interesting ideas and information to share in writing and in discussion with their peers and motivates them to continue their growth in literacy.

QUESTIONS AND TASKS FOR INDEPENDENT AND COLLABORATIVE WORK

1. Be sure that you can define each of the following terms:

   - picture books
   - traditional literature
   - fiction
   - realistic fiction
   - historical fiction
   - fantastic fiction
   - nonfiction

2. Select several books from among those mentioned in this chapter or find others that you like. Share them with several children and carefully record their responses. What do you notice? What relationships might there be among children's gender, age, and book type?

3. Find several examples of fiction and nonfiction that deal with important issues. Analyze them for content, style, and accuracy. In what ways are they good? In what ways are they inadequate?

4. Find a "chapter book," perhaps one that you remember from your childhood or one your own children enjoy. What criteria did you use to make your selection? Skim the book and determine whether it measures up to your criteria. In what ways did it disappoint you? Think about activities you would use to accompany the oral sharing of the book with young learners.

5. Gather several books and other print material that would make a good text set to use with young children. What criteria did you use in making your selections? Share your text set with another student in your class and evaluate each other's selections.

APPENDIX A

Useful References for Early Childhood Teachers

BACKGROUND AND GENERAL INFORMATION

Adams, M. J. (1990). *Beginning to read: Thinking and learning about print.* Cambridge, MA: MIT Press.

Butler, D., & Clay, M. (1987). *Reading begins at home.* Portsmouth, NH: Heinemann.

Butler, D., & Clay, M. (1988). *Writing begins at home.* Portsmouth, NH: Heinemann.

Cazden, C. B. (1988). *Classroom discourse: The language of teaching and learning.* Portsmouth, NH: Heinemann.

Chandler, P. (1993). *A place for me: Including children with special needs in early care and education settings.* Washington, DC: National Association for the Education of Young Children.

Cullinan, B. E. (Ed.). (1993). *Pen in hand: Children become writers.* Newark, DE: International Reading Association.

Cullinan, B. E. (Ed.). (1994). *Children's voices: Talk in the classroom.* Newark, DE: International Reading Association.

Edelsky, C., Altwerger, B., & Flores, B. (1991). *Whole language: What's the difference?* Portsmouth, NH: Heinemann.

Goodman, Y. M. (Ed.). (1990). *How children construct literacy.* Newark, DE: International Reading Association.

Harste, J. C., Woodward, V. A., & Burke, C. L. (1984). *Language stories and literacy lessons.* Portsmouth, NH: Heinemann.

Heath, S. B. (1983). *Ways with words: Language, life, and work in communities and classrooms.* Cambridge: Cambridge University Press.

Jones, E., & Nimmo, J. (1993). *Emergent curriculum.* Washington, DC: National Association for the Education of Young Children.

McCracken, J. B. (1993). *Valuing diversity: The primary years.* Washington, DC: National Association for the Education of Young Children.

Meek, M. (1982). *Learning to read.* London: The Bodley Head.

Meek, M., Warlow, A., & Barton, G. (Eds.). (1977). *The cool web: The pattern of children's reading.* London: The Bodley Head.

Neugebauer, B. (Ed.). (1992). *Alike and different: Exploring our humanity with young children.* Washington, DC: National Association for the Education of Young Children.

Pignatelli, F., & Pflaum, S. W. (Eds.). (1993). *Celebrating diverse voices.* Newbury Park, CA: Corwin Press.

Routman, R. (1989). *Transitions.* Portsmouth, NH: Heinemann.

Routman, R. (1991). *Invitations: Changing as teachers and learners, K–12.* Portsmouth, NH: Heinemann.

Spangenberg-Urbschat, K., & Pritchard, R. (Eds.). (1994). *Kids come in all languages: Reading instruction for ESL students.* Newark, DE: International Reading Association.

ASSESSMENT ISSUES

Barrs, M., Ellis, S., Tester, H., & Thomas, A. (1989). *The primary language record: Handbook for teachers.* Portsmouth, NH: Heinemann.

Harp, B. (Ed.). (1991). *Assessment and evaluation in whole language programs.* Norwood, MA: Christopher-Gordon.

Kamii, C. (Ed.). (1990). *Achievement testing in the early grades: The games grown-ups play.* Washington, DC: National Association for the Education of Young Children.

Valencia, S. W., Hiebert, E. H., & Afflerbach, P. P. (Eds.). (1993). *Authentic reading assessment: Practices and possibilities.* Newark, DE: International Reading Association.

LITERATURE

Cullinan, B. E. (1989). *Literature and the child.* San Diego: Harcourt Brace Jovanovich.

Cullinan, B. E. (Ed.). (1987). *Children's literature in the reading program.* Newark, DE: International Reading Association.

Cullinan, B. E. (Ed.). (1992). *Invitation to read: More children's literature in the reading program.* Newark, DE: International Reading Association.

International Reading Association & The Children's Book Council. (1992). *Kid's favorite books: Children's choices 1989–1991.* Newark, DE: International Reading Association.

Slaughter, J. P. (1993). *Beyond storybooks: Young children and the shared book experience.* Newark, DE: International Reading Association.

Stewig, S. W., & Sebesta, S. L. (Eds.). (1989). *Using literature in the elementary classroom.* Urbana, IL: National Council of Teachers of English.

Stoll, D. R. (Ed.). (1994). *Magazines for kids and teens.* Newark, DE: International Reading Association.

Trelease, J. (1985). *The read-aloud handbook.* New York: Penguin.

Trelease, J. (Ed.). (1992). *Hey! Listen to this: Stories to read aloud.* Newark, DE: International Reading Association.

TEACHER-RESEARCHERS

Bissex, G. L., & Bullock, R. H. (Eds.). (1987). *Seeing for ourselves: Case-study research by teachers of writing.* Portsmouth, NH: Heinemann.

Calkins, L. M. (1991). *Living between the lines.* Portsmouth, NH: Heinemann.

Goswami, D., & Stillman, P. R. (Eds.). (1987). *Reclaiming the classroom: Teacher research as an agency for change.* Upper Montclair, NJ: Boynton/Cook.

Olson, M. W. (Ed.). (1990). *Opening the door to classroom research.* Newark, DE: International Reading Association.

BOOKS OF GENERAL INTEREST FOR DISCUSSION AND DEBATE

Kidder, T. (1989). *Among school children.* New York: Avon.

Kotlowitz, A. (1991). *There are no children here: The story of two boys growing up in the other America.* New York: Doubleday.

Kozol, J. (1991). *Savage inequities: Children in America's schools.* New York: Crown.

Shannon, R. (1989). *Broken promises: Reading instruction in twentieth-century America.* Granby, MA: Bergin & Garvey.

JOURNALS AND NEWSLETTERS

The Reading Teacher
International Reading Association
800 Barksdale Road
P.O. Box 8139
Newark, DE 19714-8139

Language Arts and Primary Voices
National Council of Teachers of English
1111 Kenyon Road
Urbana, IL 61801

Teachers Networking: The Whole Language Newsletter
Richard C. Owen Publishers, Inc.
P.O. Box 585
Katonah, NY 10536

Young Children
National Association for the Education of Young Children
1509 16th Street, NW
Washington, DC 20036

Journals Devoted to Children's Literature

The Horn Book Magazine
The Horn Book
14 Beacon Street
Boston, MA 02108

The New Advocate
Christopher-Gordon Publishers
480 Washington Street
Norwood, MA 02062

For information and bibliographies on children's literature, contact the following:

Children's Book Council
67 Irving Place
New York, NY 10003

CHILDREN'S BOOKS

The following lists present a sample of the many excellent books available for young children. Veatch (1968) suggested a minimum of one hundred books for a permanent classroom library—and that does not include the seasonal or content-related books that rotate in and out of a classroom to meet immediate needs. Investing in books is perhaps the best step early childhood teachers can take toward making their classrooms literate—such an investment can have a long-term impact on children's attitudes toward reading and the sense of the utility of books in their lives.

Books mentioned in the text are indicated with an asterisk (*).

Narratives (including storybooks, chapter books, and classics)

*Bridwell, N. (1988). *Clifford, the big red dog* (and others in the series). New York: Scholastic .

Brando, M. W. (1926). *The velveteen rabbit.* Garden City, NY: Doubleday.

Brown, M. W. (1942/1972). The runaway bunny (and others by the same author). New York: Harper.

Brown, M. W. (1947). *Good night moon.* New York: Harper & Row.

Buckley, H. E. (1994). *Grandfather and I.* New York: Lothrop, Lee & Shepard.

Carle, E. (1971). *Do you want to be my friend?* New York: Harper.

Carlson, N. (1989). *I like me!* New York: Viking.

Cohen, M. (1967). *Will I have a friend?* New York: Macmillan.

Cohen, M. (1977). *When will I read?* New York: Greenwillow Books.

de Paola, T. (1973). *Nana upstairs and nana downstairs* (and others by the same author). New York: G.P. Putnam's Sons.

Ets, M. H. (1955). *Play with me.* New York: Viking.

Flack, M. (1933). *The story about Ping.* New York: Viking.

*Forbes, E. (1946). *Johnnie Tremain.* Boston: Houghton Mifflin.

*Fox, M. (1992). *Time for bed.* San Diego: Harcourt Brace.

Freeman, D. (1968). *Corduroy.* New York: Viking.

*Hill, E. S. (1991). *Evan's corner.* New York: Viking.

*Hoban, R. (1964). *A baby sister for Frances* (and others in the series). New York: Harper & Row.

*Huck, C. (1990). *Princess Furball.* New York: Greenwillow.

Johnson, C. (1958). *Harold and the purple crayon.* New York: Harper & Row.

*Keats, E. J. (1967). *Peter's chair* (and others by the same author). New York: Harper & Row.

Krauss, R. (1945). *The carrot seed.* New York: Harper & Row.

*Lansky, B. (1993). *The new adventures of Mother Goose: Gentle rhymes for happy times.* Deephaven, MN: Meadowbrook.

Leonni, L. (1966). *Frederick.* New York: Pantheon.

*Lobel, A. (1979). *Frog and Toad are friends* (and others by the same author). New York: Harper & Row.

*Mayer, M. (1968). *There's a nightmare in my closet.* New York: Dial Press.

McCloskey, R. (1941). *Make way for ducklings.* New York: Viking.

Minarik, E. H. (1957). *Little Bear.* New York: Harper & Row.

Ness, E. (1966). *Sam, Bangs, and Moonshine.* New York: Holt, Rinehart & Winston.

*Newman, L. (1991). *Heather has two mommies.* Boston: Alyson Publications, Inc.

*Pfister, M. *The rainbow fish.* New York: North-South.

Raskin, E. (1968). *Spectacles.* New York: Atheneum.

*Say, A. (1993). *Grandfather's journey.* Boston: Houghton Mifflin.

*Scieszka, J. (1989). *The true story of the three little pigs.* New York: Viking.

*Selden, G. (1960). *The cricket in Times Square.* New York: Dell.

*Sendak, M. (1963). *Where the wild things are* (and others by the same author). New York: Harper & Row.

*Seuss, Dr. (1940). *Horton hatches an egg* (and others by the same author). New York: Random House.

Steig, W. (1969). *Sylvester and the magic pebble.* New York: Farrar, Strauss, & Giroux.

Steptoe, J. (1969). *Stevie.* New York: Harper & Row.

*Steptoe, J. (1987). *Mufaro's beautiful daughter.* New York: Lothrop, Lee & Shepard.

Urdy, J. M. (1961). *Let's be enemies.* New York: Harper & Row.

*Viorst, J. (1972). *Alexander and the terrible, horrible, no good, very bad day.* New York: Atheneum.

*Waber, B. (1963). *Rich cat, poor cat.* Boston: Houghton Mifflin.

*Wegman, W. (1994). *Cinderella.* New York: Hyperion.

*White, E. B. (1945). *Stuart Little.* New York: Harper & Row.

*White, E. B. (1952). *Charlotte's web.* New York: Harper & Row.

*White, E. B. (1970). *The trumpet of the swan.* New York: Harper & Row.

*Wiseman, B. (1970). *Morris the Moose goes to school* (and others in the series). New York: Harper & Row.

Yashima, T. (1955). *Crow boy.* New York: Viking.

Zolotow, C. (1963). *The quarreling book.* New York: Harper & Row.

Animal, History, Science, and Other Informational Books (except dinosaurs; mostly nonfiction)

Aliki (1962). *My five senses.* New York: Harper & Row.

Aliki (1976). *Corn is maize.* New York: Thomas Y. Crowell.

Arnosky, I. (1979). *Crinkleroot's book of animal tracks and wildlife signs.* New York: G.P. Putnam's Sons.

*Balestrino, P. (1989). *The skeleton inside you.* New York: Crowell.

*Benchley, N. (1969). *Sam the Minuteman.* New York: Harper & Row.

Benchley, N. (1972). *Small wolf.* New York: Harper & Row.

Bendick, J. (1971). *How to make a cloud.* New York: Parents Magazine Press.

Bendick, J. (1975). *Ecology.* New York: Franklyn Watts.

Brenner, B. (1978). *Wagon wheels.* New York: Harper & Row.

Busch, P. (1972). *Exploring as you walk in the city.* Philadelphia: J.B. Lippincott.

Carle, E. (1969). *Very hungry caterpillar.* New York: Philomel.

Carle, E. (1975). *Mixed-up chameleon.* New York: Crowell-Collier Press.

Carle, E. (1977). *Grouchy Ladybug.* New York: Harper & Row.

*Chapman, G., & Robson, P. (1991). *Making books.* Brookfield, CT: Millbrook Press.

Chlad, D. (1982). *Matches, lighters, and firecrackers are not toys.* New York: Children's Press.

Crews, D. (1980). *Truck.* New York: Greenwillow Books.

Crews, D. (1981). *Light.* New York: Greenwillow Books.

Crews, D. (1982). *Harbor.* New York: Greenwillow Books.

de Paola, T. (1977). *The quicksand book.* New York: Holiday House.

de Paola, T. (1978). *The popcorn book.* New York: Holiday House.

de Paola, T. (1980). *The cloud book.* New York: Holiday House.

*Fritz, J. (1972). *And then what happened, Paul Revere?* (and other historical books by the same author). New York: Crowell.

Gans, R. (1964). *Icebergs.* New York: Thomas Y. Crowell.

Ginsberg, M. (1981). *Where does the sun go at night?* New York: Greenwillow Books.

Holl, A. (1965). *Rain puddle.* New York: Lothrop, Lee & Shepard.

*Horenstein, H. (1989). *Sam goes trucking.* Boston: Houghton Mifflin.

Hutchins, P. (1970). *Clocks and more clocks.* New York: Macmillan.

Hutchins, P. (1974). *The wind blew.* New York: Macmillan.

Komori, A. (1983). *Animal mothers.* New York: Philomel.

Lauber, P. (1979). *What's hatching out of that egg?* New York: Crown.

*Saville, L. (1989). *Horses in the circus ring.* New York: Dutton.

Showers, P. (1967). *How you talk.* New York: Harper & Row.

Showers, P. (1975). *Hear your heart.* New York: Harper & Row.

Showers, P. (1980). *No measles, no mumps for me.* New York: Harper & Row.

*Simon, S. (1988). *How to be an ocean scientist in your own home.* New York: Lippincott.

Wulffson, D. (1981). *The invention of ordinary things.* New York: Lothrop, Lee & Shepard.

Dinosaur Books

Aliki (1971). *My trip to the dinosaurs.* New York: Harper Trophy.

Aliki (1972). *Fossils tell of long ago.* New York: Harper Trophy.

Aliki (1981). *Digging up dinosaurs.* New York: Harper Trophy.

Aliki (1985). *Dinosaurs are different.* New York: Harper Trophy.

Jacobs, F. (1982). *Supersaurus.* New York: Putnam.

Most, B. (1978). *If the dinosaurs came back.* New York: Harcourt Brace Jovanovich.

Sattler, H. (1981). *Dinosaurs of North America.* New York: Lothrop, Lee & Shepard.

Sattler, H. (1984). *Baby dinosaurs.* New York: Lothrop, Lee & Shepard.

Alphabet Books

Alexander, A. (1971). *ABC of cars and trucks.* New York: Doubleday.

Anno, M. (1974). *Anno's alphabet: An adventure in imagination.* New York: Thomas Y. Crowell.

Barry, K. (1961). *A is for everything.* New York: Harcourt, Brace and World.

Beisner, M. (1981). *A folding alphabet book.* New York: Farrar, Strauss, & Giroux.

Brown, M. (1974). *All butterflies.* New York: Charles Scribner's Sons.

Duvolsin, R. (1952). *A for the ark.* New York: Lothrop, Lee & Shepard.

Elting, M., & Folsom, M. (1980). *Q is for duck: An alphabet guessing game.* New York: Clarion Books.

Emberley, E. (1978). *Ed Emberley's ABC.* Boston: Little, Brown & Company.

Feelings, M., & Feelings, T. (1974). *Jambo means hello: Swahili alphabet books.* New York: Dial Press.

Isadora, R. (1983). *City seen from A to Z.* New York: Greenwillow Books.

Kitchen, B. (1984). *Animal alphabet.* New York: Dial Press.

Lear, E. (1965). *Lear alphabet—Penned and illustrated by Edward Lear himself.* New York: McGraw-Hill.

*Lobel, A., & Lobel, A. (1981). *On Market Street.* New York: Greenwillow Books.

Montresor, B. (1969). *A for angel: Beni Montresor's ABC picture stories.* New York: Alfred Knopf.

Musgrove, M. (1976). *Ashanti to Zulu: African traditions.* New York: Dial Press.

Niland, D. (1976). *ABC of monsters.* New York: McGraw-Hill.

Parish, D. (1969). *A beastly circus.* New York: Macmillan.

Provensen, A., & Provensen, M. (1978). *A peaceable kingdom: The shaker ABECEDARIUS.* New York: Viking.

Sendak, M. (1962). *Alligators all around: An alphabet book.* New York: Harper & Row.

Tallon, R. (1969). *An ABC in English and Spanish.* New York: Lion Press.

Tudor, T. (1954). *A is for Annabelle.* New York: Rand McNally.

*Wegman, W. (1994). *ABCs.* New York: Hyperion.

Yolen, J. (1991). *All in the woodland early: An ABC book.* Honesdale, PA: Boyds Mills Press.

Wordless Books

Alexander, M. (1970). *Bobo's dream.* New York: Dial Press.

Carle, E. (1971). *Do you want to be my friend?* New York: Crowell-Collier.

Cristini, E., & Puricelli, L. (1983a). *In my garden.* Boston: Picture Book Studio.

Cristini, E., & Puricelli, L. (1983b). *In the woods.* Boston: Picture Book Studio.

Cristini, E., & Puricelli, L. (1984). *In the pond.* Boston: Picture Book Studio.

Knobler, S. (1974). *Tadpole and the frog.* New York: Harvey House.
Krahn, F. (1974). *Flying saucers full of spaghetti.* New York: E.P. Dutton.
Mayer, M. (1977). *Oops.* New York: Dial Press.

Predictable Books

Becker, J. (1973). *Seven little rabbits.* New York: Scholastic.
Carle, E. (1969). *The very hungry caterpillar.* Cleveland: Collins World.
Keats, E. J. (1971). *Over in the meadow.* New York: Scholastic.
Martin, B. (1970). *Brown Bear, Brown Bear* (and others by the same author). New York: Holt, Rinehart & Winston.
Mayer, M. (1968). *If I had. . . .* New York: Dial Press.
Mayer, M. (1975). *Just for you.* New York: Golden Press.
Preston, E. M. (1978). *Where did my mother go?* New York: Four Winds Press.

Books That Emphasize Language

Einsel, W. (1972). *Did you ever see?* New York: Scholastic.
Emberley, E. (1967). *Drummer Hoff.* New York: Prentice Hall.
*Emberley, R. (1994). *My day/Mi dia.* Boston: Little, Brown.
*Emberley, R. (1994). *Let's go/Vamos.* Boston: Little, Brown.
Gwynn, F. (1972). *The king who rained.* New York: Windmill.
Gwynn, F. (1973). *A chocolate mouse for dinner.* New York: E.P. Dutton.
Parish, P. (1963). *Amelia Bedelia.* New York: Harper & Row.
Spier, P. (1971). *Gobble, growl, grunt.* New York: Doubleday.
Spier, P. (1972). *Crash, bang, boom.* New York: Doubleday.

APPENDIX B

Checklists, Record-Keeping Forms, and Questions for Classroom Use

The checklists, forms, and other materials that follow should be considered only a starting point and guide for teachers. To be really effective, record-keeping materials must be developed by the teachers who will use them—to meet their own purposes and to reflect the characteristics of the students who will be assessed.

SAMPLE CHECKLISTS FOR RECORDING STUDENTS' PROGRESS

Name _____

Focus of Checklist _____

			Dates		

Selects appropriate topics:
    When given choice
    When general topic is selected					

Demonstrates strategies for planning (e.g., brainstorming)					
Demonstrates understanding of drafting processes					

Revises work:
    Adds/deletes information
    Reorganizes
    Considers vocabulary/word choice
    Considers grammar					

Sample 1
Checklist for Individual Student

Focus of Checklist: _____

Date Compiled: _____

	Susan	David	Nancy	Peter	Ana
Reads familiar material fluently					
Reads with appropriate intonation					
Reads with appropriate expression					
Self-corrects					
Uses punctuation to guide reading					
Takes risks in pronouncing unfamiliar words					
Demonstrates strategies for decoding unfamiliar words:					
Skips word and continues to read					
Rereads entire sentence					
Uses picture clues					
Uses context clues					
Sounds word out					
Asks for help					
Other strategies evident					

ETC...

Sample 2
Checklist for Group of Students

SAMPLE ANECDOTAL RECORD FORMS

Directions: This record can be kept over an extended period of time.

Student _____

Date	Reading	Writing	Oral Language	Spontaneous Uses of Literacy

Sample 1
Individual Student

Directions: This record is best limited to a single observation or observations conducted over a short period of time, such as one week.

Date(s) of Observation _____

Reading _____   Writing _____   Other activities _____

Name_____	Name_____	Name_____
Name_____	Name_____	Name_____

Sample 2
Small Group or Whole Class

INTERVIEW TO ASSESS STUDENTS' ATTITUDES TOWARD READING AND WRITING AND TO ASSESS LITERACY STRATEGIES

Ask the following questions in an informal conference and make notations about answers as unobtrusively as possible. Change questions to suit students' needs, levels of understanding, and interactional styles.

- Do you like to write? What do you like to write?
- When do you like to write?
- Do you ever write at home? What do you write there?
- Do you think you are a good writer? What makes you think so?[*]
- Do you like to read? What do you like to read about?
- When do you like to read?
- Do you ever read at home? What do you read there?
- Do you think you are a good reader? What makes you think so?[*]
- How do you select books you read? What kinds do you like?
- How does someone get to be a good reader?
- What do you do if you don't know a word in what you are reading?
- What do you do if you don't understand what you read?
- What would you say to help someone who is having trouble learning to read?
- What does someone do to get to be a good writer?
- How do you decide what you will write about?
- When you can't think of something to write, what do you do?
- When you can't think of how to spell a word, what do you do?
- What would you say to help someone who is just learning to write?

QUESTIONS TO DETERMINE YOUNG CHILDREN'S INTEREST IN AND PREPARATION FOR LITERACY INSTRUCTION

Ask the following sets of questions about each child. If answers are no, determine whether the child is fearful and reluctant or merely immature.

---

[*] Answers to these questions can be especially telling because of students' attributions. For example, they may attribute their competence or incompetence to the grades they receive, to the amount of skills they have accumulated or to their proficiency or weakness in using them, to external sources (such as in thinking, "My teacher says I am . . . "), or to their own feelings about reading and writing (such as in thinking, "I like to write, so I'm a good writer"). When students attribute competence to skills or grades, they often do not fully recognize their own contribution to achievement and do not fully appreciate the control they can have over their own learning. Discrepancies between students' assessment of their competence and teachers' assessment must be dealt with—directly and immediately, but tactfully. If students are to become truly engaged in their learning and if they are to be able to evaluate their own progress, they must become realistic about their own skills and strategies. This kind of accurate self-awareness is an aspect of metacognition.

Balance the profile that emerges about each child against age, family background, previous school experience, and general health. Evaluate children as individuals, but also evaluate the overall class situation to determine how best to support emerging literacy for all children.

Questions about Books

- Does the child seem interested in or curious about books? Does he or she know how to handle books?
- Is the child aware that books convey meaning?
- Does the child enjoy listening to stories and know how to respond to questions about them?
- Does the child reenact storybooks, either verbally or in drawing?
- Does the child ever draw, write, or talk about stories he or she has heard?
- Is there indication that the child has books at home?
- Does the child track print when he or she is read to? Is tracking left to right?

Questions about Environmental Print and Writing

- Can the child recognize some environmental print, even if he or she reads a supermarket logo as "Food Store"?
- Does the child seem to know any sight words?
- Has the child begun to "write," even if the writing is scribbles?
- What level of sophistication do the child's writing and invented spelling show?
- Is the child's drawing merely random or does it show an intended organization?
- Does the child seem to like to work with art materials, pencils, and pens?
- Does the child attend to art activities long enough to complete a finished product?
- Is there any indication of awareness of left-to-right orientation in art or writing activities?
- Does the child recognize his or her own name, even if the child cannot write it clearly?
- Can the child identify letters of the alphabet in sequence and in isolation?
- Can the child write letters of the alphabet reasonably well in sequence and in isolation?
- Does the child know any letter–sound correspondences?

Questions about Physical Capabilities

- Does the child seem able to focus near and far away?
- Can the child hold pencils and crayons comfortably and use them efficiently? Can the child use scissors?
- Has the child demonstrated hand dominance?
- Can the child sit still for a reasonable amount of time?
- Can the child stand still for a reasonable amount of time? Can he or she walk in line for a reasonable amount of time?

Questions about Concepts and Language

- Does the child have names for colors, shapes, and so forth? (Names may be in English or in child's first language if not English.) Does the child understand terms for time, space, and causality?
- Does the child seem fluent in expressing wants and needs (within normal range for age and sense of pragmatics)?
- Is the child interested in and capable of learning new vocabulary?
- Can the child stick to the point when carrying on a conversation?
- Does vocabulary in English or in dominant language seem appropriate for age and experiential background?
- Is the word order in the child's sentences relatively correct and stable?
- Is the order of syllables correct in most polysyllabic terms (e.g., not "coaster roller" for "roller coaster")?
- Does the child seem to have control of most of the consonant and vowel sounds of his or her dialect and language community? Is articulation mostly clear and easy to understand?
- Does the child seem able to understand and carry out simple oral directions?
- If the child is learning English as a second language, does this seem to be happening naturally through interactions with English-speaking peers and from direct instruction?
- Do there appear to be any hearing problems?

Questions about Emotions

- Does the child seem overly shy? How assertive or passive is the child?
- Does the child take reasonable risks? Or is he or she easily intimidated?
- Can the child attend to tasks happily?
- What is the child's apparent level of energy, stamina, and general health?
- What are the child's expectations for school?

- What are the parents' expectations? Are they reasonable and age appropriate?
- How supportive are the parents or caregivers? Do they show an interest in the school curriculum and seem to understand it?

THE SOUTH BRUNSWICK EARLY LITERACY SCALE

This scale was developed by early childhood teachers for use in scoring their students' literacy portfolios. To develop the scale, teachers stated behaviors demonstrated by beginning readers and writers, ordered the behaviors developmentally, and then compared the scale against student work to determine how well it actually reflected students' growth. Teachers developed five drafts of the scale before they were fully satisfied that they could use the scale reliably to evaluate student portfolios.

Only highlights of the scale are given here. Teachers who want to use a scale to evaluate their own students' work should discuss these behaviors, add others that they observe in their own classes, and make the scale meaningful for them. By "fleshing out" this outline, teachers can better understand the developmental nature of this set of descriptors of early literacy behavior.

THE SIX LEVELS

6   ADVANCED INDEPENDENT READER
- Uses multiple strategies flexibly
- Monitors and self-corrects
- Controls most conventions of writing and spelling

5   EARLY INDEPENDENT READER
- Handles familiar material on own but needs some support with unfamiliar material
- Draws on multiple cues to figure out unfamiliar words and to self-correct
- Uses strategies such as rereading and guessing
- Has large, stable sight vocabulary
- Understands conventions of writing

4   ADVANCED BEGINNING READER
- Uses major cueing system for word identification and self-correction
- Requires some support with unfamiliar material
- Shows awareness of letter patterns and conventions of writing, such as full stops and capitalization

3   EARLY BEGINNING READER
- Shows sense of letter–sound correspondence and concept of words
- Uses syntax and story line to predict unfamiliar words in new material
- Has small but stable sight vocabulary
- Shows awareness of beginning and ending sounds in invented spelling

2 ADVANCED EMERGENT READER
- Engages in pretend reading and writing
- Uses sense of story structure, predictable language, and picture cues in retelling stories; retellings use approximations of booklike language
- Can anticipate story elements
- Attempts to use letters in writing

1 EARLY EMERGENT READER
- Shows awareness of some conventions of book structure (such as back and front) and the distinction between pictures and text
- Shows little understanding that print conveys meaning in books and other documents; thinks meaning is external to print
- Shows little interest in reading for himself or herself, although is interested in listening to stories
- Notices some environmental print

APPENDIX C

Home–School Support

TEACHER- OR SCHOOL-MADE BROCHURE FOR CAREGIVERS ABOUT THEIR CHILD'S LITERACY DEVELOPMENT

Purpose.   To give parents a brief overview of what their children are learning

Characteristics.   Short; colorful; written in easy-to-understand language; well illustrated

Contents
- *Introduction:* State goals for children's academic work and expectations of what will be accomplished.
- *Role of parents:* Stress importance of home–school connection.
- *Steps caregivers can take:* Briefly but clearly state activities that caregivers and children can engage in; suggest routines (such as book talks or homework) that should be established.
- *Materials:* Suggest the kinds of books and materials parents should try to provide.
- *Other readings:* Either provide or suggest other sources of information about the home–school connection and reading and writing growth.

OTHER HELPFUL BROCHURES

Baghban, M. (1990). *You can help your young child with writing / Ayude a su nino con la escritura.* Newark, DE: International Reading Association.
Grinnell, P. C. (1984). *How can I prepare my young child for reading?* Newark, DE: International Reading Association.

Roser, N. L. (1989). *Helping your child become a reader.* Newark, DE: International Reading Association.

Silvern, S. B., & Silvern, L. R. (1990). *Beginning literacy and your child.* Newark, DE: International Reading Association.

Additional Brochures for Parents of Young Children

These are available for a modest charge from the International Reading Association (800 Barksdale Road; Newark, DE 19714-8139; 1-800-336-READ)

- *Eating well can help your child*
- *Good books make reading fun for your child*
- *You can encourage your child to read*
- *You can help your child connect reading to writing*
- *Your home is your child's first school*

RESOURCES FOR INFORMATION ABOUT PARENTS AND SCHOOLS

Center for Family Resources
384 Clinton Street
Hempstead, NY 11550

Family Resource Coalition
230 North Michigan Avenue, Suite 1625
Chicago, IL 60601

Home and School Institute
1201 16th Street, NW
Washington, DC 20036

National Association of Partners in Education
601 Wythe Street, Suite 200
Alexandria, VA 22314

The Parent Institute
P.O. Box 7474
Fairfax Station, VA 22039

Parents as Teachers National Center
Marillac Hall
University of Missouri (St. Louis)
8001 Natural Bridge
St. Louis, MO 63121

School-Age Child Care Project
Center for Research on Women
Wellesley College
Wellesley, MA 02181

SAMPLE LETTER TO PARENTS OF CHILDREN IN AN EARLY CHILDHOOD CLASS

Dear Parents:

This will be an exciting year for children in this class because we will all be working to develop strong reading and writing skills. Your child probably already knows a lot about reading and writing. He or she has seen you and other family members using literacy in many ways, and you have probably heard your child "read" signs and package labels or letters written for someone in the family. These behaviors are the beginnings of reading and writing skills, and we plan to build on this foundation.

Children's learning is always full of false starts and mistakes; that's how youngsters learn anything, from tying shoes to riding bikes to reading and writing. All children need support and answers to questions about what they are doing. I want to ask your help in supporting growth by continuing to answer questions your child may ask, by continuing to read to him or her as often as possible, and by engaging him or her in conversations about what is going on in school. When you show enthusiasm about what your child is doing in school, you show that you value all the hard work that goes into learning to read and write.

Your child will bring home books to share with you, and I hope that you will take him or her to the library or buy books as gifts and special treats. When your child asks to read to you, let him or her read as much of the book as possible and be sure to discuss the story. He or she will bring home beginning writing efforts, which may appear strange and misspelled to you. Don't be put off! These early efforts lead rapidly to control of the mechanics of writing, and your child will want to share them with you. Be enthusiastic and listen as your child explains what he or she has been doing in school!

I know that the duties of parents today seem at times to be overwhelming, and I may seem to be asking you to assume the role of teacher for your child. In fact, though, you have been a teacher all your child's life! We at school know that all the people in a child's home can facilitate and stimulate learning. Your interest in your child's progress is important, both to him or her and to all of us at school. You and I are really a team with the same goal for your child's learning. Your help with and acceptance of beginning literacy efforts are essential because you are an important teacher, too. Let your child see you reading and writing—show him or her that literacy is an important part of your life.

Please do not hesitate to call me or drop me a note if you have questions. I look forward to talking to you at Parents' Night and sharing with you a portfolio of your child's work.

With best regards,

ESTABLISHING A HOME–SCHOOL LIBRARY EXCHANGE

Materials
- Books to be distributed to students (at least one hundred in varied genres)
- Plastic bags
- Record-keeping forms

Procedures
1. Prepare lists of all books as permanent record; stamp all books with class designation.
2. Prepare sign-out cards for all books; insert in pockets in books.
3. Send letter home informing parents that books will be sent home and asking parents to be prepared to read to their child and fill out a brief response form; be sure to let them know how long they may keep the books and how often students will be bringing books home.
4. Orient children to the idea of taking books home, sharing them with their families, and bringing them back.
5. Prepare home report forms with space for students' names, book titles, dates read, and brief notes from parents about the experience (e.g., Did your child enjoy the book? What was his [her] favorite part? How many times did you share the book? Did the child attempt to read on his [her] own?).
6. Allow ample time on the first book distribution day for children to select a book and complete the sign-out card (with help if necessary); insert each book and a home report form in a plastic bag for protection of the book.
7. Be sure to specify the return date for the books (e.g., one day, two days, or three).
8. On the day following book selection, let children share their experiences and talk about reading the book with their families; encourage students to talk about the books they have read and make recommendations to their classmates.
9. Keep careful records on books as they are returned and on return of the home report sheets; keep track of students' responses to the books as a guide for selecting books to enlarge the library.
10. After several weeks of successful library use and sharing about book reading, reward students for their care of the books by having a party.

APPENDIX D

Terminology and Concepts about Phonetic and Structural Analysis

PHONICS

Vowels

The letters *a, e, i, o,* and *u* are vowels; *y* is sometimes a vowel.

Long Vowels.   The vowel "says its name"; long vowel sounds may be made by the letter itself alone in a word or in combination with other letters (see section on digraphs).

Short Vowels.   The vowel sounds in *cat, egg, sit, cot,* and *cut* are short.

Vowel Digraphs.   Two vowels together are digraphs when one vowel is sounded and the other is silent; usually, the first vowel is voiced, but not always, as in *build* and *fruit*; usually the voiced vowel is long, as in *boat,* but this is not always true, as in *bread.*

Examples:
- *ai* (p*ai*n); *ay* (h*ay*)
- *ea* (w*ea*ther, br*ea*d, *ea*ch)
- *ee* (tr*ee*)
- *ei* (w*ei*ght, *ei*ther, rec*ei*ve)
- *ie* (p*ie*ce)
- *oa* (b*oa*t)
- *oe* (t*oe*)
- *ow* (l*ow*)
- *ou* (t*ou*gh)
- *ue* (tr*ue*, bl*ue*)
- *ui* (b*ui*ld, fr*ui*t)

Vowel Diphthongs.   Two vowels together whose sounds make one new sound different from the sound made by either individual vowel; these can be very difficult, especially for dialect speakers.

Examples:
- *au* (h*au*l)
- *aw* (h*aw*k)
- *ew* (f*ew*)
- *ey* (th*ey*)
- *oo* (b*oo*k, sch*oo*l)
- *oi* (s*oi*l)
- *ow* (c*ow*)
- *oy* (b*oy*)

R-Controlled Vowels.   Vowels or vowel combinations that are followed by an *r* and are neither long nor short; again, children who speak dialects that drop or add *r* sounds have trouble with these sounds.

Examples:
- *star, ear, tire, ore, or, oar, lure*

Silent Vowels.   Vowels that are not voiced are silent.

Examples:
- sail (the *i* is silent)
- sale (the *a* is long and the final *e* is a "placeholder" to indicate that the previous vowel "says its name")

Medial Vowels.   Vowels that come in the middle of words; also called "middle vowels."

Examples:
- C-V-C Combinations: *c-v-c* refers to the pattern of words that begin and end with a consonant (single, digraph, or blend) with a short vowel in the middle: *cat, fish, dog*
- C-V-C-E Combinations: these demonstrate the "silent *e*" principle, as in *cape, bake, hope*

Consonants

Letters that are not vowels (or functioning as vowels) are called consonants.

Initial or Beginning Consonant Sounds.   The first consonant in a word; the "initial consonant sound" may be made by single, double, or triple combinations of consonants, as in *sit, shut,* or *school.*

Medial Consonants.   Consonants in the middle of a word.

Final, End, or Terminal Consonants.   Consonants at the end of a word.

Consonant Digraphs.   Two adjacent consonants that make one sound that differs from the sound of either consonant by itself; these are the last elements to appear in children's invented spelling.

Examples:
- *ch* (*ch*ur*ch*)
- *sh* (*sh*ip)
- *th* (*th*at)
- *wh* (*wh*at)
- *gh* (cou*gh*)
- *ph* (gra*ph*, *ph*one)

Silent Consonants.   These consonants make no sound.

Examples:
- *b* (lam*b*)
- *p* (*p*salm)
- *h* (g*h*ost)
- *w* (*w*ring)
- *l* (wa*l*k)
- *k* (*k*nife)

Consonant Blends or Clusters.   Two or more adjacent consonants whose sounds *glide* together while the individual sounds remain somewhat distinct; think of words *b-b-b-l*end, *c-c-c-l*uster, or *g-g-g-l*ide to help remember rules about consonant blends; children use blends in their invented spelling; blends can appear at the beginning, middle, or end of words and should be taught in clusters according to the first letter of the blend; teaching them as part of spelling instruction is effective.

Examples:
- *b*-blends: blue, brown
- *c*-blends: clown, crown
- *d*-blends: dress, dwell
- *f*-blends: flower, from
- *g*-blends: glue, grow
- *p*-blends: plate, pretty

- *s*-blends: skill, slow, small, snail, spin, story, swam, school, screen, shrink, splash, squash, past, crash
- *t*-blends: tree, trash, twelve, three
- *n*-blends: friend, sing, sink
- *r*-blends: work, hurt

Hard and Soft Consonants.   *c* or *g* followed by *e, i,* or *y* usually makes a "soft" sound, as in *city* or *gem*; "hard" sounds are those of *cat* and *game.*

MORPHEMIC AND STRUCTURAL ANALYSIS

Roots or Stems

These terms refer to whole words onto which an affix is added (e.g., *like* is the root of *likes, dislike,* and *likelihood*); they can also refer to Greek and Latin roots, the smaller word parts from which many of our words are built (e.g., the Latin *multus,* meaning "many," is the root for *multiply*).

Knowing the concept that affixes can be added to words is useful for word attack, but memorization of extensive lists of "word parts" serves little purpose for beginning readers; it forces them to look too closely at individual words and can slow them down; instruction as part of spelling is best.

Affixes

Word parts that are added onto the beginnings or ends of words are affixes; they change the meaning of the words in specific ways.

Prefixes

Elements added at the beginning of words are prefixes; fifteen prefixes account for more than 80 percent of all common words that have prefixes (Herr, 1982).

Examples:
- Negatives: *dis-, im-, in-, un-*
- Directional: *ab-, ad-, de-, en-, ex-, pre-, pro-, re-, sub-*
- Combinational: *be-, com-*

Suffixes

These word parts are added to the ends of words.

Examples:
- Plural markers: *-s, -es*
- Verb markers: *-s,* for third-person singular; *-ed, -d, -t,* for past tenses
- Adjective or adverb markers: *-er* for comparing two things; *-est* for comparing three or more; *-less* (meaning "without"); *-ful, -full* (meaning "full")
- Noun suffixes: *-er, -ist, -or* (meaning "one who"); *-tion, -sion, -ment, -ness* (meaning "state of")

Compound Words

Two little words put together to make one, new, longer word; children enjoy compound words because they can usually figure them out and feel proud to read big words; but care must be taken that children realize that some compounds have a cumulative meaning, as in *luncheon,* whereas some may be more deceptive, as in *hot dog* and *eggplant.* Compound words make good spelling lists.

Contractions

One word made by deleting letters from two other words, inserting an apostrophe to show the deletion; contractions are most easily learned in conjunction with oral language work. When children write contractions, they often forget which letters to leave out and where to place the apostrophe (e.g., *is'nt* for *isn't; hsn't* for *hasn't*). Some regional dialects omit additional letters in oral use of contractions, causing additional confusion as children try to spell them in their writing. Spelling instruction is the best place to study and learn contractions.

THINGS TEACHERS MUST REMEMBER ABOUT PHONICS

1. Children need extensive repetition and practice in varied situations before knowledge of these concepts and skills becomes automatic.
2. Children need to tie these concepts and skills to their oral language and learn ways their oral language may mislead them.
3. Practice that reinforces these concepts through auditory and visual channels is best; writing further reinforces these skills so long as children are using the skills purposefully rather than on fill-in-the-blank worksheets.
4. Many of these concepts and skills can best be introduced through structured "word study" as part of spelling instruction.

MAPPING ACTIVITIES

1. *Graphic organizers,* or *maps,* are useful devices to help students organize their ideas and keep track of their thinking.
2. To introduce these devices to students, teachers need to present familiar content material or a familiar story and carefully model how the map is constructed. Students should then work in small groups constructing their own graphic organizers and comparing them with those of classmates.
3. Teachers can reinforce the usefulness of graphic organizers by using them frequently to develop background knowledge, show interrelatedness about ideas, map the parts of a story, brainstorm ideas before writing, or introduce a new lesson in a content area.

NARRATIVE TEXTS
Series of Events

Story Map

Author's Name		Title		
Setting? Where?	Characters? Who?	Time? When?	Problem?Plot? What happens?	Solution? Finally

Character Map

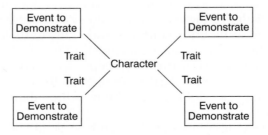

Sample 1
Some graphic organizers are useful for narratives.

EXPOSITORY TEXTS

Concept Maps

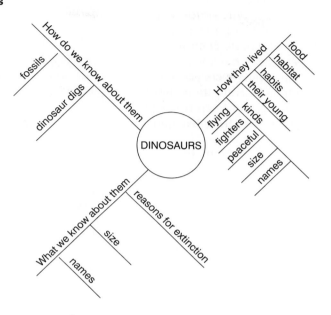

Time Line

Dates or sequence (1st, 2nd, 3rd steps, etc.)

Cause/Effect

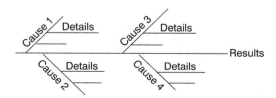

Sample 2

Some graphic organizers are useful for informational, expository writing.

Sample 3

The Know–Want to Know–Learned (K–W–L) graphic organizer helps students determine their extent of background knowledge, set goals for their learning in content areas, and keep track of what they have learned.

K-W-L Chart.

| Name _____ Date _____ |
| Topic _____ |

This is what I already KNOW	This is what I WANT to learn	This is what I LEARNED

These are my sources of information

1.
2.
3.
4.
5.

BIBLIOGRAPHY

Aaron, I. E. (1987). Enriching the basal reading program with literature. In B. E. Cullinan (Ed.), *Children's literature in the reading program* (pp. 126–138). Newark, DE: International Reading Association.

Adams, M. J. (1990). *Beginning to read: Thinking and learning about print.* Cambridge, MA: MIT Press.

Alexander, F. (1987). California Reading Initiative. In B. E. Cullinan (Ed.), *Children's literature in the reading program* (pp. 126–138). Newark, DE: International Reading Association.

Anderson, R. C., Hiebert, E. H., Scott, J. A., & Wilkinson, I. A. G. (1985). *Becoming a nation of readers: The report of the commission on reading.* Washington, DC: National Institute of Education, U.S. Department of Education.

Atwell, N. (1987). *In the middle: Writing, reading, and learning with adolescents.* Portsmouth, NH: Heinemann.

Au, K., & Jordan, C. (1980). Teaching reading to Hawaiian children: Finding a culturally appropriate solution. In H. Trueba, G. P. Guthrie, & K. Au (Eds.), *Culture in the bilingual classroom.* Rawley, MA: Newbury House.

Baghban, M. (1984). *Our daughter learns to read and write.* Newark, DE: International Reading Association.

Banks, J. A. (1989). Multicultural education: Characteristics and goals. In J. A. Banks & C. A. McG. Banks (Eds.), *Multicultural education: Issues and perspectives.* Needham Heights, MA: Allyn & Bacon.

Banks, J. A. (1991/1992). Multicultural education: For freedom's sake. Educational Leadership, 49(4), 32–36.

Barrs, M. (1990). The primary language record: Reflections on issues in evaluation. *Language Arts, 67,* 244–253.

Barrs, M., Ellis, S., Tester, H., & Thomas, A. (1989). *The primary language record: Handbook for teachers.* Portsmouth, NH: Heinemann.

Beers, C. S., & Beers, J. W. (1981). Three assumptions about learning to spell. *Language Arts, 58,* 573–580.

Bissex, G. L. (1980). *Gnys at wrk: A child learns to write and read.* Cambridge, MA: Harvard University Press.

Bissex, G. L. (1984). The child as teacher. In H. Goelman, A. Oberg, & F. Smith (Eds.), *Awakening to literacy* (pp. 87–101). Portsmouth, NH: Heinemann.

Bissex, G. L. (1987). What is a teacher researcher? In G. L. Bissex & R. Bullock (Eds.), *Seeing for ourselves: Case study research by teachers of writing.* Portsmouth, NH: Heinemann.

Boute, G. S., LaPoint, S., & Davis, B. (1993). Racial issues in education: Real or imagined? *Young Children, 49*(1), 19–23.

Boute, G. S., & McCormick, C. B. (1992). Avoiding pseudomulticulturalism: Authentic multicultural activities. *Childhood Education, 68,* 140–144.

Bredekamp, S., & Rosengrant, T. (Eds.). (1991). *Reaching potentials: Appropriate curriculum and assessment for young children.* Washington, DC: National Association for the Education of Young Children.

Britton, J. (1987). A quiet form of research. In D. Goswami & P. R. Stillman (Eds.), *Reclaiming the classroom: Teacher research as an agency for change* (pp. 13–19). Upper Montclair, NJ: Boynton/Cook.

Brown, A. L., Armbruster, B. B., & Baker, L. (1986). The role of metacognition in reading and studying. In J. Orasanu (Ed.), *Reading comprehension from research to practice* (pp. 49–75). Hillsdale, NJ: Erlbaum.

Brown, A. L., Palinscar, A. S., & Armbruster, B. B. (1984). Instructing comprehension-fostering activities in interactive learning situations. In H. Mandl, L. Stein, & T. Trabasso (Eds.), *Learning and comprehension of text* (pp. 255–285). Hillsdale, NJ: Erlbaum.

Brown, C. S., & Lytle, S. L. (1988). Merging assessment and instruction: Protocols in the classroom. In S. M. Glazer, L. W. Searfoss, & L. M. Gentile (Eds.), *Reexamining reading diagnosis: New trends and procedures* (pp. 94–102). Newark, DE: International Reading Association.

Bruner, J. (1984). Language, mind, and reading. In H. Goelman, A. Oberg, & F. Smith (Eds.), *Awakening to literacy* (pp. 193–200). Portsmouth, NH: Heinemann.

Busching, B. (1981). Readers theatre: An education for language and life. *Language Arts, 58,* 330–338.

Bussis, A. M., Chittenden, E. A., Amarel, M., & Klausner, E. (1985). *Inquiry into meaning: An investigation of learning to read.* Hillsdale, NJ: Erlbaum.

Butler, D., & Clay, M. (1979). *Reading begins at home.* Exeter, NH: Heinemann.

Butler, D., & Clay, M. (1988). *Writing begins at home.* Portsmouth, NH: Heinemann.

Calkins, L. M. (1981). When children want to punctuate: Basic skills belong in context. In R. D. Walshe (Ed.), *Donald Graves in Australia: "Children Want to Write"* (pp. 89–96). Rozelle, New South Wales: Primary English Teaching Association.

Cazden, C. B. (1981). Language development and the preschool environment. In C. B. Cazden (Ed.), *Language in early childhood education* (rev. ed.) (pp. 3–16). Washington, DC: National Association for the Education of Young Children.

Cazden, C. B. (1982). Contexts for literacy: In the mind and in the classroom. *Journal of Behavior, 14,* 413–428.

Cazden, C. B. (1983). Adult assistance to language development: Scaffolds, models, and direct instruction. In R. P. Parker & Frances A. Davis (Eds.), *Developing literacy* (pp. 3–18). Newark, DE: International Reading Association.

Cazden, C. B. (1988). *Classroom discourse: The language of teaching and learning.* Portsmouth, NH: Heinemann.

Chittenden, E. (1991). Authentic assessment, evaluation, and documentation of student performance. In V. Perrone (Ed.), *Expanding student assessment* (pp. 22–31). Alexandria, VA: Association for Supervision and Curriculum Development.

Chukovsky, K. (1963). *From two to five* (M. Morton, Trans.). Berkeley, CA: University of California Press.

Clay, M. M. (1976). *What did I write?* Portsmouth, NH: Heinemann.

Clay, M. M. (1979). *Reading: The patterning of complex behaviour.* Portsmouth, NH: Heinemann.

Clay, M. M. (1979). *The concepts about print test.* Auckland: Heinemann.

Clay, M. M. (1985). *The early detection of reading difficulties* (3rd ed.). Portsmouth, NH: Heinemann.

Clay, M. M. (1987). *Writing begins at home.* Portsmouth, NH: Heinemann.

Clay, M. M. (1993). *Reading recovery: A guidebook for teachers in training.* Portsmouth, NH: Heinemann.

Cochran-Smith, M. (1984). *The making of a reader.* Norwood, NJ: Ablex.

Davey, B. (1983). Think aloud: Modeling the cognitive process of reading comprehension. *Journal of Reading, 26,* 38–41.

Davey, B. (1985). Helping readers think beyond print through self-questioning. *Middle School Journal, 16*(3), 38–41.

DeFord, D. (1981). Literacy, reading, writing, and other essentials. *Language Arts, 58,* 652–658.

DeGroff, L. (1990). Informational books: Topics and structure. *The Reading Teacher, 43,* 496–501.

Delpit, L. C. (1990). Language diversity and learning. In S. Hynds & D. L. Rubin (Eds.), *Perspectives on talk and learning* (pp. 247–266). Urbana, IL: National Council of Teachers of English.

Delpit, L. D. (1988). The silenced dialogue: Power and pedagogy in educating other people's children. *Harvard Educational Review, 58,* 280–298.

Drew, N. (1987/1994). Learning the skills of peacemaking. Rolling Hills Estate, CA: Jalman Press.

Durkin, D. (1984). Is there a match between what elementary teachers do and what basal manuals recommend? *The Reading Teacher, 37,* 734–745.

Durkin, D. (1990). Dolores Durkin speaks on instruction. *The Reading Teacher, 43,* 472–477.

Dyson, A. H. (1984). Who controls classroom writing contexts? *Language Arts, 61,* 618–625.

Dyson, A. H. (1986). Transitions and tensions: Interrelationships between the drawing, talking, and dictating of young children. *Research in the Teaching of English, 20,* 379–409.

Dyson, A. H. (1987). The value of "time off task": Young children's talk and deliberate text. *Harvard Educational Review, 57,* 396–420.

Dyson, A. H. (1988). Negotiating among multiple worlds: The space/time dimensions of young children's composing. *Research in the Teaching of English, 22,* 355–387.

Dyson, A. H. (1989). *"Once-upon-a-time" reconsidered: The developmental dialectic between function and form.* Technical Report No. 36. Berkeley, CA: Center for the Study of Writing.

Dyson, A. H. (1992). *Whistle for Willie,* lost puppies, and cartoon dogs: The sociocultural dimensions of young children's composing. *Journal of Reading Behavior, 24,* 433–462.

Dyson, A. H. (1994a). Sociocultural aspects of learning to write. Presentation at Reading Research '94, May, Toronto, Canada.

Dyson, A. H. (1994b). Viewpoints: The word and the world: Reconceptualizing written language development or, Do rainbows mean a lot to little girls? In R. R. Ruddell, M. R. Ruddell, & H. Singer (Eds.), *Theoretical models and processes of reading* (pp. 297–322). Newark, DE: International Reading Association.

Eckhoff, B. (1983). How reading affects children's writing. *Language Arts, 60,* 607–616.

Edelsky, C. (1986). *Writing in a bilingual program: Habia una vez.* Norwood, NJ: Ablex.

Edelsky, C., Altwerger, B., & Flores, B. (1991). *Whole language: What's the difference?* Portsmouth, NH: Heinemann.

Engle, B. (1990). Keeping track: Evaluation of literacy learning in the early years. In C. Kamii (Ed.), *Achievement testing in the early grades: The games grown-ups play.* Washington, DC: National Association for the Education of Young Children.

Englert, C. S., & Palinscar, A. S. (1991). Reconsidering instructional research in literacy from a sociocultural perspective. *Learning Disabilities Research and Practice, 6,* 225–229.

Epeneter, S., & Chang, C. (1992). Exploring diversity through the arts. In B. Neugebauer (Ed.), *Alike and different* (rev. ed.) (pp. 61–68). Washington, DC: National Association for the Education of Young Children.

Ferreiro, E. (1984). The underlying logic of literacy development. In H. Goelman, A. Oberg, & F. Smith (Eds.), *Awakening to literacy* (pp. 154–173). Portsmouth, NH: Heinemann.

Ferreiro, E. (1986). The interplay between information and assimilation in beginning literacy. In W. H. Teale & E. Sulzby (Eds.), *Emergent literacy* (pp. 15–49). Norwood, NJ: Ablex.

Ferreiro, E. (1990). Literacy development: Psychogenesis. In Y. M. Goodman (Ed.), *How children construct literacy: Piagetian perspectives* (pp. 12–25). Newark, DE: International Reading Association.

Ferreiro, E., & Teberosky, A. (1982). *Literacy before schooling.* Portsmouth, NH: Heinemann.

Fitzgerald, J. (1993). Literacy and students who are learning English as a second language. *The Reading Teacher, 46,* 638–647.

Flood, J., & Lapp, D. (1989). Reporting reading progress: A comparison portfolio for parents. *The Reading Teacher, 42,* 508–517.

Flood, J., & Lapp, D. (1990). Reading comprehension instruction for at-risk students: Research-based practices that can make a difference. *Journal of Reading, 33,* 490–496.

Flores, B., Cousin, P. T., & Diáz, E. (1991). Transforming deficit myths about learning, language, and culture. *Language Arts, 68,* 369–379.

Ford, S. A. (1993). The facilitators' role in children's play. *Young Children, 48*(6), 66–69.

France, M. G. (1992). Personal communication.

France, M. G., & Hager, J. M. (1993). Recruit, respect, respond: A model for working with low-income families and their preschoolers. *The Reading Teacher, 46.*

Fredericks, A. D., & Rasinski, T. V. (1989). Dimensions of parent involvement. *The Reading Teacher, 43,* 180–182.

Fredericks, A. D., & Rasinski, T. V. (1990a). Lending a (reading) hand. *The Reading Teacher, 43,* 520–521.

Fredericks, A. D., & Rasinski, T. V. (1990b). Resources for parents. *The Reading Teacher, 44,* 266–268.

Freeman, D. E., & Freeman, Y. S. (1993). Strategies for promoting the primary languages of all students. *The Reading Teacher, 46.*

Fromberg, D. P., & Driscoll, M. (1985). *The successful classroom.* New York: Teachers College Press.

Garvey, C. (1977). Play with language and speech. In S. Ervin-Tripp & C. Mitchell-Kernan (Eds.), *Child discourse* (pp. 27–48). New York: Academic Press.

Geller, L. G. (1985). *Wordplay and language learning for children.* Urbana, IL: National Council of Teachers of English.

Gentry, J. R. (1981). Learning to spell developmentally. *The Reading Teacher, 34,* 378–381.

Gentry, J. R., & Henderson, E. H. (1978). Three steps to teaching beginning readers to spell. *The Reading Teacher, 31,* 632–637.

Gilyard, K. (1991). *Voices of the self.* Detroit: Wayne State University Press.

Glazer, S. M., & Brown, C. S. (1993). *Portfolios and beyond: Collaborative assessment in reading and writing.* Norwood, MA: Christopher Gordon.

Gomez, M. L., Graue, M. E., & Bloch, M. N. (1991). Reassessing portfolio assessment: Rhetoric and reality. *Language Arts, 68,* 620–628.

Goodman, Y. M. (1984). The development of initial literacy. In H. Goelman, A. Oberg, & F. Smith (Eds.), *Awakening to literacy* (pp. 102–110). Portsmouth, NH: Heinemann.

Goodman, Y. M. (1985). Kidwatching: Observing children in the classroom. In A. Jagger & M. Smith-Burke (Eds.), *Observing the language learner* (pp. 9–17). Newark, DE: International Reading Association.

Goodman, Y. M. (1986). Children coming to know literacy. In W. H. Teale & E. Sulzby (Eds.), *Emergent literacy* (pp. 1–14). Norwood, NJ: Ablex.

Goodman, Y. M. (1987). Foreword to *Supporting literacy: Developing effective learning environments,* by C. E. Loughlin & M. D. Martin. New York: Teachers College Press.

Goodman, Y. M. (1989). Evaluation of students: [Evaluation of Teachers]. In K. S. Goodman, Y. M. Goodman, & W. J. Hood (Eds.), *The whole language evaluation book* (pp. 3–14).

Goodman, Y. M. (1990). Discovering children's inventions of written language. In Y. M. Goodman (Ed.), *How children construct literacy: Piagetian perspectives* (pp. 1–11). Newark, DE: International Reading Association.

Goodman, Y. M. (Ed.). (1990). *How children construct literacy: Piagetian perspectives.* Newark, DE: International Reading Association.

Goswami, D., & Stillman, P. R. (Eds.). (1987). *Reclaiming the classroom: Teacher research as an agency for change.* Upper Montclair, NJ: Boynton/Cook.

Grant, J., & Azen, M. (1987). *Owner's manual: 5 year olds.* Rosemont, NJ: Programs for Education.

Graves, D. H. (1983). *Writing: Teachers and children at work.* Portsmouth, NH: Heinemann.

Green, M. (1993). Perspective and diversity: Toward a common ground. In F. Pignatelli & S. W. Pflaum (Eds.), *Celebrating diverse voices: Progressive education and equity* (pp. 1–20). Newbury Park, CA: Corwin Press.

Hansen, J. (1983). Authors respond to authors. *Language Arts, 60,* 970–976.

Harp, B. (Ed.). (1991). *Assessment and evaluation in whole language programs.* Norwood, MA: Christopher-Gordon.

Harste, J. C. (1990). Foreword to *Opening the door to classroom research,* M. W. Olson (Ed.) (pp. iii–viii). Newark, DE: International Reading Association.

Harste, J. C., Short, K. G., & Burke, C. (1988). *Creating classrooms for authors.* Portsmouth, NH: Heinemann.

Harste, J. C., Woodward, V. A., & Burke, C. L. (1984). *Language stories and literacy lessons.* Portsmouth, NH: Heinemann.

Heald-Taylor, G. (1989). *The administrator's guide to whole language.* Katonah, NY: Richard C. Owens Publishers, Inc.

Healy, M. K. (1980). *Using student response groups in the classroom.* Berkeley: University of California/Bay Area Writing Project.

Heath, S. B. (1982). What no bedtime story means: Narrative skills at home and school. *Language in Society, 11,* 49–76.

Heath, S. B. (1983). *Way with words: Language, life, and work in communities and classrooms.* London: Cambridge University Press.

Henderson, E. (1985). *Teaching spelling.* Dallas: Houghton-Mifflin.

Hilliard, A. (1989). Teachers and cultural styles in a pluralistic society. *NEA Today, 7,* 65–69.

Hills, T. (1993). Assessment in context: Teachers and children at work. *Young Children, 48,* 20–28.

Holdaway, D. (1979). *The foundations of literacy.* Sydney: Ashton Scholastic.

Holdaway, D. (1986). Guiding a natural process. In D. R. Tovey & J. E. Kerber (Eds.), *Roles in literacy learning* (pp. 42–51). Newark, DE: International Reading Association.

Hubbard, R. (1989). Inner designs. *Language Arts, 66,* 119–136.

Huck, C. S., Hepler, S., & Hickman, J. (1987). *Children's literature in the elementary school* (4th ed.). New York: Holt, Rinehart & Winston.

International Reading Association & Children's Book Council. (1992). *Kids' favorite books: Children's choices, 1989–1991.* Newark, DE: International Reading Association.

Irvin, J. J. (1990). *Black students and school failure: Policies, practices, and prescription.* Westport, CT: Greenwood Press.

Johnston, P. (1987). Teachers as evaluation experts. *The Reading Teacher, 41*(8), 744–748.

Jordan, C. (1985). Translating culture: From ethnographic information to educational program. *Anthropology and Education Quarterly, 16,* 105–123.

Kagan, S. L. (1990). Readiness 2000: Rethinking rhetoric and responsibility. *Phi Delta Kappan, 72,* 272–279.

Kagan, S. L. (1992). Readiness past, present, and future. *Young Children, 48*(1), 48–53.

Kamil, M. L. (1984). Current traditions of reading research. In P. D. Pearson (Ed.), *Handbook of reading research* (pp. 39–62). White Plains, NY: Longman.

Kidder, T. (1989). *Among school children.* Boston: Houghton Mifflin.

Kotlowitz, A. (1991). *There are no children here.* New York: Doubleday.

Lamme, L. L., & Hysmith, C. (1991). One school's adventure into portfolio assessment. *Language Arts, 68,* 629–640.

Lara, S. M. G. (1989). Reading placement for code switchers. *The Reading Teacher, 42,* 278–283.

Lipson, E. R. (May 22, 1994). What the children are reading. *New York Times Book Review,* 26–27.

Lloyd-Jones, R., & Lunsford, A. A. (Eds.). (1989). *The English Coalition Conference: Democracy through language.* Urbana, IL: National Council of Teachers of English.

Lyons, C. A., Pinnell, G. S., & DeFord, D. E. (1993). *Partners in learning: Teachers and children in Reading Recovery.* New York: Teachers College Press.

MacGillivray, L. (1994). Tacit shared understandings of a first grade writing community. *Journal of Reading Behavior, 26,* 245–266.

Marriott, D. (1993). Parents and teachers together: An assessment partnership. *Assessment Matters: Newsletter of Exemplary Assessment Practices, 2*(3), 1, 3.

Marshall, M. M. (1988). Work or learning: Implications of classroom metaphors. *Educational Researcher, 17*(9), 9–16.

Martin, N. (1987). On the move: Teacher-researchers. In D. Goswami & P. R. Stillman (Eds.), *Reclaiming the classroom: Teacher research as an agency for change* (pp. 20–27). Upper Montclair, NJ: Boynton/Cook.

Mason, J. M., & Au, K. H. (1984). Learning social context characteristics in prereading lessons. In J. Flood (Ed.), *Promoting reading comprehension* (179–203). Newark, DE: International Reading Association.

May, S. A. (1993). Redeeming multicultural education. *Language Arts, 70,* 364–372.

McCracken, J. B. (1993). *Valuing diversity: The primary years.* Washington, DC: National Association for the Education of Young Children.

Meek, M. (1982). *Learning to read.* London: The Bodley Head.

Meisels, S. (1987). Uses and abuses of developmental screening and school readiness testing. *Young Children, 42*(2), 4-5, 68-73.

Meisels, S. J. (1993). Remaking classroom assessment with the Work Sampling System. *Young Children, 48*(5), 34–40.

Moffett, J., & Wagner, B. J. (1993). What works is play. *Language Arts, 70,* 432–436.

Moll, L. C. (1986). Writing as communication: Creating strategic learning environments for students. *Theory into Practice, 25,* 102–108.

Monson, D. (1982). The literature program and the arts. *Language Arts, 59,* 254–258.

Morris, D. (1980). Beginning readers' concept of words. In E. H. Henderson & J. W. Beers (Eds.), *Developmental and cognitive aspects of learning to spell: A reflection of word knowledge* (pp. 97–111). Newark: DE: International Reading Association.

Morrow, L. M., & Paratore, J. (1993). Family literacy: Perspective and practice. *The Reading Teacher, 47,* 194–200.

Moss, E. (1977). The "Peppermint" Lesson. In M. Meek, M. A. Warlow, & G. Barton (Eds.), *The cool web: The pattern of children's reading* (pp. 140–142). London: The Bodley Head.

Myers, C. (1983). Drawing as prewriting in preschool. In M. Meyers & J. Gray (Eds.), *Theory and practice in the teaching of composition* (pp. 75–85). Urbana, IL: National Council of Teachers of English.

Nagy, W. E. (1988). *Teaching vocabulary to improve reading comprehension.* Newark, DE: International Reading Association.

National Association for the Education of Young Children & National Association of Early Childhood Specialists in State Departments of Education. (1991). Guidelines for appropriate curriculum content and assessment in programs serving children ages 3 through 8. *Young Children, 46*(3), 21–38.

National Association of Early Childhood Specialists in State Departments of Education. (1987). *Unacceptable trends in kindergarten entry and placement: A position statement.* Chicago: Author.

National Center for Educational Statistics. (1993). *Language characteristics and schooling in the United States, a changing picture: 1978–1989.* Washington, DC: U.S. Department of Education.

Nelson, K. (1973). *Structure and strategy in learning to talk.* Chicago: University of Chicago Press. Monograph of the Society for Research in Child Development, Series No. 38.

Neugebauer, B. (1992). Reflecting diversity: Books to read with young children. In B. Neugebauer (Ed.), *Alike and different* (rev. ed.) (pp. 163–174). Washington, DC: National Association for the Education of Young Children.

Neugebauer, B. (Ed.). (1992). *Alike and different.* Washington, DC: National Association for the Education of Young Children.

Newkirk, T. (1982). Young writers as critical readers. *Language Arts, 59,* 451–457.

Norton, D. E. (1990). Teaching multi-cultural literature in the reading curriculum. *The Reading Teacher, 44,* 28–41.

Ogle, D. M. (1989). The know, want to know, learn strategy. In K. D. Muth (Ed.), *Children's comprehension of text* (pp. 205–223). Newark, DE: International Reading Association.

Olson, M. W. (Ed.). (1990). *Opening the door to classroom research.* Newark, DE: International Reading Association.

Paley, V. G. (1979/1989). White teacher. Cambridge, MA: Harvard University Press.

Paley, V. G. (1987). Listening to what children say. *Harvard Educational Review, 56,* 122–131.

Palinscar, A. S., & Klenk, L. (1992). Fostering literacy learning in supportive contexts. *Journal of Learning Disabilities, 25,* 211–215, 229.

Parsons, L. (1990). *Response journals.* Portsmouth, NH: Heinemann.

Patterson, L., Santa, C. M., Short, K. G., & Smith, K. (Eds.). (1993). *Teachers are researchers: Reflection and action.* Newark, DE: International Reading Association.

Pearson, P. D., & Raphael, T. E. (1985). Increasing students' awareness of sources of information for answering questions. *American Educational Research Journal, 22,* 217–235.

Pearson, P. D., & Valencia, S. W. (1987). Assessment, accountability, and professional prerogative. In J. E. Readence & R. S. Baldwin (Eds.), *Research in literacy: Merging perspectives* (pp. 3–16). Rochester, NY: National Reading Conference.

Pignatelli, F., & Pflaum, S. W. (Eds.). (1993). *Celebrating diverse voices.* Newbury Park, CA: Corwin Press.

Protheroe, N. J., & Barsdate, K. J. (1991). *Culturally-sensitive instruction and student learning.* Arlington, VA: Educational Research Service.

Purcell-Gates, V. (1988). Lexical and syntactic knowledge of written narrative held by well-read-to kindergartners and second graders. *Research in the Teaching of English, 22,* 128–160.

Purcell-Gates, V. (1989). What oral/written language differences can tell us about beginning instruction. *The Reading Teacher, 42,* 290–295.

Reed, S., & Sautter, C. (1990). Children of poverty: The status of twelve million young Americans. *Phi Delta Kappan, 71,* 1–12.

Rioux, W., & Berk, N. (January 19, 1994). The necessary partners: Tips from research on creating parent involvement programs that work. *Education Week,* p. 31.

Ritty, J. M. (1991). Single-parent families: Tips for educators. *The Reading Teacher, 44,* 604–606.

Rosenblatt, L. M. (1938/1978). Literature as exploration. New York: D. Appleton.

Rosenblatt, L. M. (1979). *The reader, the text, and the poem.* Carbondale, IL: Southern Illinois University Press.

Rosenblatt, L. M. (1985). Language, schooling, and society. In S. N. Tchudi (Ed.), *Proceedings of the International Federation of Teachers of English* (pp. 64–80). Portsmouth, NH: Boynton/Cook.

Rosenblatt, L. M. (1989). Writing and reading: The transactional theory. In J. M. Mason (Ed.), *Reading and writing connections* (pp. 153–176). Boston: Allyn & Bacon.

Rosenblatt, L. M. (1991). Literature—S. O. S.! *Language Arts, 68,* 444–448.

Routman, R. (1989). *Transitions.* Portsmouth, NH: Heinemann.

Routman, R. (1991). *Invitations: Changing as teachers and learners, K–12.* Portsmouth, NH: Heinemann.

Sage, C. (1993). One hundred notable picture books in the field of social studies. In M. Zarnowski & A. F. Gallagher (Eds.). *Children's literature and social studies* (pp. 5–11). Washington, DC: National Council for the Social Studies.

Salinger, T. (1988). *Language arts and literacy for young children.* Columbus: Merrill.

Salinger, T. (1993). *Models of literacy instruction.* Columbus, OH: Merrill/Prentice Hall.

Salinger, T., & Chittenden, E. (1994). Analysis of an early literacy portfolio. *Language Arts, 71,* 446–452.

Sardy, S. (1985). Thinking about reading. In T. L. Harris & E. J. Cooper (Eds.), *Reading, thinking, and concept development* (pp. 213–229). New York: College Board.

Saul, E. W. (1989). "What did Leo feed the turtle?" and other nonliterary questions. *Language Arts, 66,* 295–303.

Sawyer, W. (1987). Literature and literacy: A review of research. *Language Arts, 64,* 33–39.

Schweinhart, L. (1993). Observing young children in action: The key to early childhood assessment. *Young Children, 48*(5), 29–33.

Sebasta, S. L. (1993). Creative drama and language arts. In B. E. Cullinan (Ed.), *Children's voices: Talk in the classroom* (pp. 33–46). Newark, DE: International Reading Association.

Shannon, P. (1989). *Broken promises: Reading instruction in twentieth-century America.* Granby, MA: Bergin & Garvey.

Simmons, J. (1990). Portfolios as large-scale assessment. *Language Arts, 67,* 262–268.

Siu-Runyan, Y. (1991). Learning from students: An important aspect of classroom organization. *Language Arts, 68,* 100–107.

Sloan, G. (1984). *The child as critic* (2nd ed.). New York: Teachers College Press.

Smith, F. (1988). *Joining the literacy club.* Portsmouth, NH: Heinemann.

Smith, F. (1992). Learning to read: The never-ending debate. *Phi Delta Kappan, 73,* 432–441.

Smith, G. B. (1988). Physical arrangements, grouping, and ethnographic notetaking. In S. M. Glazer, L. W. Searfoss, & L. M. Gentile (Eds.), *Reexamining reading diagnosis: New trends and procedures* (pp. 169–177). Newark, DE: International Reading Association.

Smith, N. B. (1965). *American reading instruction.* Newark, DE: International Reading Association.

Smitherman, G. (1977). *Talkin and testifyin: The language of Black America.* Boston: Houghton Mifflin.

Spangenberg-Urbschat, K., & Pritchard, R. (Eds.). (1994). *Kids come in all languages: Reading instruction for ESL students.* Newark, DE: International Reading Association.

Squire, J. R. (1983). Composing and comprehending: Two sides of the same basic process. *Language Arts, 60,* 581–589.

Stahl, S. (1992). Saying the "P" word: Nine guidelines for exemplary phonics instruction. *The Reading Teacher, 45,* 618–625.

Stewig, J. W. (1988). *Children and literature* (2nd ed.). Boston: Houghton Mifflin.

Stoll, D. R. (1994). *Magazines for kids and teens.* Newark, DE: International Reading Association.

Strickland, D. S. (1987). Literature: Key element in the language and reading program. In B. E. Cullinan (Ed.), *Children's literature in the reading program* (pp. 68–76). Newark, DE: International Reading Association.

Strickland, D., et al. (1989). Research currents: Classroom dialogue during literature response groups. *Language Arts, 66,* 192–200.

Sulzby, E. (1985a). Children's emergent reading of favorite storybooks: A developmental study. *Reading Research Quarterly, 20,* 458–481.

Sulzby, E. (1985b). Kindergartners as writers and readers. In M. Farr (Ed.), *Children's early writing development* (pp. 127–200). Norwood, NJ: Ablex.

Sulzby, E. (1986). Writing and reading: Signs of oral and written language organization in the young child. In W. H. Teale & E. Sulzby (Eds.), *Emergent literacy* (pp. 50–89). Norwood, NJ: Ablex.

Taylor, D. (1983). *Family literacy: Young children learning to read and write.* Portsmouth, NH: Heinemann.

Taylor, D. (1989). Toward a unified theory of literacy learning. *Phi Delta Kappan, 70,* 184–193.

Taylor, D., & Dorsey-Gaines, C. (1988). *Growing up literate: Learning from inner-city families.* Portsmouth, NH: Heinemann.

Teale, W. H. (1984). Reading to young children: Its significance for literacy development. In H. Goelman, A. Oberg, & F. Smith (Eds.), *Awakening to literacy* (pp. 110–121). Portsmouth, NH: Heinemann.

Tierney, R. J., Carter, M. A., & Desai, L. E. (1991). *Portfolio assessment in the reading-writing classroom.* Norwood, MA: Christopher-Gordon.

Torbe, M., & Medway, P. (1981). *The climate for learning.* Montclair, NJ: Boynton/Cook.

Trelease, J. (1985). *The read-aloud handbook* (rev. ed.). New York: Penguin.

Trousdale, A. M. (1990). Interactive story-telling: Scaffolding children's early narratives. *Language Arts, 67,* 164–173.

Valencia, S. W., McGinley, W., & Pearson, P. D. (1990). Assessing reading and writing. In G. G. Duffy (Ed.), *Reading in the middle school* (2nd ed.) (pp. 124–153). Newark, DE: International Reading Association.

Vandergrift, J. A., & Greene, A. L. (1992). Rethinking parent involvement. *Phi Delta Kappan, 5*(1), 57–59.

Vasquez, J. A. (1990). Teaching to the distinctive traits of minority students. *The Clearinghouse, 63,* 229–304.

Veatch, J. (1968). *How to teach reading with children's books* (2nd ed.). New York: Richard C. Owen.

Vygotsky, L. S. (1962). *Thought and language* (E. Hanfmann & G. Vakar, Trans.). Cambridge, MA: MIT Press.

Vygotsky, L. S. (1978). *Mind in society* (M. Cole, V. John-Steiner, S. Scribner, & E. Souberman, Eds. and Trans.). Cambridge, MA: Harvard University Press.

Walker, B. (1988/1994). Diagnostic teaching of reading: Techniques for instruction and assessment. Columbus, OH: Merrill/Prentice Hall.

Walker-Dalhouse, D. (1993). Beginning reading and the African American child at risk. *Young Children, 49*(1), 24–28.

Ward, R. (1985). Final exam, ECED 3455. El Paso: University of Texas-El Paso.

Weed, J. (1991). Living daily in a whole language classroom. In Y. M. Goodman, W. J. Hood, & K. S. Goodman (Eds.), *Organizing for whole language* (pp. 84–94). Portsmouth, NH: Heinemann.

Wells, G. (1985). *The meaning makers.* Portsmouth, NH: Heinemann.

Willert, M. K., & Kamii, C. (1985). Reading in kindergarten. *Young Children. 40*(6), 3–9.

Workman, S., & Anziano, M. C. (1993). Curriculum webs: Weaving connections from children to teachers. *Young Children, 48*(2), 4–9.

INDEX

ABOUT THE AUTHOR

Terry Salinger began teaching in the New York City public school system immediately after obtaining her masters degree from the Bank Street College of Education. Many of the writing samples used in this book are treasures that she kept from her nine years of teaching young children. She completed her doctoral work at New Mexico State University and has been a teacher educator in New Mexico, Texas, and Ohio.

Dr. Salinger is currently the director of the Research Division of the International Reading Association. Before joining IRA, she worked at Educational Testing Service where she was involved in several school-based research projects. Dr. Salinger is the author of numerous books and articles, including *Models of Literacy Instruction*, published by Merrill/Prentice Hall in 1993.

Terry Salinger and her husband live in Wilmington, Delaware; they share their home with a dog, three cats, and several fish. Terry's interests include cooking, gardening, reading, and renovating old houses. One of her biggest goals in life is to write a novel.